973.7

They Died
to Make Men Free

They Died to Make Men Free

A history of The 19th Michigan Infantry in the Civil War

William M. Anderson

Foreword by John Y. Simon

Hardscrabble Books
Berrien Springs, Michigan
1980

FIRST EDITION

For
Hattie Anderson Timpy
My Aunt, Teacher and Mother

INTRODUCTION

Despite many similarities, each Civil War regiment was different, its unique cast of characters accounted for much of the difference. This is a story of a group of civilians about a thousand or so) who agreed to help fight a war. The only saving grace was that the other side was doing it the same way. The bulk of them went to work for room and board (certainly not all one could eat) and $13.00 a month. They were motivated by a variety of reasons, some straight out of the textbook, many just swept along, and others went simply to "see the elephant". No question, the Civil War was the central experience in their lives. The volume of correspondence generated attests to their literacy. And being conscious of their great experience, many carefully preserved these family archives.

This then, is a history retold by the participants, where the major contributors are officers and enlisted men who wrote letters to families and friends and to home town newspapers, and conscientiously recorded entries in personal diaries and journals. In all, the author has become aware of 823 letters written by 16 officers and 33 enlisted members of the 19th Michigan Infantry Regiment. Additionally, the recollections of 10 members were preserved in diaries and journals. Among the letters, almost 90 percent were written by enlisted men, a heavy portion, 533, emanating from B Company alone. Eight local newspapers had "correspondents" within the regiment, one of them being a former editor. Some of these knew they were writing for publication but most wrote very privately and personally, often instructing wives to keep the content confidential. One soldier wrote an incredible total of 300 letters. Taken as a whole, these "epistles" described their collective experiences, antics, heroics and complaints.

The volume of correspondence and other primary source material has given the author some special opportunities. It allowed me to make judgments about the motivation of people and to get inside their minds. Names became people and people take on personality and reenact the experience of thousands of Americans during the Civil War. One gets to know Sergeant Phinehas Hager after reading and studying 84 letters to his wife, the first written the day his company arrived at the rendezvous camp in August, 1862 and the last just days before his life was claimed by a sniper's bullet before Atlanta in August, 1864. A history so dependent on the accounts left by participants takes on another dimension of life with characters dropping in and out of the story. Thus, when Sergeant Hager died on August 9, 1864, Sherman lost a top-notch veteran and I lost his discerning eyes and descriptive pen. Access to hundreds of letters also allows the historian to reconstruct relationships and understand command and personnel problems. Finally the availability of several observations of the same event enhances objectivity, understanding and awareness of its significance.

In a project like this one certainly calls upon friends for a great deal of assistance. But a writer also makes new friends and discovers wonderful people whom he has never met, yet they willingly come to his aid. That is one of the nicest parts of the experience.

Beyond acknowledgements already made, there are many others I wish to thank for their contributions to this study. Bernice Vanderburg, Dowagiac and Cass County historian, frequently dug into her reservoir of knowledge and provided information and suggestions. I asked Archivist Wayne Mann, University Archives and Regional History Collections at Western Michigan University for help so often that I began to feel embarrassed. He and his secretary Phyllis Barnham are due special thanks. Gratitude is especially extended to Dorothy Ivey for reading the entire manuscript and offering many helpful suggestions, to John Y. Simon for writing the forward, to publisher John Gillette for encouragement and years of continued assistance, and to Archie Nevins who kindly allowed me to use the Charles Prentiss letters, diary and photograph.

I also want to thank the following persons for providing valuable assistance and information: Thomas Krasean, Indiana Historical Society; Robert Schultz; Lee Dodd; Richard Hathaway, Michigan State Library; Mary Jo Pugh, Bentley Historical Library, Michigan Historical Collections; The

University of Michigan; David Johnson, State Archives of Michigan; Douglas Wilson, Knox College Library; Sydney Kerksis; Phyllis Holbrook; C. William Pearson; Donald Allen; Jo Anna Appleby; Charlotte Wentz; Southwestern Michigan College Library; Ruth Anderson, and Paul Carlson.

Most of all I want to thank my wife Anna for doing most of the typing and for being so supportive of this family project. Similarly, I appreciate the patience of our three children, Dave, Dan, and Susan. It appears that "the book" will be finished before the beginning of the back yard football season.

WILLIAM M. ANDERSON

Galesburg, Illinois - September 17, 1978

vii

Foreword

After the Civil War had ended, many veterans could not or would not forget the climactic event in their lives. Prominent officers on both sides conducted continuing literary skirmishes with the enemy, now not confined to those they had fought against, but including rivals for whatever glory war had brought to their side. Many regiments -- though not the 19th Michigan -- found a regimental historian in the ranks, someone eager to memorialize the group by paying tribute to gallant officers and brave men. Often the nineteenth century regimental history contains valuable factual information or colorful vignettes of army life, but most suffer from a relentless emphasis on the positive aspects of the careers and service of officers and men. Authors did not forget that the potential customers were either fellow-soldiers or their survivors.

Not all regiments were covered, and some were covered in a way that did not begin to exhaust the subject. In the past dozen years, probably inspired by Bruce Catton, who found so much of his most trenchant material in long-neglected regimental histories, and by Bell I. Wiley, who explored the rich variety of the soldier letters, new enthusiasts have revived the practice of writing regimental histories, among them John J. Pullen, Leslie Anders, John W. Rowell, and Stephen Z. Starr. With his study of the 19th Michigan, Bill Anderson joins their ranks.

Often the old regimental history benefited from the ability of the author to tap the memories of his surviving comrades, but the passing years carried off the last veterans. The new regimental history is based instead on the accumulated documentary evidence, including both archival sources and the personal letters and diaries of the troops. The latter often provide -- as do those of the 19th Michigan -- more insight into the tensions within the group, a better basis for understanding the effects of the long stretches between battles, and a perspective on the Civil War with heroics and glory stripped away. Much of this personal material is only now emerging from attics to become available in libraries.

Historians often complain that so much history is written about so few people: kings, generals, statesmen, and other leaders. The story of a Civil War regiment should satisfy the most strident demand for history from the bottom up, though it will not please those who insist that it reveal class-consciousness or proletarian resentment. This does not mean that the men of the 19th Michigan were always cheerfully obedient soldiers; in fact they complained throughout the war about one thing and another, but they used much the same tone for inferior food and incompetent officers. Generalizations fail to encompass them, except perhaps their basic American individualism and independence.

Anderson presents a fairly typical Civil War regiment, not far from the average in total casualties, engaging in about its fair share of combat, and far from the worst in morale. For this reason, readers somewhat jaded with accounts of generalship and strategy have much to learn by following the Civil War from the ranks. From this viewpoint, it is easier to see what the experience of war was really like.

John Y. Simon
Ulysses S. Grant Association

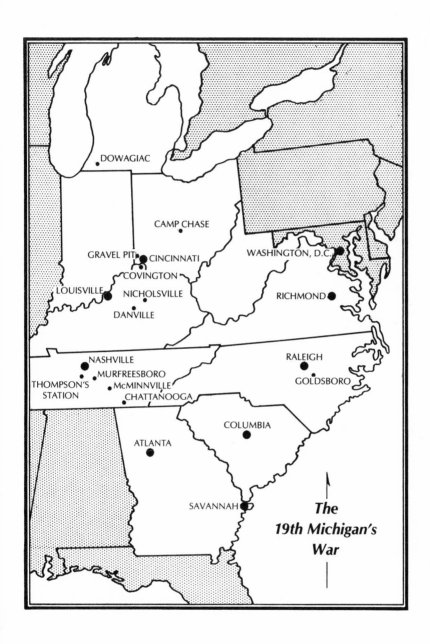

The
19th Michigan's
War

A CALL TO ARMS: *1*

"THREE HUNDRED THOUSAND MORE"

"We are coming, Father Abraham - three hundred thousand more." And the Civil War reached out again and touched new people. For Michigan, the significant number was 11,686, its share of President Lincoln's July 2, 1862 call for 300,000 additional troops. The Michigan legislature promptly authorized the organization of six new infantry regiments, one from each congressional district, among which was the Nineteenth Michigan Infantry. [1]

The second congressional district, comprising the counties of Allegan, Berrien, Branch, Cass, Kalamazoo, St. Joseph, and Van Buren, encompassed the southwestern corner of the State. It offered a population base of 140,324 resident from which to recruit a regiment. By 1860 standards and considering that the state's population was just slightly under three quarters of a million, southwestern Michigan was a major population base of the state. The regiment's ten companies were organized at Allegan, Coldwater, Constantine, Dowagiac, Kalamazoo, South Haven, St. Joseph and Sturgis with Coldwater and Kalamazoo supporting two companies each. Kalamazoo was the big town in the district with a population of over 6,000; Coldwater with its 2,905 residents was easily the second largest community. [2]

Officially, recruitment began on July 15, with the issuance of General Order number 154 by Adjutant General John Robertson. The order set forth the task of raising six infantry regiments, each under the general direction of a commandant charged with supervising recruitment and initial organization of the regiment at its rendezvous camp, yet carefully establish-

1

ing that the assignment did not automatically lead to future commission as a regimental field officer.[3] Governor Austin Blair made the appointments and selected a 44-year-old attorney from Coldwater to direct the organization of the 19th Michigan. Born July 14, 1818, in Onondaga County, New York, Henry Clark Gilbert first came to Michigan in 1841. Settling in Coldwater, he was soon joined by his brother and father, like himself members of the legal profession. Prior to the war, Gilbert enjoyed a prominent legal and political career. He served first as Branch County prosecuting attorney for a period of six continuous years. In 1850, he was employed as an attorney for the Michigan Southern Railroad Company with the assignment of procuring a right-of-way through Branch and adjoining counties. During President Franklin Pierce's administration, Gilbert was named Indian Agent for the Northwest Territory. Apparently he was also a highly successful businessman who managed his financial affairs shrewdly for he amassed considerable wealth. According to the 1860 Census, Gilbert's property and capital amounted to $61,000 making him the wealthiest man in Coldwater. By comparison, his brother's net worth was a meager $7,000 accumulated over a very similar period of time. Henry Gilbert invested in several enterprises including a saw mill, flour mill and newspaper. He owned a farm too, but in the opinion of at least one observer, his attempt to operate a nursery on his property was less than a successful venture. Married in 1843, Henry and Harriet Gilbert reared a large family of four boys and four girls.[4]

Politically, Gilbert was a staunch Democrat. His newspaper, the *Sentinel*, was considered a strong party organ. When the war commenced, he served as a member of the Democratic State Committee.[5] Despite his party affiliation, Gilbert clearly aligned with those urging a vigorous prosecution of the war. Significantly, he was appointed commandant by a Republican Governor. Since Gilbert was already accustomed to shouldering responsibility, it was only natural that he be cast in a role of leading men in a war so dependent upon volunteers and citizen-soldiers. There is little question that he possessed the requisite courage to be a successful commander. He had strength, yet at times his aggressive and forceful manner strained relationships within the regiment. There would be other occasions when his political background and savvy would seemingly dictate his leadership style. The "good colonels" were a highly skilled lot. They possessed a delicate balance among strength, compassion and finesse. In Gilbert's case, strength overshadowed other leadership traits. Henry Gilbert was at his best when the 19th Michigan was engaging the enemy; to his credit, not once would his regiment break and run.

Robertson's communique instructed that recruitment would be conducted in accordance with Federal regulations dated July 8, 1862. The Adjutant General made some modifications to make the procedure fit the local situation. Basically, a person was empowered by the Governor to raise a company subordinate, of course, to the overall organizational responsibility of the commandant. Additionally, there were a number of recruiting lieutenants appointed within each district charged with mustering in volunteers as they were enlisted. The Federal regulations envisioned recruits being sent on a weekly basis to the rendezvous camp where they would be sworn in and physically examined; however, this procedure was altered, probably for convenience sake, so that recruits were enlisted and then later assembled as companies and moved as a unit to their initial encampment for processing. Transportation expenses were borne by the government. Anticipating that recruiting officers would compete to fill their companies as quickly as possible, recruiters were cautioned against enlisting unfit men. A lack of scrutiny in mustering an obviously unfit volunteer could result in the officer making good any expenses incurred in the process plus the forfeiture of pay. Surgeons were instructed to identify those with clearly apparent physical limitations. As a recruiter, there were other risks as well. The failure to fill a company within what was considered a reasonable length of time was a very real possibility. If that happened, the recruiter was just out; his recruits would be transferred to another company and the government under no obligation to pay him.[6]

Although recruitment did not officially begin until July 15, 1862, the company organized at South Haven, got the jump on the rest by enlisting four men on July 14. The first four 19th Michigan volunteers were John Wilson, William Breed, Thomas Carroll, and Osmer Letson.[7] But their uniqueness ended there; within eight months both Breed and Carroll were dead, victims of disease. Wilson was wounded during the war yet he and Letson made it back to Michigan.[8] Despite an early start enlistments were slow; only 29 volunteered during the first two weeks.[9] But then the effort became organized. The press in southwestern Michigan began to have an impact as editorial proclamations of "Three Hundred Thousand More," "Our County Calls Now!" and "Arise, Fellow Men, Our Country Yet Remains" stirred an anxious citizenry. War meetings to adopt patriotic resolutions, generate enthusiasm, encourage enlistments and raise bounty money were held throughout the district. One of the first meetings called was held in Sturgis on July 26 and the appeal of the *Journal* editor was stated with conviction:

> No Brother Wait, we are not. We are going to work. We are going to put our hands, hearts and heads together, raise a company in short order, provide for its health, food and comfort, and send it up to camp at Dowagiac in short metre. One good, big company is about our quota, and we are going to recruit, officer, feed, clothe, nurse, and if need be, equip it from all parts of the county. There is no time to be lost either. We are going to hold war meetings all over the county . . . Let the long roll sound, and men rush to arms. The president and generals have promised that we may fight and - - let us fight.[10]

The groundswell of a free people had been set in motion. Sturgis' example was followed two days later with meetings at Galesburg and Schoolcraft; others convened at Kalamazoo on July 30, at Alamo on August 1, Dowagiac on August 2, and

4

Centreville on August 5. [11] The results were immediate and effective; in a week's time beginning August 6, over 500 enlisted. [12]

The mass meeting held at Dowagiac on Saturday, August 2, was typical of the others, resembling perhaps a kick-off rally, except that the stakes were higher. During the morning, the population of this small village swelled as people from neighboring communities gathered for the occasion. Amidst the blare of music and flying banners, war enthusiasm was building. By noon the streets were overflowing with excited visitors. "At half past one o'clock a procession was formed on Front street and marched to the School House Square . . ." where the meeting was held judged to have drawn the largest crowd in the village's history. [13] Local newspaperman W. H. Campbell, owner and operator of the *Cass County Republican* and chairman of the County Republican Committee, strongly supported the cause urging merchants and manufacturers to close their doors to observe the spirit and seriousness of the occasion. [14]

The meeting began with prayer and the election of the town's leading citizen Justus Gage as chairman. Musical selections were presented by the Buchanan Glee Club. The singing of patriotic music was a standard part of every war meeting program.

Following the meeting at Centreville, a local newspaper editor called attention to the appropriateness of a new and popular song which had been sung entitled "The Battle-Cry of Freedom."

The honorable Charles E. Stuart, United States Senator from Kalamazoo, was the first of three distinguised political figures to address the audience. He apprised the gathering of the crisis facing the nation and urged support of the war effort. "He was in favor of a vigorous prosecution of the war, willing to sacrifice the last dollar he had in the world and even life itself, to sustain the Government . . ." Great applause followed and then Dowagiac's own Glee Club stirred emotions with a patriotic song. A prominent Coldwater resident, Congressman Charles Upson was the second speaker. He was followed by

U.S. Senator Jacob M. Howard from Detroit. In general, his remarks reinforced what had already been said except that he emphasized the country's need with a vivid and stirring illustration. Senator Howard reported that he had just returned from visiting General George McClellan's army on the Peninsula. There he had witnessed three proud Michigan regiments, numbers reduced to scarcely a third of their original strength yet still occupying a precarious and advanced position.

The message was clear; the war advocates were not just talking about defending an intangible called Union, but some Michigan boys needed help. "Had he the power, that little band of heroes should be reinforced at once, even if it should make every women in the land a widow." The audience listened with fixed attention, only spontaneous cheers interrupted the magnetic hold of Senator Howard's words. Henry Gilbert anchored the program with a strong appeal that those in attendance declare their support. As might be expected, Gilbert frequently appeared on these war meeting programs. [15]

One hundred and twenty-six persons pledged to contribute $4,040 in bounty money to entice enrollments. Six major donors contributed $3,000 of the total. Typically, the largest bounties pledged were intended to go to the first group of men who enlisted from a particular township. Although the donations became smaller following these substantial contributions, the same spirit carried through. Thus a man named Jones contributed . . ."$50 to the first ten men enlisting from Silver Creek Township." A while later Daniel Larzelere of Dowagiac offered ". . .$50 to the first five men enlisting in the 19th regiment after this date." Still later in the day, a gentleman from Wayne Township announced that he would pay " . . .$50 each to the next ten enlisting after the five mentioned by Daniel Larzelere." The number of contributors and sizes of their gifts indicate rather clearly that support for the war was broadly based. Twenty-eight contributed a dollar, one offered 50 cents. Contributions like cows offered by four different persons, a rent free house for a soldier's family and a pair of socks

6

demonstrated that people were giving whatever they could afford. Certainly the war was touching the "little people in Cass County, Michigan.[16] Similar "fund drives" were occurring in each of the other communities where a company was being raised for the 19th Michigan Infantry. Citizens of Kalamazoo County set their sights high, promising $50 per enlistee. The meeting held at Centreville in St. Joe County netted $6,000. [17]

Even so, *Republican* editor Campbell was dissatisfied. Editorializing on page two, he lashed out at the absence of contributions from the wealthier members of his community. He urged that the bounty be uniform and if the needed funds could not be raised voluntarily, then a tax should be imposed. "There is but one way to reach the sympathies of this class . . . and that is by a direct war tax. This will reach them in proportion to their abundance." [18]

Three hundred thousand more - for the nation, 11,000 more - for Michigan, and 200 more - for St. Joseph County. Thus Lincoln's call for additional men was translated until it reached the point from which the needed response, volunteers, would spring. When St. Joseph County echoed President Lincoln's call, it went even further to break down its share into township quotas. The *Three River Reporter* carried the announcement of the number of volunteers expected from each community. [19]

Lockport	20	Constantine	18
Sturgis	17	White Pigeon	16
Mendon	15	Nottawa	14
Colon	12	Florence	12
Flowerfield	11	Park	11
Burr Oak	11	Leonidas	9
Mottville	7	Sherman	6
Fabius	6	Fawn River	5

Late in July, Governor Blair announced his appointments of regimental commandants and those authorized to raise companies. For the 19th Michigan, the recruiting team consisted of George Peck, Cassopolis; Hazen Brown,

Constantine; George White, Coldwater; Phelix Duffie, Kalamazoo; Charles Lincoln, Coldwater; Martin McKinney, Buchanan; Joel Smith, Dowagiac; Charles Thompson, Kalamazoo; John Stafford, Decatur; Julius Cross, Three Rivers; and Henry Ford, Kalamazoo.[20] Since infantry regiments were composed of ten companies, a quick tally of the list reveals the makings of a problem at the very onset; it was simply not possible for all of these recruits to successfully organize a company and have it accepted.

Once the recruitment process had been set in motion, the Governor had more men, more companies, and more would-be commanders than he could use. Competition for acceptance into the 19th Michigan was sharp and the Governor's many promises along with authorizing too many men to raise companies intensified the rivalry. The system got out of hand in Berrien County. At one point five companies were being raised in the county, all unassigned and all vying for volunteers and acceptance into the same regiment. Supposedly only one company from Berrien County would be admitted into the 19th Michigan Infantry. A war meeting had been held in Niles during which the town's mayor, Robert Landon, wired the Governor and asked if he would commission persons selected at the meeting to raise a company. After receiving an affirmative response, the group named a captain and two lieutenants to direct their recruitment. The major then wrote to Governor Blair asking that he officially authorize these men to begin enlisting recruits. Several days passed yet no further confirmation was received. One of the lieutenants, Arthur Twombly of Niles, went to Jackson to confer with the Governor. His alleged conversation illustrates the potential for confusion when military and political decisions become mixed. Supposedly, Twombly questioned the Governor as to whether he had:

> . . . received a letter from Landon stating the Action of the Meeting the Gov said no he had received no Such letter Twombly told him he knew better, he then turned to the clerk and asked him if he had ever Seen any Such

letter he told him he had and reached out on the table before which the Gov was sitting and picked up the letter. the Gov then Said he believed he did recollect reading the letter, but had forgotten all about it. he then made out the commissions and handed them to him and told him to report to Col Gilbert at Dowagiac when his Company was full. [21]

A satisfied Lieutenant Twombly returned to Niles and in a week's time he and his comrades had completed the enlistment of a full company. Reporting to Gilbert at Dowagiac, his unit was accepted. Still another Berrien County officer went to Jackson and was on the verge of having his company accepted when Gilbert showed up and informed the Governor of his prior commitment to a company from Niles. Supposedly, Blair commented that this would not work at all for he had already taken another company from St. Joseph also located in the county. Ultimately, the only Berrien County company to join the 19th Michigan was the one organized at St. Joe. [22]

This surplus of companies led to the organization of the 25th Michigan Infantry. Two of those commissioned to recruit 19th Michigan companies, Martin McKinney and Julius Cross, ended up commanding companies in the 25th Michigan. Men who volunteered for service with the 19th Michigan accidently became members of an entirely different regiment when they were mustered into service [23]

An examination of the Descriptive Books reveals that a variety of persons became involved in recruiting soldiers for the regiment. Although in most instances the bulk were enlisted by the officer authorized to raise a company, at least twelve others assisted, some of whom never had any further affiliation with the regiment and in a few cases were responsible for bringing in just one soldier. [24] A $2.00 premium was paid to either citizen, soldier or officer when each recruit was mustered.

As an inducement, volunteers were offered their first month's pay plus $25.00 of a $100.00 bonus upon enlistment. It is hard to believe that either wages or bounty made up a man's mind to volunteer. The experience of a young farm hand from St. Joseph County is probably representative of the circumstances which brought many into the Union Army. According to Frank Rice, until he attended a war meeting at Centreville, he had given very little thought to enlisting. In fact, he had no idea that there was a critical need for additional troops. But Rice caught the "war fever" and the very next day, went to Sturgis and volunteered his services. At the time, he was employed on his uncle's farm earning $12.50 a month.[25] Joel Smith, who recruited most of the company organized at Dowagiac, even offered to throw in his $2.00 enlistment premium to "sweeten the pot." His advertisement announced his intentions to "muster the first and best Company in this Regiment . . ."[26] War enthusiasm, the ever present threat of a conscription law and to some extent bounties, combined to help fill companies. Lawmakers and newspapermen frequently reminded the citizenry that the alternative to voluteerism was a draft. One editor suggested that an appropriate slogan for a recruiting office might be: "Come in out of the draft."[27]

By mid-August most companies were full. They began training and taking on the assemblage of organization while waiting the call to report at Dowagiac. War fever, as Rice called it, was spreading like a contagion throughout southwestern Michigan. Although the nation was embroiled in a terrible Civil War, the hard realities as well as the impact must have seemed far removed to folks living in this western state. Just twenty-five years before, Michigan was a territory and even in 1862 much of the State resembled frontier. Most of the men who joined the 19th Michigan were born in another state or in some other country. Among those who were Michigan natives, many had birth dates reaching back to territorial days. Now, however, the raising and arming of a local regiment swelled a new spirit of nationalism and the preservation of the Union became a personal cause. Each community naturally felt great pride in its men sent forth to defend the nation, in every instance of course representing the flower of its youth. As they left their homes for Dowagiac they carried with them best wishes, affecttion and high expectation. These men, particularly the officers, were instant heroes. Before B Company departed Allegan for its rendezvous camp the Free Masons held a special meeting to honor Captain Elisha B. Bassett, their lodge master, and now commanding officer of the local company. Captain Bassett was presented a sword, sash and belt described as a costly and elegant gift. The occasion was serious with the gathering bidding Bassett farewell and an exaggerated charge "to save our government from peril and country from ruin."[28] That intangible but mighty force called patriotism was stirring.

Aside from Dowagiac's own company, the first units to arrive in camp came from St. Joe and South Haven. Company B was next, arriving by rail in the late afternoon, August 19.[29] Their procession from the depot through town must have resembled a parade as they brought along the Allegan and Martin Brass Bands to accompany their march. The journey to Dowagiac was an exhilarating experience for all these units for their passing through each village evoked enthusiastic cheers and the waving of flags and handkerchiefs. The companies from Constantine and Sturgis traveled in wagons and both reached Cassopolis, the next town east of Dowagiac, about noon. Here they were provided a free meal at one of the hotels.[30] The account of their arrival at Dowagiac bears a remarkable similarity to the reception given the first western regiments which came to Washington D.C. in 1861 to defend the nation's capital. The circumstances and significance were entirely different yet the same feeling was present. "When we arrived within sight of the village, we dismounted from the wagons, and proceeded by the band, marched in double file through the village to the camp . . .As we marched through the village, and even from the officers in the camp, we heard many remarks that it was the best company that had arrived, which reputation we still retain."[31] Not surprisingly, almost every other company believed it too was the best. Their arrival brought to six the number of companies in camp. Two more came in from Coldwater on the 22nd, another from Kalamazoo on the 25th and the last, Company K, reached Dowagiac on August 27. All were pleased to see the regiment completed and although

Company K from Kalamazoo brought up the rear, it was accorded a warm greeting upon its arrival, as the regiment was drawn up into two long lines to receive it. [32]

X The camp of the 19th Michigan was located about a half mile southwest of the village near Dowagiac Creek, just east of the railroad tracks, and at the site of a racetrack. [33] It was the commandant's job to select the site mindful of healthy location, availability of fresh water and preferably one with sandy soil and rolling terrain which would provide good drainage. [34] Based on these criteria, Gilbert chose an excellent spot for the camp. The ranks were favorably impressed and appreciative of the numerous shade trees. And as for sand, Dowagiac had more than its share; its abundance was bound to leave an impression. A couple of years before the war, Grace Greenwood, then a well-known writer, visited her brother, Dr. William E. Clark, in Dowagiac. Dr. Clark later became surgeon of the 19th Michigan. Her less than favorable impression of the village was recorded in a Philadelphia literary publication, the *Evening Post*. "The bare white houses reminded the writer of rocs' eggs lying on the desert sand." [35] A layer of five or six inches of loose sand in the roads made traveling around Dowagiac disagreeable, particularly when the wind was gusting. Colonel Gilbert's feelings about Dowagiac and his recently established camp are revealed in a lieutenant's letter: "As the Colonel jocularly remarked the other evening, in allusion to the abundance of sand of this region, 'It is a capital place to make mortar,' but he thinks it is an indifferent location for a camp." [36]

It is hard to imagine a civil war regiment organizing in such an unlikely place. This observation could have easily been made against a backdrop of 116 years of history focused upon a little village in Cass County, Michigan during the late summer of 1862. Yet the presence of the railroad and its central location within the congressional district must have been determining factors. More important still, the Civil War eventually involved nearly everyone, even those in remote places, on the farms and in the small villages across the land; they were not exempt, nor did they want to be.

12

Founded in 1848, Dowagiac was an infant when the Civil War began. Its origin was directly tied to the construction of the Michigan Central Railroad completed through Cass County in 1848. The tracks ran diagonally through town causing the main street to be laid out parallel with it. Here along Front Street, the business community was concentrated, including merchants dealing in dry goods, groceries, drugs and hardware. The Dowagiac House, up on the corner of Main and Front competed with several other hotels for railroad and stage coach passenger traffic. The village was a developing manufacturing center comprising a foundry established by P.D. Beckwith, destined soon to be an industrial magnate, a flour mill, brewery, saw mill and several factories including one producing baskets and another down on the creek below town manufacturing chairs. The village also had its own newspaper, post office and bank. A little place with a little more than a thousand residents was about to serve as a military base for the 19th Michigan Infantry Regiment. Its visitors nearly outnumbered the home folks. [37]

On July 31, an advertisement appeared in the *Cass County Republican,* soliciting bids for the provision of rations and wood for the regiment with contracts issued by the U.S. Disbursing Office at Detroit. [38] All logistical concerns involved in setting up a camp were the responsibility of the commandant. Gilbert decided it was more than one quartermaster could handle so he employed a friend, Harvey D. Miller, to help out on a temporary basis. Miller was promised $2.00 a day for his 30 days of service. During this period of organization, Colonel Gilbert and any staff he employed were not on the regular army payroll. Compensation for services rendered depended upon filing a successful claim. Represented legally by his brother, Colonel Gilbert submitted Miller's claim for services rendered along with one of his own. Gilbert's bill included payment for 45 days service as commandant at $5.00 per diem and $66.83 for expenses incurred. Whether either ever got paid is unknown. This first attempt was rejected because it was submitted to the wrong office; military red tape was as old as the army. [39]

As commandant, Colonel Gilbert was prohibited from expending funds to construct or rent buildings. [40] The intent was clear; the regiment was to be billeted in tents. As the companies began to arrive at Dowagiac, Gilbert and his staff were ready to receive them. Tents were erected in rows generally about five being assigned to a company. Most were the famed Sibley tents capable of housing 20 or so men in relatively comfortable fashion. Additional tents were provided for cooks and commissioned officers. Tables where the ranks ate were constructed of boards some 25 to 30 feet in length. Each company was alloted two. The men liked what they had to eat, particularly the fresh bread made locally at Niles by Colby and Company. [41] Tin eating utensils were provided by the quartermaster. A separate facility, referred to as the Colonel's dining room, established an officer's mess. It was simply a canopy-like affair with canvas stretched over poles, anchored to the ground with ropes. [42]

The 19th Michigan began with an initial strength of 995 officers and men. A tough physical examination administered by regimental surgeons had weeded out those recruits least capable. [43] An innocent soldier reported: "We had to take off our shirts." [44] The officers and men were typical volunteers in nearly every respect. Characteristically, they were primarily agrarians, green, naive and enthusiastic. Many had family relationships within companies. Based on a preliminary examination of census records and other evidence, brothers, brother-in-laws, father-son and cousin relationships have been identified. Three Baird brothers from Allegan, Ancil, Edward and George were all members of Company B. Likewise there were three brothers in Company A: Alexander, Thomas, and William Kirkwood. Phelix Duffie commanded Company K; his son was a drummer and belonged to his father's outfit. [45]

Although unfamiliar with the army, the regiment was not totally void of prior military experience. Generally though, it is very difficult to determine how many of the enlisted men had previous experience.

Some basic information regarding principal officers is

14

summarized below: [46]

Officer	Age	Home Town	Occupation
Col. Henry C. Gilbert	44	Coldwater	Lawyer
Lt. Col. David Bacon	33	Niles	Lawyer
Maj. William R. Shafter	27	Galesburg	Teacher
Adj. Hamlet B. Adams	26	Coldwater	Lawyer
QM Warren Chapman	50	St. Joseph	Lumberman
Surgeon William E. Clark	44	Dowagiac	Doctor
Asst. Surgeon John Bennett		Centreville	Doctor
2d Asst. Surg. Leander Tompkins	45	Cassopolis	Doctor
Chaplain Isreal Cogshall	42	Coldwater	Methodist Minister
Company Commanders			
A Capt. Joel H. Smith	42	Pokagon	Methodist Minister
B Capt. Elisha Bassett	40	Allegan	Merchant
C Capt. Charles P. Lincoln	20	Coldwater	Lawyer
D Capt. Hazen Brown	44	Constantine	
E Capt. John J. Baker	27	Sturgis	
F Capt. Charles Thompson	25	Kalamazoo	Lawyer
G Capt. Charles Bigelow		South Haven	
H Capt. George H. White	34	Coldwater	Nurseryman
I Capt. Richard Lysaght	45	St. Joseph	Grocer
K Capt. Phelix Duffie	47	Kalamazoo	Hotel Keeper

A quick glance reveals that this cadre was highly educated, maybe more so than the officers who led most Civil War regiments. Their backgrounds demonstrate that officers who organized companies and regiments were usually very influential people in their home communities. Joel Smith is a good example. When he and brother Ezekiel came to Dowagiac they began one of the first businesses. About the same time, Ezekiel established the *Cass County Advocate*, the village's first newspaper. When Dowagiac was incorporated in 1857, Joel Smith was elected a charter trustee. In the next two elections, he was chosen village president. The year the war began, Dowagiac boasted a newly constructed brick Union School; Joel Smith was the builder. Additionally, he served as assessor and school board members. In recruiting and organizing a volunteer company in and around Dowagiac, Captain Smith was a natural. [47]

When a company arrived at Dowagiac, it was assigned its quarters, cooks were designated, and other men detailed for guard duty. Then the regimental surgeons began conducting physical examinations. For the first few days at least, life in camp was very relaxed and sort of unmilitary. Men moved about rather freely and were assigned little duty. [48] With eight companies in camp, Colonel Gilbert called his first formation for the evening of August 23. Addressing the regiment, he named the encampment, Camp Willcox in honor of Michigan's first Civil War hero Colonel Orlando Willcox. Gilbert's timing was such that at that very moment the city of Detroit was planning a hero's welcome for Willcox, commander of the First Michigan Infantry at Bull Run, and recently released from a Confederate prison. [49] The occasion must have been especially meaningful to Captain Charles Lincoln and First Lieutenant Smith W. Fish since both had been with Willcox at Bull Run as members of the First Michigan. And now the new regiment got down to business. Part of the shakedown and organizational process involved selecting junior officers and all non-commissioned officers. Given a volunteer army, a little politics necessarily intervened into the process. Company B is representative. Within the make-up of the Company, Allegan,

16

Colonel Henry C. Gilbert of Coldwater organized the Nineteenth Michigan in 1862 and served as its first commanding officer until May 15, 1864. [Machinac Island State Park Commission]

Otsego and Martin were the principal communities. A newly elected sergeant from Otsego reported the election results to his wife saying: "We had to give Martin first duty sergeant." [50]

17

Along with noncoms to stratify the ranks, the schedule changed too:

5:00 A.M.	Reveille
6:30 A.M.	Roll Call
7:00 A.M.	Breakfast
8:00 A.M.	Clean up tents
9:00 - 11:00 A.M.	Drill
12:00 noon	Dinner
2:00 - 4:00 P.M.	Drill
4:00 P.M.	Half hour swim and supper
6:30 P.M.	Dress parade
	("as long as the Colonel likes")
9:30 P.M.	Tattoo and lights out [51]

And, oh, the adjustments; for Camp Willcox was a Civil War recruit camp with nearly a thousand would-be soldiers still all just plain citizens. The transition would be both amusing and painful while men got used to new relationships, lost their freedom, learned to sleep on the ground and adjusted to new diets with the accompanying side effects of diarrhea and other disorders. An even more common ailment was referred to as the "summer complaint" or in non-medical terms, laziness.[52] A perimeter guard was established around the camp to control traffic in both directions. Naturally, some people had to learn the hard way. Within the first week disciplinary action was taken against several men, and the regiment experienced its first court-martial. Allegedly, a man on guard decided to call it quits one evening; "stuck his gun in the ground & run away, he was caut 4 miles west on the railroad asleep what will be done with him I cant tell the rest that run guard has to care a large stick of wood (weight about 60 lbs) on their sholders ½ day & the Reg. bee laghing at them so you see that it stands an hand to behave him-self." [53] A less expected aspect of camp which adversely impressed many soldiers was the amount of noise. Having been thrown together with a lot of strange people, noise deterred the opportunity to get away even to the privacy of their own thoughts. "We have all sorts of noises here some

*Teams lined up on Beeson Street in Dowagiac on wheat
day in 1860. Grain elevator, not shown, was at right.
[Bernice Vanderburg]*

are singing some fiddling some dancing and a good many of
them are swearing." [54] The initial correspondence of soldiers
leaves the impression that those vocabularies seemed
limited to four letter words were pretty common. Thanks to a
soldier's descriptive letter to a friend back home, we have a
good view of life in camp in Dowagiac:

I have been on guard twice before to day. I was on
one week ago last Sunday and it did not seem hardly
right to be pacing up and down my beat with a gun in
my hand but here in camp there is but little difference
between Sunday and other days. We hear a great deal
of profanity here in camp and a great deal of nonsense
too. I expected to have been home this week but the
mustering officer did not come Tuesday as expected but
will be here Friday if nothing happens and then I shall
be home if I can get a furlough but if they will not give
me a furlough I shall have to stay or run away. Last
night one of our company got put into the guard house
the first one that has been in his name was Jones and
came from Allegan. They are pretty strict in their rules
in camp and no one is allowed to go out without a pass
or being passed out by a commissioned officer or

Sergeant of the guard and consequently some of the unruly boys run the guard and if they get caught they go into the guard house to pay for it. We see a great many girls here at dress parade as they come down from the village of Dowagiac to see us perform and it would well pay the folks of Martin to come out here and see how things are carried on here in Camp Willcox as to see eight or ten hundred men drawn up in two lines would be something of a sight to a great many but presume no one from Martin will think it worth while to come out here to see. [55]

Presumably some of the Dowagiac girls got too close for a couple of them were confined to the guard house and later sent packing down the tracks. [56] There were plenty of authorized visitors too; numerous families and friends came to camp since passes were relatively easy to secure. During their last week at Camp Willcox, a delegation of ladies came over from St. Joseph to enterain their company with a picnic. [57] It would appear that the military still had great faith in the "minute-man myth" for despite a very short training period of just 17 days when the entire regiment was present, many men were permitted to return to their homes on furlough. Though not so for one old "veteran"; he recognized the seriousness of preparing to fight and told his wife not to expect him back home because he did not " . . . want to get behind in drill." [58]

Soon a new institution called the sutler was introduced to these recruits. The sutler was an early version of the present day military's post exchange. Sulter and soldiers quickly got acquainted. On one occasion, a soldier received sutler's tickets instead of cash as his change after making a purchase. Shortly thereafter, he attempted to use these tickets in another purchase but they were refused. "At this the boys commenced an attack upon his shanty which was soon demolished, so now we are minus a sutler. After this the 19th Mich. will be a poor place for Sulters". [59] He too, was learning his role.

Time passed quickly as the date for their departure drew

nearer. On September 5, the regiment was mustered into Federal service. Against the backdrop of enthusiasm and surplus enlistments in 1862, Private Delos Lake described some very contradictory and unexpected behavior. No one else exposed the very unmilitary conduct of several members of the regiment the day they were mustered into U. S. service. According to Lake, the colonel had just announced that there would be no more card playing on Sundays. One can surmise that some of these independent soldiers bent on having a good time in the military, decided they were not going to join any "chicken outfit" where you were not allowed to play cards on Sundays. Anyway, eight members of Company E refused to be mustered. They took their places in the ranks only after the mustering officer drew his sword and swore at them. Two of the most recalcitrant then refused to raise their hand during the swearing in ceremony. They were marched off to the guard house, tied up, and confined for the night. By morning they had a change of heart. 60

A week later on Friday, September 12, they received a $25.00 advance bounty and marched to a large open field north of the village where they were reviewed by a U.S. Mustering Officer. Captain M. Mayer was pleased with the level of their training and soldierly bearing. That evening Governor Blair arrived in town. On Saturday he too reviewed the troops, offered his praise, gave a pep talk, and announced that the regiment would soon be starting south. The 19th returned the compliment with the usual "hip, hip, hurray." 61 Time was running out for lovers too. That same day, a lieutenant from Centreville married his sweetheart repeating their vows at a Dowagiac church. 62

In anticipation of the regiment's departure on Sunday, hundreds of people from surrounding communities flocked to Dowagiac. The streets were congested with wagons and teams as an estimated 3,000 gathered to say goodbye. If editor Bill Campbell's appraisal was reflective of general opinion, the 19th Michigan Infantry Regiment had made a good first impression and it left Michigan with high expectations:

21

The regiment has been with us but a short time, but during that brief period has won hosts of friends. The people of this county will watch with interest the career of the Nineteenth, which from what we have seen of both officers and men, we shall be disappointed if it is not a brilliant one. As a general thing the men are drawn from the intelligent and educated portion of the population and are prepossessed of that moral worth and stamina that is the highest characteristic of the patroit and soldier. We shall be sadly mistaken if they do not render a glorious account of themselves.[63]

2

GETTING INTO THE WAR

While the 19th Michigan organized and trained at Dowagiac, the Confederates were driving north through Kentucky threatening Cincinnati and Louisville. From Cincinnati on August 30, 1862, Major General Horatio G. Wright, commander of the Department of the Ohio, wired an urgent appeal to Michigan Governor Austin Blair stating: "General Halleck telegraphs me that some regiments from your State were ordered East. Please send rest of quota here as fast as possible. We want troops in Kentucky at once. Let me know how many regiments I may expect from your State and when."[1]

Similar messages were sent to the governors of Illinois and Indiana; Cincinnati was facing a crisis. The possibility that the Confederates would sweep into Ohio seemed very real. On September 2, martial law was declared in Cincinnati and a very concerned Ohio Governor called out the home guards.[2] With school suspended, even the teachers had organized a company and were drilling.[3] In addition to the "Squirrel Hunters" and newly organized western regiments, other more seasoned forces were being diverted to threatened Ohio River cities. U. S. Grant sent Major General Gordon Granger's division from Corinth and later, Major General Don Carlos Buell's army marched north from Nashville.[4]

By September 14, when the 19th Michigan departed Camp Willcox and headed south for the Ohio River, the Confederates

23

had already defeated a Union army at Richmond, Kentucky and seized control of the state capital at Frankfort. Three days earlier General Kirby Smith had pressed to within five miles of Cincinnati with an army estimated at more than 15,000.[5] The regiment's specific destination was in Ohio at a place called Gravel Pit, located 18 miles west of Cincinnati. The river was exceptionally low, and the 19th was being called upon to help prevent Rebels from fording it.

With their brief induction completed, the 19th Michigan boarded the Michigan Central passenger cars enroute to Cincinnati. The occasion produced mixed emotions as a large crowd gathered for the send-off. The editor of a southwestern Michigan newspaper recounted that sad but proud moment stating: "We shall never forget the scene. Hundreds of mothers, wives and sisters on that day whispered words of love and cheer to the departing ones, while their tears betokened their deep sorrow in thus parting . . ."[6] It was nearly 4:00 P.M., the train was moving and the 19th Michigan departed for the war. By rail the regiment passed through Indiana via Michigan City, Lafayette, Indianapolis, Shelbyville, and Lawrenceburg on its journey to the Ohio River. The train stopped briefly at Indianapolis where some of the men carelessly got off and were temporarily left behind as the train departed. Their absence soon noted, the train stopped and waited as these embarrassed soldiers ran on foot to catch up. At Shelbyville, they were greeted by young ladies who filled their canteens with fresh water as the train paused briefly. Another stop was made about 14 miles from Cincinnati and here an officer boarded, reporting that the Rebels were only a short distance away. His announcement caused plenty of anxiety among these green Michigan troops.[7]

The train reached Cincinnati about 8:00 P.M. on September 15. The regiment's arrival brought cheers and praise as ". . . the nicest Reg. that they had seen."[8] A lieutenant fondly recalled hearing ladies remark that the "Michigan boys were the prettiest that ever passed through their city."[9] It is doubtful that they accepted these accolades at face value. Hospitable citizens prepared the evening meal which was served at the 5th

Street Market. During their first night in the Queen City, the 19th Michigan was quartered indoors at the Commerical Chamber and the Merchant's Exchange. The Exchange had nothing but a dirt floor. [10]

X On the following day, the regiment rode the rails west to Gravel Pit on the Ohio-Indiana border. Here they relieved the home guards and occupied a campsite on a narrow strip of terrain some 30 feet above the river which they fronted while the Ohio and Mississippi Railroad ran behind their position. Their camp ground was a recently harvested wheatfield tucked into a valley with high ground to the rear and forest covered hills towering above and south of the river. There was no community at Gravel Pit, just a station and a few dwellings strung out along the river. The regiment's mission was to protect against a crossing along some 22 miles of river stretching from west of Lawrenceburg, Indiana, to Cincinnati. [11] Companies and details were assigned picket duty up and down the river. At Lawrenceburg, the Miami River empties into the Ohio and there the regiment had a major responsibility of guarding an important railroad bridge. Another detachment provided security for a ferryboat crossing. Back up the river at Cincinnati, a detail of 55 men from Company B was stationed high above the city providing security for the artillery at Fort Jones. Across the river in Kentucky, Union cavalry scouted along the Ohio, providing yet another line of defense. [12]

Accounts of the failures and follies of green troops mark the annals of any war, particularly of a nation which relies on volunteer soldiers. Following the Union debacle at Richmond, Kentucky on August 30, attention was again called to the shortcomings of citizen-soldiers. General Wright urged Henry Halleck to send him a force of seasoned troops stating that ". . . Richmond shows that newly raised troops are not reliable. ." [13] In performing its duty along the river, the 19th would do little to dispute history or Wright's conclusion. The regiment arrived at Gravel Pit during the day on September 16. The mixture of advancing Rebels, imagined Rebels, spooky river sounds and darkness all contributed to an anxious state of mind. According to one lieutenant, the observation of Rebels reconnoitering the

25

river caused Colonel Gilbert great concern. Finally at midnight, he made a decision, roused the regiment and issued ammunition. Fumbling in the dark and without prior instruction, these men learned to load their weapons. The rest of the night they slept on their arms. [14]

But this was only a beginning. Their second night in camp, the regiment fought its first "big battle" against darkness, strange noises and ghostly Confederates. Many soldiers mentioned the incident in their correspondence. Lieutenant Samuel Hubbard left a vivid description of a wild evening filled with excitement and fear:

Wednesday night we had an alarm. It was very dark and stormy. About 11 o'clock at night the officer of the day, Capt. Bigelow, called out the regiment. He said that a message had arrived, informing him that skirmishing was going on at Miami bridge 2 miles west on the R. R. between our pickets and the rebels who were trying to force a passage across the Ohio. In five minutes the regiment was thrown into the wildest excitement. Guns had to be loaded and companies formed in the pitchy darkness. Capt. Bassett was acting Lieutenant Col. and displayed remarkable judgement and coolness. He arranged the companies and got them in shape for action. I had charge of what remained of our Company. Some of our men were intensely excited, were ready to do anything, every-thing, and nothing in particular. In a few moments I succeeded in getting their attention, and they obeyed my orders, which I endeavored to give in a cool manner, without show of fear. The men wondered why I was so deliberate. The safety and efficiency of soldiers depends almost entirely upon the self possession and courage of the officers in command. The company with the Col. was sent immediately to the bridge where skirmishing was reported, the rest of the regiment remained in camp. After an hour's watch we found ourselves safe, and lay down to sleep on our arms. After about one hour

26

more we were aroused by firing of sentinels; the regiment rallied from their tents like a nest of yellow jackets. By this time we were assured that an immediate attack by the rebels was upon us, and that they had taken advantage of our ignorance of the vicinity, exposed situation, inexperience as well as the impenetrable darkness. I called the company to our quarters, took in a fresh supply of ammunition, got them in battle array ready for instant action - Capt. Bassett acting commander of the regiment shouted "where is Company B?" I replied "here, on hand." The regiment showed the wildest excitement. Sentinels under fright, fired at imagined enemies. One sentinel in rear of our tent, wandered 20 or 30 rods into a cornfield, another fired at corporal Paterson as he was taking around the relief guard. Captains swore and screamed at their men, telling them a hundred things at once, assuring them of their imminent danger, that it was certain that the rebels were about to enter into a wholesale butchery of the entire regiment. The regiment made noise enough for 30,000 men in a charge. The whole affair was a ridiculous farce. There may have been rebel scouts in the vicinity, but of this I have serious doubts. The only wonder is that we had not killed some of our own men. It had one very satisfactory result, by way of showing the native fighting qualities of the men. Some men cried like babies, others acted like maniacs, others showed promptness, coolness and courage, whilst a few showed contemptible humiliation and cowardice. Some feigned illness, others that their guns were out of order and useless, others had to undergo a change of linen, the next day. [15]

Fear was not restricted to the ranks for according to one account, Captain Phelix Duffie, commanding Company K, ". . . was so scart he — — — — *his britches*". [16]. Private Prentiss figured that wind blowing against the tightly drawn sides of tents caused a howling sound which was thought to be Rebels attacking the bridge and that expectation spooked the sentinels.[17] Casualties were limited to one dead hog and one bayonet wound to a soldier, both accidently inflicted.[18]

Duty at Gravel Pit or as it was later named, Camp Hooker, consisted primarily of picketing in small squads along the river. Generally a picket would include four men, two watching and two sleeping. Every two hours they rotated. Especially for these unseasoned soldiers, this was a dreary and monotonous experience. Sleeping was hardly better than watching. "How to lay on the stony beach" was no small problem to Sam Hewitt. "After turning over the feathers (stones) and fixing them smooth side up, I spread my blanket on the stony beach and with my canteen for a pillow, I Streached out my weary limbs to dream of the fortunes of war and $13 a month, but to go to sleep in such a place and under such circumstances it requires considerable nerve."[19] These conditions, along with noisy steamboat traffic on the river, denied Hewitt of sleep and before he could settle down, it was time to stand guard. "Half froze and unrefreshed we poor cusses took their places, dark as blazes, with only the barking dogs on Kentucky's shore to relieve the monotony."[20] After another rotation, a miserable sleepless night had passed. Thankfully daylight finally came, but then it was time to begin the daily training routine.

Becoming a soldier was a painful transition. At Camp Hooker, the men were readied in the school of the soldier and as combatants. A day of training ". . . consisted of shooting with ball cartridges at a mark; also shooting with blank cartridges by the Co. in the afternoon; dress parade, and practicing firing by companies, by files, by right and left oblique at will; and also as fast as we could load and shoot by the whole regiment."[21]

On the first day of October the regiment's camp was moved to higher ground above the river.[22] Perhaps feeling more secure, the men were becoming more adventuresome in exploring the surrounding area. They also began learning how to forage. Foraging was considered basic to survival and often practiced with discretaion, amounting to little more than

28

*Captain Felix Duffie of Kalamazoo, commanding
Company K, after his release from Libby Prison.
[Michigan History Division]*

stealing. Unless checked by officers, most men helped
themselves to whatever they wanted. On an early occasion,
Charley Prentiss and Jim Batchelder, buddies from Allegan

County persuaded a cow to stand still long enough to fill two canteens with milk. Another party slipped across the river into Kentucky and brought back six horses and a mule. Apparently Colonel Gilbert went along with the requisition as he selected one of the horses for his own personal mount.[23]

These experiences helped enliven camp life. And scouting the area was not restricted to soldiers, for civilians would sometimes come to the camp with a variety of motives. On one such occasion, the regiment ". . . had the pleasure of drumming 2 laydes out of camp & set them a drift on the rail road."[24] To protect his men, Gilbert would have to tighten his security knowing some of his sentries would not find these floozies so objectionable. Anyway, it was all part of being a Civil War soldier and a commander of volunteer troops.

The regiment suffered its first losses here along the river as several men died of disease. At its height, those who were afflicted with sickness and disease numbered upwards of 200.[25] Although some of the men contracted measles, diarrhea was the more serious problem. According to the Assistant Surgeon, Dr. John Bassett, the local source of well and spring water contained large quantities of sulphates which helped produce diarrhea. The alternative was to drink river water and it was far from an appetizing choice. Bassett explained that ". . . the men can hardly bring themselves to drink river water, because they have seen a dead horse in it a mile or two above, and they say we are drinking the washings of the sewers of Cincinnati."[26] Their plight caused many a soldier to dream longingly of a drink from a fresh clear Michigan stream.

Early in October, Braxton Bragg's army began retreating, the immediate threat to Louisville and Cincinnati had passed. Federal forces were then concentrated in Covington in preparation to pursue the Confederates south. Buell had orders to drive the Confederates from Kentucky and seize control of east Tennessee. Greatly concerned about protecting Nashville, he began pushing southwesterly, positioning units along the Louisville and Nashville Railroad.[27]

The 19th Michigan was a part of this general movement. Relieved of its duties of guarding the Ohio, the regiment was ordered to Covington. It broke camp around noon on October 14 and rode the train to Cincinnati. Here again, the regiment drew favorable attention, this time from the *Cincinnati Times* when it reported: "Gone Forward - The Nineteenth Michigan Regiment passed through the city yesterday. They are a splendid body of men and look as though they would do good service in the field."[28] The regiment marched across the pontoon bridge onto "Confederate soil" and took up camp some two miles from Covington. Here a great build up of troops was in the making. There were no cheers, flag waving or complimentary editorials when the regiment marched into Kentucky. In fact, the reception was noticeably cool.[29]

The 19th Michigan camped in a pleasant grove of walnut trees awaiting its orders to march south. As the concentration of union troops continued, the 19th was first introduced to the 33rd Indiana, a regiment with whom it would see considerable service in the future. The arrival of this regiment made a profound impression on the members of the 19th Michigan Infantry. Nearly every letter written from Covington at this time, included some reference to the appearance of this Hoosier regiment. The 33rd Indiana was already a veteran regiment, having fought at Wild Cat, Kentucky and recently withdrawn under heavy pressure from the Cumberland Gap. Along with several Kentucky regiments, the 33rd had marched to Cincinnati under very adverse conditions. When they arrived many were shoeless and some wore only their underwear. In short, they were a tough looking lot. To a sergeant in Company A, "They are the hardist looking men that I ever saw"[30] Most others would agree. "They teach a valuable lesson to our inexperienced and still 'independent' recruits . . . I tell you sir, the sight exhibits the shady side of soldiering and shows us who are just facing the realities of war, to what we are coming."[31] Their indoctrination continued.

The stay at Covington was brief for during the afternoon of October 18, the regiment struck tents and began marching toward Lexington. This was its first sustained march, covering 125 miles in eleven days. The men were broken in quickly as the terrain immediately south of Covington was especially

rugged and difficult to traverse. The hills were so steep that the
mule teams had to be doubled in order to haul the wagons up
the precipitous slopes. "We went up, up and the thought
struck me that we were going to Heaven; the idea of starting
from Dixie Land to go to that grand place!" [32] According to a
young first sergeant from Sturgis ". . . nothing but a
government mule and a United States soldier could have made
the journey, carrying the load we were compelled to . . ." [33]
That load was vividly described by another member of the
regiment when he wrote:

> . . . tell Martin that if he feels as though he would
> like to be a soldier to take a bushel of corn and travel
> twenty miles some day and see whether he likes it or
> not. I tell you what we have to carry we have a knapsack
> in which we put our clothing consisting of two chances
> of unde clothes, a heavy blanket dress coat and some
> little trinkets that (to a soldier) are indispensible and
> then we have our gun weighing about ten pounds and
> a cattridge box containing 40 rounds of cattridges and a
> haversack containing three days rations of hard crackers
> and meat and a canteen filled with water. . . [34]

The Nineteenth marched from Covington to Florence, to
Crittendon and then on to Falmouth, arriving there on October
21.

Falmouth was located on the Kentucky Central Railroad
where the Rebels had recently burned the bridge. When they
camped at Crittendon along the way, a family took their well
bucket off the rope, reminding these Yankees that there were
many Kentuckians who preferred the Confederacy. [35] Shortly
after arriving at Nicholsville a similar incident of defience
occurred. A black man was sent for water at a nearby well.
After drawing a pailful, a citizen appeared and ran him off. He
soon returned with an armed escort and the "freedman"
pumped the water while three southern civilians helplessly
looked on. [36] The regiment was also learning that if you did not

like the menu provided through the mess, there were other ways to supplement diet. Quantities of pork, beef, and poultry were consumed. At Falmouth " . . . we confiscated 25 sheep 100 gees & hens, 6 or 8 hogs & I think 8 horses." [37] Put another way, the regiment " . . . pressed into the service sheep and hogs enough each night to furnish us a good breakfast." [38] And all legitimized under the pretense of foraging.

The march took its toll as fatigued men left the ranks, units were detailed to pick up stragglers, others became ill, and in general, many suffered with sore feet. For certain, new socks were a highly sought item following the march. From Falmouth the regiment marched southwesterly following the course of the railroad. It passed through Cynthiana and Paris, arriving at Lexington on October 28.

The stop at Lexington was a welcome opportunity to rest. The regiment's campsite was located in a beautiful grove of trees. Among those who suffered most during the march were two of the regiment's company commanders. Both Captains Elisha Bassett and Hazen Brown were overcome by sickness. Bassett, apparently suffered with typhoid fever. Both were confined to a private home with orderlies detailed to care for them.[39] The family in whose home Captains Basset and Brown convalesced illustrated the philosophical division among Kentuckians. The soldier assigned to care for Captain Bassett described these divided loyalties:

> The family where we are stopping have four sons in the rebel army. The father is a union man, but the mother and all the children are seceshionists. The old lady appears to be a Christian, but she thinks the South has been oppressed. The bible upholds slavery, and it is therefore right; and any thing that has a tendency to do away with slavery, is so much towards robbing them of their property, and about here they stop reasoning and commence assertions that the south will never submit to have their property taken from them, that the difficulties can never be settled at the point of

33

the bayonet, that if Lincoln carries out his proclamation every Ky soldier in the union army will return home or go into the rebel army; and things will go wrong generally. [40]

In sharp rebuttal Phinehas Hager expressed his strong Union sentiments stating: "That proclamation is just what will be the salvation of the country. Just as I said several months ago, as you remember. I don't believe even the Kentucky soldiers will make any fuss about it when the time comes. Slavery will die hard of course, but that we must expect."[41]

It is not uncommon to read references to suspected faking or goldbricking in letters written by soldiers describing the conduct of other men. Like any other group of people, some soldiers and commissioned officers were just lazy. Inactivity and monotony probably cultivated that characteristic. John Howard, a twenty-year-old private from Allegan County, represented the opposite extreme being a very dutiful soldier. This first march would separate the men from the *men* and Howard was a *man*. The night before they reached Falmouth, he pulled guard duty. According to his first sergeant: "In the morning he complained of being unwell, and during the afternoon got permission to have his knapsack carried and before we got through rode himself. The last I saw of him he came to the Lieut. for a permit to ride. Poor boy! his marches are over."[42] John Howard died of disease in a Cincinnati hospital, 11 days later.

The weight of suffering was especially heavy during the Civil War. A man could be eliminated in so many ways and because he likely knew so many people in the military, he could not escape the agony of death. The war had just begun for Sergeant Hager but already he received painful news that his step son serving in another Michigan regiment had died. [43]

If anything characterized military life during the Civil War it was the prevalence of rumor. Soldiers often complained that they campaigned and marched ignorant of either their mission or destination. Yet they were never without speculation and rumor. As they became more experienced, soldiers placed less and less credence in forecasts of troop movements, impending battles and peace. Unquestionably, the most commonly heard rumor was that the war would soon be over. That possibility was being speculated about camp here at Leximgton and some of the officers were obviously trying to take advantage of the assumed naivety of the men. "Our officers are trying to speculate out of the poor soldiers by saying that they will give them 50 cents a day after 50 days as long as the war will last, if the soldiers or anyone else will give them 6 cents a day the first 50 days . . . A great many make their brags of being home to eat Christmas dinner. . ."[44]

Perhaps rumors were just wishful thinking because for some men, the war had already lasted too long. Charley Prentiss lamented his situation in a letter to his wife stating: "Just 3 months ago to day I put my name to the enlistment roll. It seems as though it was 3 years, & I am sorry a thousand times for I am not doing any earthly good here & haven't since I enlisted & don't think I shall, nor this Regt. we all want to come home."[45] Other men expressed this attitude in more drastic ways as several had already deserted. Writing to the editor of the *Kalamazoo Gazette*, Lieutenant Henry Ford threatened to expose these men publically. Some of whom according to Ford ". . . are well known in certain circles in Kalamazoo. I may furnish their names for publication in a roll of infamy should they not be caught and returned as they probably will".[46]

Dissatisfaction took many different forms not the least of which was frequently heard grumbling concerning the ineptness of certain officers. Most of course were handicapped by a total lack of military training. Their knowledge of the military and soldiering would be learned the hard way through experience and trial and error. Naturally opinions would change; sometimes for the better, which probably reflected the growing abilities of some officers. Seemingly this must have been the case with Sam Hubbard. With Bassett bedridden and First Lieutenant William Darrow assigned to headquarters staff, command of Company B evolved upon Second Lieutenant Hubbard. First Sergeant Phinehas Hager had grave doubts whether he was equal to the task. In a stinging remark to his wife he wrote: "He don't know what to do half so well as some of the men. The company is in bad condition."[47] Yet in the subsequent months, Hubbard would gain the confidence of the company and be one of the most respected officers in the regiment.

Others fared less favorably and probably with good cause. The unit's surgeon was particularly disliked. Negative feelings were strong enough to prompt the circulation of a petition calling for his dismissal. All three regimental doctors were indicted for being unsympathetic by a private when complaining to his wife that " , , , we have some of the worst, hard hearted, Doctors you ever saw." Supposedly paraphasing Surgeon William E. Clark, Private Prentiss reported that ", , , he says he had rather burry 150 men than to furlow 50 to go home. The boys are quite up about it." Before he could finish his letter ", , , a particion came in the tent to have our old hee Doctor removed from the Regt. His name is Clark. A brother-in-law to the Cor. he has been drumed out of 2 other Regiments before this we have 76 names in Co. B their will be about 800 names in the Regt. Woe be unto Doct Clark & Cor. Gilbert if we ever get into action." [48] There would be other strong expression of contempt voiced, and especially for Surgeon Clark; his relationship with the ranks would never improve.

The regiment settled in at Lexington uncertain as to whether it would move again prior to spring. The troops had not prepared winter quarters giving at least one strong indication that their stay would be short. Charley Prentiss aptly described life in a Sibley tent when he wrote:

. . to begin with we all set flat on the ground like so many taylors, my big drum at my right hand, me next with my portfolio writing a letter to my wife, & Dave at my left writing to his Brother Juleus, 3 or 5 scratching around in the straw a making their bed like so many hogs. V. Rose writing a letter to some one, Ike Kenney, Tim Dagget, Ed. Baird & John Duel haveing a gaim of

cards & the rest telling stories, the center of the tent is
a stack of guns & our Candle sticks is a baynet stuck in
the ground, but a little while ago Hubbard was in here &
we had a sing. [49]

Prentiss was one of the regimental drummers and enjoyed
music a lot. Soldiers often gathered at his tent for a sing. While
most soldiers requested food and articles of clothing from
home, Prentiss asked his wife to send the "words to burry me
not in the deep deep see, & . . the Miss Brown song." [50]

Seemingly wherever the Union army moved, bands of
Negros followed along. Despite Kentucky's prearious balance
in the Union and support of the Union, these slaves were now
being retained and used as servants and laborers. The 19th
Michigan had attracted a sizeable caravan of blacks on its
march from Covington. "Our company of contrabands appears
to be on the increase. They have one or two about the hospital
the Col. and Major each have one, and I don't think there is a
company in the regiment whose officers have not one or more,
Other regiments I think have more than we have, and I hear of
none being sent back to their masters; indeed that thing is
'played out.' " [51]

Winter was approaching as the evenings turned cold, and
temperatures dropped below freezing; so cold that " . . . the ice
frose hard enough . . . to bare up a mule." [52]

3

GARRISONED AT
NICHOLSVILLE

While at Lexington, the 19th Michigan, 33rd Indiana Infantry, 85th Indiana Infantry, and the 22nd Wisconsin Infantry joined to form the 1st Brigade, 3rd Division, Army of Kentucky.[1] Commanded by Colonel John Coburn, these four regiments would remain brigaded for the rest of the war and often be referred to as Coburn's brigade. Coburn, a native of Indianapolis, entered military service as the first commander of the 33rd Indiana Infantry. Coburn was then 36 years old. He was a graduate of Wabash College and, like his father, was a lawyer. He had spent several years prior to the war in public service as a representative in the Indiana Legislature and later as Judge of the Court of Common Pleas at Marion, Indiana. Following his resignation in 1864, Coburn distinguished himself in Congress during four consecutive terms. Among other measures, he was a leading proponent for publication of the *Official Records*.[2]

In addition to Colonel Gilbert, his regimental commanders included Colonel James P. Baird, 85 Indiana; Lieutenant Colonel James M. Henderson, 33rd Indiana; and Colonel William L. Utley, 22nd Wisconsin.

Like most volunteer officers in the Civil War, Coburn and his regimental commanders were short on military experience. Coburn, Baird, and Gilbert had all been members of the legal profession prior to the war. "Utley was a veteran of political

39

wars only." He had served as a state senator and adjutant-general prior to the war. Jim Henderson was teaching at the Morton Academy, Princeton, Indiana, when the hostilities began. [3]

The regiments they commanded were do different. Only the 33rd Indiana had experienced combat previously. The rest would be initiated soon.

Henderson, at 26, was the youngest among Coburn's subordinates; Utley was senior having reached his 48th birthday. None would see the war to its end. Yet all but Gilbert would survive it. When Coburn's term expired in 1864, he returned to political life. Both Baird and Henderson resigned due to disability during the same year. Utley too, ended his military service in 1864, following a bitter quarrel with his second in command, Lieutenant Colonel Edward Bloodgood.

Striking tents early on the morning of November 13, 1862, the regiment began its movement to Nicholsville. On its way it passed the camp of the 18th and 22nd Michigan Infantry Regiments. Upon learning that it was the 19th Michigan passing, these fellow Wolverines gave "three rousing cheers . and the 10th Kentucky (they were camped on the fair ground) called out loudly 'Bully for Michigan.' "[4]

Coburn's brigade covered the 15 mile trek without incident arriving by mid afternoon Nicholsville was the southern terminus of the Kentucky Central Railroad making it militarily significant. Its 2,000 residents contained a high proportion of slaves. Unlike other parts of Kentucky, members of the regiment expressed a low opinion of the town. Sergeant Ira Carpenter felt Nicholsville manifested a "funeral like aspect." In similar fashion, Samuel Hewitt described the town as "a poor looking place. There are very few good looking buildings here. The most of the buildings were put up when Adam was a boy I should think." [5]

Once again, there was plenty of discussion whether this was going to be the regiment's winter quarters. Camp life went on as usual except for increasing frequency of funerals. Death caused by disease was striking a frightening number of men. The regiment had suffered its first casualty back at Gravel Pit on October 5. Six others died during October and four more in November. Yet the worst was to come in December as the 19th Michigan was fighting an unexpected foe. The enemy was disease and the frequency of death during this time must have had a dreadful impact on those who survived, naturally wondering and worrying about who would be next. The December casualty list with ages indicated in parenthesis underscores the shuddering consequence of just getting sick: December 5 - Albert Baker (25) and Alonzo Berry (20); December 6 - John Barrett (26), John Benedict (18) and Obediah Wright (23); December 12 - John Davis (23); December 13 - Charles Miller (20); December 15 - Charles Brown (18); December 17 - William Furney (25); December 18 - Julius Lease (45), Luther Miller (26) and Samuel Shafer (22); December 20 - Norman Wilson (38); December 25 - Sargent Whaley (23); December 27 - Guilford Hare (19); December 30 - Clark Brainard (20). The death rolls totaled 16 for December and most occurred at Nicholsville. Charles Connor must have expressed what many others were thinking when he wrote: "We have not been in any fight yet but the fighting don't trouble me half so much as the Devilish Decesses in camp."6

Digging graves became a common work detail, reminding the grave diggers of the odds of their own death. The men felt a real concern about the proper care and internment of deceased soldiers. After his friend Guilford Hare died, Private Judson Austin wrote: "They are talking about sending the corps home. If they can raise money enough. I have got 1 dollar & they can have it. When I see him on the cares with a good honest man to go with it. I will give my last shilling to send any of the boys home out of this Co. and think they would do the same for me."7

What a soldier knew of the war was based primarily on what he read in the newspaper. On the other hand many men like Sam Hewitt sought to keep folks back home informed by writing to the editor of the local newspaper. He was often facetiously called the editor of the *Allegan Journal*. Unquestionably Hewitt took great pleasure in seeing his letters produced in print. And if the editor did not send him a complimentary copy, he would complain. Many did not receive a newspaper but copies were shared and in some instances, one would read aloud as others gathered to hear the news. [8]

Like drill and guard duty, inspection was a part of a soldier's training routine. Frequently these inspections were conducted by higher commands and it gave the men in the ranks an opportunity to get a look at some of the general officers. Their frank impressions written to family and friends provide interesting glimpses of many high ranking officers. During its stay at Nicholsville, the unit went through a brigade inspection conducted by Brigadier General Henry M. Judah and Colonel Coburn. General Judah was a graduate of West Point in the same class with U.S. Grant. His assignment at the time was that of Acting Inspector General.[9] According to Private Hewitt, the General took a close look. "He is a fine looking fellow about 5 feet 10 inches in height, and a German I should say. Company B carried off the palm for the guns and for neatness of dress and packing their knapsacks. Not wishing to brag but Co. B has carried off the palm every time." [10] Within ten days the regiment was examined again, this time by Generals Absalom Baird and Horatio Wright. Brigadier General Baird was the regiment's division commander. To his sweetheart back home in Martin, Private Henry Noble described General Wright as ", . . a very ordinary looking man and were it not for this uniform he would not look much like a gan." [11] Noble was certain that his girl was really missing something. As he described it: "There were four Regs of infantry and two Batteries I wish you could have been here and seen them drill. It is quite a sight to see nearly five thousand men all armed and equipped and formed into companies of from fifty to one hundred each." [12] His enthusiastic impression was shared by Hewitt. Their comments reflected a growing esprit de corps and despite obvious bias, indicated that the regiment was becoming proficient on at least the drill field. Hewitt reported that:

> . . . when the Michigan boys had to pass into Review they did so with a bold front, a still upper lip and heads erect and when the tail end of the Regiment passed by (which is company B) they came on with a heavy tread,

a right dress and a step with the music every time and Gen. Wright complimented our company and said ours was the best line and our marching was ahead of any company. After the review we returned to camp and formed in a line and soon the General rode through our company street and gave the Regiment the credit of having the cleanest quarters and being the best looking and sized Regiment he had seen in a long time. The batteries fired a salute in the evening in honor of the General. . . 13

As for Company B's superiority, comments from soldiers of other companies are not available. Regardless of its validity, it made for good reading back in Allegan.

Nearly three months had passed since the regiment had been organized and received its only pay. By Thanksgiving Day, the enlisted men were broke. Like many other soldiers, Charley Prentiss wrote home to his wife asking her to send some money. Assuming that she was in similar financial straits, he suggested that she borrow some for both of them. He informed her that "'. . . there is no money in the Regt. that most of the officers have sent home for money for their own use, and growl a great deal because they are not paid off." Strangely enough he requested Confederate currency, stating "'. . . if you send me any be *sure* and send Southern money in one dollar bills, our northern money is of no account here. . ."' 14 A sergeant in Company F compensated for his poverty by using counterfeit currency or as some called it, Kalamazoo money. His treachery was soon exposed:

The boys are getting hard up for cash and a few of them resort to the shameful crime of passing off bad money on the nonsuspecting citizens that bring privisions into camp. One of these rascals bought a hog of a poor ignorant fellow that could neither read nor write. He paid him two dollars for the hog in Kalamazoo Railroad money. He gave him five dollars of this worthless stuff and received three dollars of good money in return. But he got his reward or is getting it fast now. He was caught at it and brought up before the Colonel and when at night we went out on dress parade he was marched up before the Reg and his sentence was read. He was denounced as a villain and unfit to associate with honest men and he was to be paraded in front of the Reg and have the rogues march played for his special benefit and was to be kept under guard and do the manual labor of the camp for one month and live on bread and water half of the time. This may seem hard but it was just. [15]

Ⅹ Basically this non-commissioned officer's actions were deceitful; it was fraudulent and the same as stealing. In many regiments foraging was also considered stealing, yet sometimes the difference between what was legal and illegal represented a very fine distinction. It apparently made a difference whether one was an officer or just one of the ranks. Regardless of the decision, it mattered most whether or not one got caught. The disparities are illustrated by an enlisted man's account of an incident which occurred at Nicholsville while he served as corporal of picket. With apparent pride he wrote: "We stole a lot of stuff from Secesh pedlers that they was going to sell to our soldiers. We stopped one man and found out that he favored the South. We took 125 warm biscuits from him a lot of butter, a lot of apples pies and pickles and in fact we stripped his wagon and told him we would put him in the guard house if he did not start off." [16]

The regiment experienced its first holiday away from home in November. For those who stayed in camp, Thanksgiving dinner was not exactly a feast. Hewitt wrote that governor Austin Blair had urged regimental commanders to make the day a festive occasion, yet the 19th Michigan lacked the means of doing it. As he put it, they lacked "the ready John Davis." [17] In camp the men ate boiled salt beef and hard crackers and drank coffee. Many of them secured passes, left camp, and enjoyed Thanksgiving dinner as guest of Kentucky families. [18]

Mail call was always a big event as soldiers waited eagerly

and impatiently for letters. "Some of them crowd & stand with their mouth & eyes stretched open anxious to hear their name called. When last name is called some of the boys go off feeling light hearted & happy. They got a letter. Others go off swearing; saying they will not write another letter home till they get one from home. Others say nothing to any body but turn & walk back to their tent with a sober look & wate for tomorrow night."[19] And if a package arrived, it was a celebrated occasion. Given the general shortage of cash, soldiers were making increased demands on their families for clothing, food and other items. Sergeant Hager even wrote fewer letters because he was forced to economize on postage. Writing appreciatively to his wife for sending a package filled with goodies, Charley Prentiss began:

> In reply to your letter in a red shirt pocket without dated I will let you know that the box arrived here yesterday It would be amuseing to you to see the anxious eyes that watched the contence as we over-halled it. onely 20 in the tent 16 ft in circumference. It arrived here safe except one thing. that is the honey box spring a leak & run through the box some. my shirts was not dobed very much. the box was mark rong side up, I never had anything come & looked so good as the contence of that box. I would like to know how much the charges were. you need be scared I shant eat it up to fast. I shall string it out as long as we can. Those shirts are tiptop no fault to find. Dave likes mine the best. when we get our pay you will have some money to pay for this job The fruit cake we will not cut yet a while that has got to last also the butter, when we cut it I will tell you how good it is. That pillow is the nicest thing yet, that has got to go with me where ever I go. I layed awake most all night last night athinking, of what you know. you cant imagine how a fether pillow feels under my head, The butter we shall leave in the can. I can keep it frose farther than that we have nothing els to keep it in. I will resk it, the cakes was passed around this

morning in the squad, (our squad consists of 16 men) & the tast of them allmost brought the tears to their eyes, put them in mind home, when the boys get their box they will devide I am sorry that I did not send for a par of boot taps. I dont care how large a cheese we get, we can take care of it. Chese is a great treat to have to eat with our army bread, that dont get cut wright off. I am satesfied with the tobaco I did not think it was so high. It will be the last that I shall buy. this will last me untill I get home If it would send me the tribune evry week after you get done with it if you can pay the postage. I dont know but I am asking to much of you. but you must excuse me for begging so much. [20]

Despite the routine of military life, there was still enough novelty to cause soldiers to write vivid accounts of their daily activities. They explained to wives and friends how weapons functioned, the details of military exercises and a variety of other occurrences involving the life of a soldier. Henry Noble wrote of a long cold night on picket duty at Nicholsville and decided he had better explain to his lady friend what was involved. "I will tell you a number of men are detailed every morning and they are sent out in groups of from ten to fourteen and about a mile from camp to intercept all wandering soldiers and citizens that have no papers and to give alarm in case of an attack This is the duty of pickets during the day only one stands at a time. But at night they generaly send out two or three more in different places." [21]

One evening at formation, the Colonel introduced a new officer. First Lieutenant Timothy Turner had just been mustered in as the Regiment's first Quartermaster. Turner from Coldwater, ". . . made a short speech and the Regiment gave him 3 rousing cheers. He was and will be well received by the Regiment." [22]

Since November 17, Company E had been detailed to guard the Hickman Creek Bridge spanning the Kentucky River some eight miles south of the village. They remained at the river until Thanksgiving Day. A part of their experience was

46

reminiscent of the regiment's performance during the first few nights at Gravel Pit. Supposedly its pickets were fired on, the long roll was sounded and the company sprang to arms. The incident even led to extra and "secret" pickets. But "the whole confounded thing was a sham made up by some of the boys." [23]

While located at Nicholsville, members of the regiment gained increased awareness of the divided loyalties of Kentuckians. Some Kentuckians would attempt to hide their Rebel sentiments yet their Negroes would regularly give them away.[24] This was a tactic used by southerners to protect their property from foragers. Politically, Kentucky had to be handled carefully and the practice of guarding southern Property really rankled some Union soldiers and officers. Ira Carpenter compained that: "The same old routine of guarding rebel property and allowing the owners all the rights of Union men, is being pursued . . . (for) we are under Generals who seem bound to keep Kentucky in the Union after the President's proclamation of freeing the slaves in the rebel States goes into operation." [25] Personally, Carpenter was convinced that the majority of Kentuckians were Confederates at heart. "Many persons in Michigan have an idea that there are but few Kentuckians in favor of the rebel cause, but it is not so. Probably along the Ohio River a good share of the inhabitants are for the Union, but hereabouts they are scarce. The men that live near our camp profess to be friendly but if you visit their homes the women, being less guarded in their conversation express in the strongest terms their hatred of the north." [26] But one of the officers saw it the opposite way. Lieutenant George Shaffer eagerly sought out Kentuckians and became acquainted with several families. "There are as good Union men in Kentucky as there are anywhere but they are not abolitionists; they do not like Abraham's proclamation." [27]

In their correspondence, soldiers frequently vented their feelings about comrades. Officers, both non-commissioned and commissioned, were most often the targets of their criticism. At least among the correspondence of this regiment, negative comments far outweigh words of praise. Perhaps it is human nature to complain more often about shortcomings than to commend admirable behavior. Many of the men and their wives were probably acquainted before the war due to the practice of recruiting companies from a particular locale. In many instances they were undoubtedly neighbors, friends or relatives. Yet the military with its system of rank imposed some new relationship Given an egalitarian citizen-based and volunteer army, adjustments were not easy. There was jealousy and distrust to overcome. There were some men who played by the rules, and others who preferred to play. One of these relationships which is gleaned from correspondence, involved three members of Company B. The threesome included a private, sergeant and second lieutenant, all from Otsego. Private Charley Prentiss was in a squad commanded by Sergeant Phinehas Hager. Both were subordinate to Lieutenant Samuel Hubbard. These men were a little older than most soldiers; Prentiss was 31, Hubbard 33, and Hager the senior at 42.[28] Prior to the war, Prentiss earned a living farming. Lieutenant Hubbard had served as justice of the peace and Hager taught school. During the war, the three crossed sabers on more than one occasion. As a drummer Prentiss enjoyed the privilege of being exempt from most duties. Faking a malady was not beneath his dignity. In a letter to his wife he confessed that "when the regiment left us at Nicholsville I was not able to march (at least I pretended so(& I did not want to leave the company & if I stayed with the Co. I would have easy times. . ."[29] No questions, he liked a good time. He must have been one of the regiment's best foragers, often arrogantly confiscating property. Two of his tent mates were relatives, David Anderson and Ancil Baird. To top it all off, he had a very familiar relationship with Lieutenant Hubbard.

Sergeant Hager also shared the same squad tent with Prentiss but there was no affection between the two. Hager's approach to life and especially soldiering was decidedly different. He was a "Puritan" who possessed a strong sense of morality. Indeed Hager was a strick disciplinarian who wanted his company to run in an efficient and orderly manner. Charley

Portrait of Charles Prentiss still preserved in its ornate case. [Archie Nevins]

Prentiss believed that his sergeant was too strict and exceeded his authority. "What I have said about Mr. H. please keep it to yourself. All there is about it He tryed to use to much authority, more than belongs to him."[30] And he might have been right. A least on one occasion, Lieutenant Hubbard thought so. While the regiment was at Nicholsville, Sergeant Hager received a

49

letter from Mrs. Stephen Knapp inquiring of her husband's whereabouts. His suggestion to Hubbard that he attempt to locate Private Knapp provoked the lieutenant:

Perhaps I ought to say nothing but I felt myself more abused by Hubbard a day or two since than by any officer since I enlisted. I took the liberty to say to him that as he now had the entire command of the company he ought to try and ascertain where Mr. Knapp was. He said he was not going to write a dozen letters for such a purpose. I told him I should feel as though an officer ought to do what he could to relieve the anxiety of the friends of men under his command. He told me that he knew his own business, and did not wish to be instructed, and of course I said no more. I think he was sorry for what he said, for he did commense to make inquiries . . . [31]

Hager felt affronted yet he partially excused the lieutenant stating ". . . I presume he did not feel well at the time." [32] In the same context; however, he made his feelings very clear. "You must not say anthing about it in Otsego. There are men in the company I prise more highly than Hubbard, David Anderson, or Charley Prentiss. If I ever go home I can tell you why." [33]

In his correspondence Prentiss more often than not referred to Lieutenant Samuel Hubbard as "Hubbard" yet Sergeant Phinehas Hager was always "Mr. Hager." Unquestionably, "Mr. Hager" possessed a high sense of duty; he was also a man of strong conviction. His views on slavery were clear; it was morally wrong and ought to die. He believed in prosecuting the war with vigor. He despised drunkenness and laziness. He lacked patience with those who were selfish. Consistent with his principles, he would prefer to eat a meager Thanksgiving meal in camp rather than breach his honor by "begging" a Kentucky family to include him.

Relationships did improve. At least Sam Hubbard grew to respect his top sergeant referring to him on one occasion as "the father of the company." Hager was promoted to first sergeant in May, 1863, while Hubbard became the company commander and earned the rank of captain a month later.[34]

To his wife, Sergeant Hager speculated about where he might go next: "I hear it rumored that the Regt. will go into winter quarters at Danville . . ."[35] On the next day, December 12, rumors became orders and the regiment moved farther south.

THEY DIED TO MAKE MEN FREE

4

WINTER QUARTERS AT DANVILLE

The regiment got an early start on its march to Danville. Crossing the Kentucky River at Boone Cave, it covered the 14 mile journey to Camp Dick Robinson in about seven hours, arriving there at noon. Camp Dick Robinson had recently been occupied by Confederates under General Braxton Bragg; they left behind large stores of pork and several spiked cannon. This trip toward Danville caused Sergeant John Griffis to seek a little sympathy from his brother Tom as he challenged: " . . . if you think Soulgering funn Suppose you bild up a fire in the field and lay thare all nite and then take fifty three lbs and march the next day and if it don't take the fighing propencity out of you are a hed of me that all I can say." [1]

The 33rd and 85th Indiana Regiments were a day ahead having departed Nicholsville on the 11th. The 22nd Wisconsin and 19th Michigan marched together and reached Danville on December 13.[2] Confusion reigned as the men tried to set up camp. Each exercise of pitching tents was followed by an order to break camp and move. The futility was repeated three times taking up most of the day until finally the tents stayed up at a location a good mile and a half from the regiment's first campsite. [3]

On the day the regiment reached Danville, General Order Number 24 appointing a General Court Martial to try Captain George H. White was issued by Division Headquarters. White who commanded Company H was charged with contemptuous and disrespectful behavior toward his commanding officer. The specifications as drawn by Colonel Gilbert charged that Captain White:

> . . . did, on or about the 18th day of November, A.D. 1862, in the presence of several men and officers of Co. H of said Regiment, use harsh, reproachful, and abusive language of and concerning Col. H. C. Gilbert, commanding said Regiment, and did among other things say in substance: "Go tell the Col. he has made a fool of himself; he has made a (here using a word too obscene and vulgar to be written) of himself; tell him to go to hell with his guardhouse," which language the said Capt George H. White requested a private in his said Co. H to repeat to said Col. H. C. Gilbert. [4]

Yet, interestingly enough, this was the second charge brought against Captain White, the first having been dropped. The first charge stemmed directly from the strained relations between Surgeon William Clark and the regiment as a whole. If appears that Clark was perceived as a heartless hard-nosed doctor showing little compassion for the ailments and sickness experienced by these soldiers. Contrary to Prentiss' accusation, Dr. Clark was not the colonel's brother-in-law and had not been dismissed from two other regiments. The two officers were cousins and Clark had served previously as surgeon in the 4th Michigan Infantry. [5] His being related to the colonel caused some to assume that the Doctor would be given special consideration and that probably happened. In fairness to Clark, he surely saw enough cases of shirking duty and faking sickness to make him very disgusted and insensitive. In addition, he was probably victimized by rumor and exaggeration. Yet whether real or imagined, Clark had acquired a horrible reputation. After digging a grave, Private Austin related the circumstances of the soldier's death in which Surgeon Clark appeared very negligent:

Captain William E. Clarke of Dowagiac served as the regiment's first surgeon. [Chicago Historical Society]

This man was sick & not able to march when we came from Lexington here he get so bad before he got here that he stopped & layed down on the way side. The Doctor Mr. Clark came along & told him to get up & walk or he would run over him with his horse the man did not get up & the Doc did not run over him the Col. cam along & the old Doc happened to see him before he get quite to him so the Doc jumped & when the Col. came up Doc was trying to help the man up & put him on his own horse. They got him on after a while & got him here. Today the man died. What dou think the old Doc cares about. You never will hear of my getting so far gon that I cant get onto a horse before I get to a stoping

place & then if any of the Doctors want to ride over me
they most take what follows. dont'know as I ought to
write such a letter about my officers over me. If they
shoued get hold of this they would put me in the guard
house likely as not. Wonder if any the rest of the boys
say anything about their officers. 6

That relationship deteriorated beyond repair in November
while the regiment was stationed at Nicholsville. According to
Charley Prentiss, 840 signatures were affixed to a petition
calling for Clark's dismissal.[7] His figure seems incredibly high;
however, Lieutenant Shaffer also related that the petition
contained over 800 signatures.[8] Colonel Gilbert was obviously
upset and anxious to squelch this uprising. Whatever his role,
George White became the scapegoat. He was first charged
with ". . . conduct prejudicial to good order and military
discipline." More specifically that he ". . . did, on or about the
15th and 17th days of Nov., 1862, allow and permit to be
circulated among the privates and men under his command, for
their signatures, a certain written paper, containing
reproachful, ungentlemanly, and seditious language of and
concerning William E. Clark . . ." [9] Now in order for 800 plus
men to sign a petition it must have circulated freely among all
companies. Seemingly all company commanders would have
been guilty of the same offense. Captain White was under
arrest for this offense when he compounded his problems by
lashing out at Colonel Gilbert. The fact that Gilbert was himself
a lawyer and promptly dropped the first charge suggests that
he knew it was a flimsy allegation. The situation was tense, and
unquestionably men feared reprisals for participating in a
campaign to dispose of Surgeon Clark. This whole affair must
have been the talk of the regiment, yet men were guardedly
silent in their correspondence. Even Chaplain Cogshall, who
was called as a character witness for Chaptain White made no
mention of the episode in his private journal. Among the
correspondence and accounts examined, only four men;
Lieutenant Shaffer, Sergeant Griffis, Private Austin and
Private Prentiss referred to the affair. [10]   Shaffer carefully

instructed his wife to burn his letter; fortunately for history she did not comply.[11] It appears significant that Shaffer and Griffis, both members of Company A, were the only ones who mentioned their comrade "Jerry" who sought to expose the shortcomings of both Captain Clark and Colonel Gilbert. It is reasonable to speculate the "Jerry" was a member of Company A. Because of the risks involved, he wrote under an assumed name publicly criticizing Clark and Gilbert. His letters were printed in the *Cass County Democrat*, a newspaper published in the same county where Caompny A was raised.[12] Shaffer agreed with "Jerry's" attack stating: "This much I can say, that what he wrote in regard to Dr. C is most of it, if not all true. The Col is a relative of his, so of course he will favor him and keep him in the service if he can. The Dr. treats the men very differently since over eight hundred men in the regiment signed a petition to have him dismissed from the service; and since Jerry came down on him so hard. So these things have done some good." Lieutenant Shaffer went on to include an evaluation of the colonel's performance:

> The Col is not a military man but he is exerting himself tremendously lately to make this a crack regiment. He is learning to drill pretty fast and is gaining the good will of his men. They think a great deal more of him now that they did a few months ago. If he does stand (sometimes when he does not know what to do) like the paddy waiting for the water of a mighty river to run down so he could cross (as Jerry said) I think he will make a pretty good Colonel with a sufficiency of experience. [13]

Shaffer also hinted that he knew "Jerry" but denied speculation that he was the ghost writer. He cautioned his wife about discussing the contents of his letter saying, "I don't want anybody to know that I have an idea who wrote those letters."[14] There is evidence that at least one man took serious exception to "Jerry's" appraisal and offered a stern rebuttal in a letter to the editor of a rival newspaper, the *Cass County*

Republican. He rebuked the editor of the *Democrat* for accepting the validity of "Jerry's" charges and publishing two of his letters. This 19th Michigan correspondent, known as "Tyro," then censured "Jerry" calling him a "villian" and "lazy shirk"while indicating that "Jerry's" accustations were made in retaliation after being punished for stealing sheep. Crediting his commander for having "superior executive ability," "Tyro" forecefully defended Colonel Gilbert. He recalled the praise of two reviewing officers as evidence of the regiment's condition and level of readiness. "Major Gen. Wright expressed himself highly pleased with the order and discipline of our camp and regiment. This you may say should be placed to the credit of our Major. True, he gets his share, but without the executive ability and energy of the commanders, the experience of the Major would be insufficient. Remember always that men from civil life have much to learn, to become good military men, and none should fail to learn that order and discipline must be preserved." 15

Finally, in regard to Shaffer and this incident, he informed his wife that he had been Colonel Gilbert's dinner guest and on another occasion, socialized with the colonel and General Baird.16 Since there is no indication that Lieutenant Shaffer was the colonel's fair-haired boy, this fraternizing causes one to wonder about its motivation.

The court convened on December 22 with Lieutenant Colonel Edward Bloodgood, 22nd Wisconsin, serving as President and Lieutenant Henry Ford, 19th Michigan, as Judge Advocate. The court as sworn in included major William Shafter, 19th Michigan, Major Robert Craig, 85th Indiana, Captain Joel Smith, 19th Michigan; Captain Charles Smith, 22nd Wisconsin; and Captain Abner Floyd, 85 Indiana. Absent members were Major Levin Miller, 33rd Indiana, Captain George Williamson, 22nd Wisconsin, and Captain William Reeder, 85th Indiana. 17   As is abundantly clear, Captain White was tried by his own brigade. Captain White pleaded not guilty to the charges that were read. The Judge Advocate commenced his prosecution by calling three witnesses, all of whom were present at the time Captain White allegedly behaved in a contemptuous and disrespectful manner, Lieutenant James Shoecraft, an officer in White's company, took the stand first. His testimony strongly confirmed the prosecution's charges. According to Shoecraft, the incident occurred at the headquarters of Company H. Supposedly the colonel's orderly came to the company commander's tent and Captain White began querying him as to who was at regional headquarters and what he had heard about his case. This conversation led to Captain White's alleged outburst toward Colonel Gilbert. White, serving as his own legal counsel, began cross-examining the witness. His questions were intended to shift the responsibility to Harrison Rockafellow, the colonel's orderly, by establishing that he (White) had not instructed him to carry a message but instead left that decision to his judgement Shoecraft did not remember it that way. He maintained that Captain White's language clearly communicated his desire that Rockafellow deliver the captain's sentiments to Colonel Gilbert. The court then asked the witness whether Rockafellow had expressed any concern that Captain White and his company would be upset with him if he followed through and carried the message to the colonel. Lieutenant Shoecraft recalled the Rockafellow said: "If I should go and tell the colonel what you have said, you and the whole company would be down on me for it." According to Shoecraft, the captain responded by stating: "No, I would not; what I say, I say openly; I would say it to Col Gilbert as soon as to you."[18] Captain White continued to question his lieutenant hoping to show that the colonel's orderly had used initiating language and that his own response was made during a moment of anger. The lieutenant did not agree that Rockafellow's language was provoking. He did acknowledge that the captain ". . . was speaking pretty warmly . . ."

Next, Lieutenant David Anderson Company H was called as a witness for the prosecution. His testimony generally followed the pattern of the first witness. White countered by asking the lieutenant to comment on whether he (Captain White) was angry and as to his character as an officer. Anderson did not sense that Captain White was particularly angry. He attested that the captain had generally tried to fulfill his duties.

Rockafellow followed Anderson to the stand. Along with affirming the prosecution's case, he claimed to have warned Captain White that his statements could get him in trouble. "I told him they would shove him in the guard-house if he didn't look out." [19] Captain White's cross-examination followed the course applied to previous witnesses. Nothing Rockafellow said in response helped White's case.

The court reconvened on Tuesday morning, December 23 with Colonel Henry C. Gilbert called as a witness for the defense. White first asked his commander to explain the circumstances of his initial arrest. He then asked the colonel to recall a subsequent conversation in which he apologized for his actions. The colonel answered that he remembered such a meeting. "At that interview Capt White denied having used the language imputed to him in the manner in which it is stated in the specifications. He admitted that he had used improper language, and said something by way of apology but what I cannot now recollect particularly.'[20] In response to another query, the colonel acknowledged receiving a written apology from Captain White about two weeks after the incident. Apparently White had also apologized to Surgeon Clark. This written apology was presented to the court. It concluded with a plea of forgiveness. "I trust this apology, freely made will be sufficient to have the past forgotten, letting the *future* be my record.'[21] At this point, Captain White sought to stand on his past performance asking the colonel if he had not set a good example and faithfully carried out his responsiblities. As a witness for the defense, the colonel was not cooperating. He responded "No . . Capt White is one of the class of officers that may be called *troublesome* - indisposed to obey orders conflicting with his notions, without argument, frequently violating military rules that were well known and understood by the whole regiment." [22] White challenged him to recall a single incident of this nature. Colonel Gilbert obliged by recounting the captain's actions the day following the regiment's arrival at Gravel Pit. According to Colonel Gilbert, White, without authorization, left his company, crossed the river and walked around most of the morning examining the Kentucky side.

The defense then called Lieutenant William Darrow, Chaplain Israel Cogshall, Captain Charles Bigelow, Lieutenant Hamlet Adams, and Lieutenant Lucius Wing each as a character witness. All spoke of his good character even though Lieutenant Adams and Wing may have offered some damaging testimony in referring to incidents which illustrated less than exemplary conduct.

The afternoon session opened with the submission of an "address" presented by Captain White. His statement was read to the court. After summarizing the arguments in his defense and apparently anticipating the court's decision, he stated: " . . . allow me to say that I would not think of remaining in a regiment when the Col was my enemy - as I am sorry to say Col Gilbert appears to be - for in such a place I could not serve my country which is my earnest desire to do - But I hope I may never be obliged to have it disgraced."[23] The court reached its decision: Captain George H. White was guilty. It sentenced him to be dismissed from the service. The findings and sentence were approved and on March 1, 1863, George White was again a civilian.

When the regiment departed Nicholsville, Company B was left behind to serve as provost guard. Their duties entailed providing security for the railroad and commissary stores. They also loaded railroad cars and guarded prisoners. On one occasion a detail escorted nine prisoners to Lexington. Duty was easy and they enjoyed being separated from the regiment.[24] Charley Prentiss and Dave Anderson attended church but found the service a little strange and the singing disappointing. ". . . The way they do here is to stand up to pray and sit down to sing . ."[25] In his next letter, Prentiss told his wife that: "They have the worst singing that I ever hurd. When we go in and sing it makes them stair. I wish you all could come down here and show them how to sing. . ."[26]

Prentiss and others were also busy foraging. One morning they had a yearning for milk and set out to find some. Prentiss colorfully described the details of their adventure in a letter to his wife.

At daylight we started out for a real jenuine secesh
farmer 1½ mile from and just as we arrived there we
saw a wench with a bucket of milk on her head, we met
her, halt, was the command, ground arms, was the
command. The bucket of milk was set before us, the
next in was to fill our containers. Some 15 or 20-
appeared to us from the house but dare not say a word,
we were busy filling our containers we saw the old he
one coming from the one house back with a gun in his
hand. He road up to the gate dismounted came storming
in with his gun. thinking to scare us. I drew my revolver
and cocked it, and stood before him. He soon cooled
down we got milk and piked to the camp and had a good
breakfast besides a good bunch of fun . . . [27]

Prentiss was making a game out of confiscating southern
property. In haughty terms he boasted: "The secesh are affraid
of the Michigan soldiers. We make them do just as we want
them to. They dare do no other way. If they refuse down comes
their shanty." [28]   On another occasion Prentiss and Dave
Anderson appropriated a railroad hand car and took a ride.
When the train crew showed up at camp to complain, the
officers denied knowing them. Again he vainly explained to his
wife that " . . . somehow every thing that comes in reach of a
soldier it freesees to him & very often he has the cramps in his
hands especially when they get their hand over a turkey
head." Prentiss noted that he had never seen so many dogs
yet the reason should not have puzzled him. Southern farmers
were simply trying to protect their property. According to
Charley Prentiss, if a dog approached them while they were
foraging ". . the next thing he knows he knows nothing." [29]
Squad leader Phinehas Hager was concerned about other
matters as well as Prentiss and Anderson. He observed
astutely how a unit's strength and fighting effectiveness were
reduced by death, sickness and duty assignments. He
accounted for a loss of 21 men in his company's present for

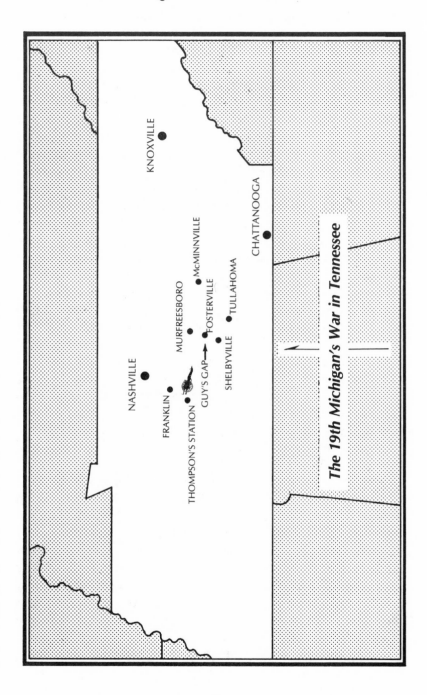

KNOXVILLE

CHATTANOOGA

McMINNVILLE

MURFREESBORO

FOSTERVILLE

TULLAHOMA

GUY'S GAP

SHELBYVILLE

NASHVILLE

FRANKLIN

THOMPSON'S STATION

The 19th Michigan's War in Tennessee

duty strength, eight being sick in hospitals and another nine assigned to various duties. He was also bothered by drunkenness and irresponsible behavior. To his wife he related the occurrence of a slave celebration lasting from Christmas Day to New Year's. With typical Hager morality, he remarked: "I don't see much difference between whites and blacks when filled with whiskey. Either of them are fools when intoxicated."[30] And he was growing weary of the attitude of Privates Prentiss and Anderson. "Dave Anderson is just now thinking hard because I ordered him to go and help draw rations. Hubbard pets him and mads the whole company. Dave will get reduced to the ranks if he is not careful. Dave and Charley Prentiss annoy me more than any other men have in our squad. They are both of them afraid they shall do a little more than their share. I despise a shirk. We have three or four in our squad."[31]

Christmas was a gala affair for the 19th Michigan; the colonel favored the men with quantities of oysters and a half keg of beer for each company. Regardless of its purpose, it was one way of fostering good will. Anyway, it was an event mentioned in nearly every soldier's letter after the holiday. "The provisions were devoured with a relish made keen by long living on 'hard tack' and Cincinnati sidewalk."[32] Amidst the merriment, orders came directing the 19th Michigan, another infantry regiment, and an artillery battery to proceed on the following day to Munfordsville, located on the Louisville and Nashville Railroad.[33]

Once again the Confederates were making a dash into Kentucky, this time aimed at breaking the railroad in General William Rosecrans' rear.[34] General John Hunt Morgan began his raid from Alexandria, Tennessee on December 22, 1862. On the following day he crossed the Cumberland River and by the 24th, Morgan was in Kentucky. His command of over 300 men and seven pieces of artillery was divided into two brigades. On Christmas eve Morgan first encountered Union troops as he skirmished briefly with the advanced guard of the 2nd Michigan Cavalry near Glasgow. During the next day, he broke contact, moved his command

64

through Glasgow and north toward Munfordsville and crossed the Green River near dusk. On the following day, he struck suddenly at Bacon Creek compelling nearly a hundred members of the 91st Illinois Infantry Regiment to surrender. The torch was put to the stockade and trestle bridge. In concert with this action, Morgan's other brigade seized the garrison at Nolin, manned by another detachment of the 91st Illinois. The seizure resulted in 76 more prisoners and another stockade and bridge reduced to ashes. They also started fires alongside the tracks intended to heat and warp the rails, a procedure William T. Sherman would perfect in a couple of years. Driving hard on the 27th, Morgan reached Elizabethtown and demanded its surrender. Colonel H.S. Smith commanding, initially refused but following a half hour engagement, he was forced to change his mind. Here 652 prisoners were taken.[35]

Morgan's raid was causing much excitement. Colonel William Haskins was certain that he could not hold Lebanon without immediate reinforcement. General Baird answered his appeal for help by sending two regiments of infantry and an artillery battery. This relief force covered about half of the distance to Lebanon on December 26. Wet and weary, the 19th Michigan camped near the Perryville battlefield. During breakfast the next morning, orders came to return to Danville.[36]

But alas for the uncertainty of all human calculations, particularly if such calculations are based upon anything pertaining to this war. In the morning, in place of rushing forward surrounding the whole southern Confederacy in general, John Morgan and friends in-particular, and crushing the last breath out of succession in the folds of this "Anaconda" we "forced by the rear rank",[37] and advanced upon Danville, pitching our tents upon the identical ground from which they had been taken the day before. No one seems to know why we were ordered back, not even the General himself. Guess the whole move was one incident upon the many health's drank to Santa Claus on Christmas. [38]

Yet the regiment had new orders to march toward Lebanon on December 28. Reveille sounded at 4:30 A.M. that morning with departure planned for 7:00 A.M. But at 5:30 A.M. these orders were countermanded and in its place, the 33rd Indiana and 22nd Wisconsin were instructed to proceed toward Lebanon. The following day these two regiments marched to within five miles of their destination and then were ordered back to Danville. After marching about three miles in the direction of Danville, these orders were countermanded and back toward Lebanon they went! The chaplain of the 19th Michigan emphazied the frustration of the situation in recording: ". . . Have just gone to bed get up and dress think it hardly prudent to Sleep with clothes off."[39]

Seemingly the only "solider" not confused was John Hunt Morgan. Following the capture of the garrison at Elizabethtown, Morgan turned toward Bardstown attacking Muldraugh's Hill on December 28. He easily overpowered the military defenses there and burned two tremendous trestle bridges. Morgan had achieved his mission: "The destruction of the Louisville and Nashville Railroad from Munfordsville to Shepardsville, within 18 miles of Louisville . . ."[41] By January 2, 1863, Morgan was south of the Cumberland; he had also escaped.[42]

Relieved of its assignment back at Nicholsville, Company B rejoined the regiment on January 2, 1863. It returned just in time for pay day. The men received pay for August and September with the Government owing them for two additional months. Going without pay since August had forced many to borrow on their anticipated wages. By the time Private Frank Rice paid his debts, he was left with just $7.00. His biggest creditor had been the Sutler.[43] And the folks at home needed money too.. Conscious of responsibility to their families, soldiers sent a remarkably large portion of their pay home. Sergeant Hager expressed a sum of $175.00 from his squad alone and considering that a sergeant drew a month salary of $17.00, corporal $14.00, and private $13.00, the amount was substantial.[44]

Almost on his company's first day back with the regiment,

ᴗergeant Hager drew command of the straw detail, his instructions being to take two men with a team and wagon and bring in a load.

I first had to report to the Division QM to get directions where to go. He was just drinking with some of his friends, and was cross as a drunken man usually is; but finally told me to get it where I could find it. That was enough for me so we started out, inquiring of the negroes, until we found where there was straw. We turned off the road, and went back a half mile, when we came to a pretty good specimen of a Kentucky gentleman farmer's residence. I went into the yard, on one side of which was the large house where the owner lived, and all around on all sides were little offices as they call them for the kitchen, store room etc. This was the first time I had had any business of this kind to do; and I felt a little anxious, but just as I was going to the house I discovered a man in one part of the yard, and made up to him and inquired if he was the man of the house "Yes". "Well sir I have a team here for straw." "Well, there is the straw but I think it is strange doings" "Why you get your pay I suppose?" "No they have taken the straw of thirty acres, and I get no pay." Poor old fellow he thought he was being taxed very hard. They told me to give him a receipt, but he did not seem inclined to take any . . . [45]

This system of reimbursements was inoperative and unevenly applied.

Contrasted with Nicholsville, the men were favorably ᴊmpressed with Danville; several compared it to Kalamazoo. Danville with 4,000 residents was the county seat and the location of a state deaf and dumb asylum as well as ". . . a very nice female academy. . ." [46]

The regiment had recently taken on a new dimension with the organization of an attached battery of "mounted howitzers" manned by members of the regiment and commanded by Captain Charles Bigelow. Its firepower consisted of six brass twelve pound howitzers mounted on carriages each pulled by a single horse. If the situation dictated, these guns could be broken down and carried on a horse's back.[47] The guns impressed Prentiss as a "savage machine . . .desined for clost fighting space they are use for shel shot the distance from 40 to 100 rods."[48]

Accidents are difficult to explain, yet a greater mystery may be why there are not more. Certainly any military unit is accident prone. The regiment experienced some typical examples of carelessness while stationed at Danville. One evening while on picket duty, Shepard Curtis accidentally discharged his gun. the slug ripped through his left forearm but fortunately left is bones intact.[49] Curiosity and foolishness overcame several other men early in January when they picked up an unexploded artillery shell. Eager to determine what was inside, a black servant and Private Ira Dexter tried to unscrew the shell but when that failed, they began to pound on it. The inevitable occurred. The round exploded knocking down one man, injuring Dexter and literally exploding the black man who had been holding the shell with both hands.[50]

The 19th Michigan had enlisted the services of a number of blacks most of whom worked as servants and laborers. To Private Austin's way of thinking, the accident with the shell demonstrated the need to keep Negroes away and restrict their activities. Judging that their actions were childlike, he wrote: "It almost makes me mad to think of the way negrows are allowed to run around the camp ground cuting up all kinds of capers."[51]

One day the local sheriff apprehended a black teamster who was out on a hay detail. "The Col was told of the circumstances, appeared desirous to be kept in ignorance. He dont care much about the negro but he did not like the idea of having one of his teamsters taken, when out with them."[52] Taking matters into their own hands, a relief expedition comprised of several corporals was soon organized. Mounting up, they rode into town bent on springing their black comrade. The sheriff offered no resistance, the man was released from jail and promptly returned to the unit. [53]

Idleness may have contributed to accidents; at least the men had little to cheer them. They had recently received the depressing news of the Federal defeat at Fredericksburg and their futile participation in pursuing Morgan could hardly have improved their morale either. Finally some good news came (even if it was a rumor) General Bragg was dead:

> . . . we were called out to give three cheers for the death of Rebel Gen Bragg some cheered and some did not I was among the last named It was contrary to my bringing up to rejoice over the downfall of a fellow being although an enemy And I kinder think that perhaps he might turn up somewhere by and by and then you see the cheering would be all for nothing. [54]

News of a victory at Stones' River helped too. Sergeant John Griffis found encouragement in a letter from his two young daughters: "I think thare is good news in them if I could read them. . . [55]

Although these incidents helped break the monotony of camp life, they were generally shared by only a small portion of the regiment. Such was the experience of Sergeant Griffis while on picket one cold January evening. According to the Sergeant, he found a bee tree occupied by a couple of swarms. When the free fell, probably as a result of being pushed over, it was the soldier's turr to swarm:

> " . . . some of them was so fast for the honey that they ate bees and all and got so badly stung on the tongue that they could hardly talk and at mid night when the officer of the day came . . . the men was roling the ground with the cholic the colonel of the twenty Second Wisconsin acosted us thus Sergeant what in hell is the matter with the men.   got the colick Colonel eating honey. Whare did you find it.   found a bee tree well I want you to find Some cows dam quick and See iff that wont fetch the bloat out of them if it dont I will keep

every one of you on picket for one week. Colonel would you like to have the colic no but I would like Some of the honey. So he ate about two pounds and then made for camp on double quick . . . [56]

One of the stock methods of the military for maintaining general readiness was to conduct inspections. Typically, these were held on Sundays. Different from most soldiers, Private Austin provided a fairly detailed description of what happened during a regimental inspection. Sunday, January 11, 1863:

scrubbed my old gun bright as a dollar. go at my catrage box & belt. (on another occasion Austin explained that the soldiers generally used sand to polish their brass. When it was not available they substituted ashes) pack all my clothes into my napsack except what was on my back. all had to fly around to get ready to fall in at 11 . . all sholdered our napsacks & guns & fell in line right dressed counted toes. that is for both wranks to count ½ 1-2 till we get the whole length of the line. after this we right faced in files of four & forward march- ed to whare the music was playing & took our place in the reg. faced & dressed to the right, ordered arms sholdered arms present arms then sholder arms & right wheel halt to the reer open order prepare for inspection when we get this order we all pull our ramrod out & put it in the gun & place the gun back by our side. Cap takes the front wrank & the Lt. the reer Cap. examins the orderly & Sargeants fun 1st then goes to the head of the Co. & comes along down examining every mans gun after this is over get the order close order march, stack arms to the reer open order march front rank about face . . . [57]

Two company commanders were attracting attention with their pending resignations. Both Captains Bassett and Brown had earlier been too sick to perform their duties for a period of time. Upon his request, Captain Bassett's wife joined him in the field. He was left behind at Lexington and soon went home to Michigan on sick leave. After rejoining the regiment, he submitted his resignation. In this regard, he asked each sergeant in the company to sign a statement recommending acceptance of the resignation. Sergeant Hager was hesitant:

> They have all signed but me The reasons he gives are his health, and his business. I have no doubt but there are plenty of men who can leave their business much better than he can, who would be glad to go for the pay he gets, and would perhaps do nearly as well as he; but the boys say that he told them he should never ask them to go any further than he went. I don't remember just what he said, nor would it have made any difference with me. . .As to his health, I know he was very sick; but whether he can endure camp life, or not, I can't say. [58]

Apparently Captain Bassett had emphasized the idea of sticking the war out together when he recruited his company because Prentiss also makes reference to this kind of commitment. Seemingly many men in Company B believed he was reneging on a promise which had enticed men to volunteer. Nevertheless, Prentiss still thought he was the best captain in the regiment. Always a man of high principles and conviction, Sergeant Hager continued to balk and was affronted by the captain's attempts to encourage his support. "I did not thank him for trying to tickle me with the prospect of soon getting a commission if he resigned saying what he did to induce me to sign his paper." [60] Bassett also suggested that a leave to go home could probably be secured for the Sergeant. With firmness Hager wrote ". . .I won't do anything which will be a detriment to the company or country to secure my own ends." [61] It was all for naught anyway as Colonel Coburn refused Bassett's request.

Captain Brown fared better, perhaps because his request was based solely on medical reasons which were convincing. The colonel obviously had high regard for Brown because in an unusual gesture he sent a card to the captain's local newspaper expressing his commendation. In addition to the tribute paid him, Colonel Gilbert stressed that the captain's resignation was honorable. "His resignation is not voluntary to escape the service, but from utter physical inability after repeated trials to endure the labor demanded from an officer. He carries with him our warmest wishes for his future welfare." [62]

Amidst strife, boresome details and spurts of excitement, the war had its quiet, gentle side too, so tranquil that an old noncom could feel a day passing and write: "The boys are just singing a piece, composed in memory of the soldiers who were killed in Baltimore, when the war just broke out. It is called 'Send them home tenderly.' Find the piece if you can, and hear it sung." [63]

5

"I AM TIRED OF A
SOLDIER'S LIFE"

"I do not feel exactly homesick yet I have a sort of undesernable yearning to visit home and friends once more I rather think I should appreciate the luxuries of home should I be spared to come back at the close of the war Did a man but know what he would have to put up with what privations he would have to endure could he but learn this before he enlisted nothing but the strongest of patriotic feelings would induce him to become a soldier."[1]   This was an atypical expression for the usually positive Henry Noble but it reflected an attitude that was becoming increasingly common within the ranks of the 19th Michigan Infantry. Their correspondence during late January and February, 1863, communicated a new low in unit morale. Seemingly their attitudes paralleled those of the nation during this particularly difficult time which Wood Gray called "The Period of Despair."[2]   This was the time from Ambrose Burnside's failure at Fredericksburg until the great Union victories at Gettysburg and Vicksburg. It was a period of defeatism and hopelessness. Among northerners, only the copperheads were winning. Almost every week brought a new cry for peace. The wisdom of the emancipation proclamation was being seriously challenged. War weariness was being stimulated among the military by letters from home and the press.[3] "Open justification of disertion by certin Democratic newspapers on the grounds that volunteers had been deceived as to the purpose of the war and that oaths of enlistment which they had taken were tacitly dissolved by the issuance of the proclamation was an important factor in the situation." 4 In remarkably similar fashion, the 19th Michigan Infantry reflected the mood of the time.

It was Charlie Prentiss who remarked "I am tired of a soldier's life." 5 Prentiss wrote frequently to his wife and their mutual disenchantment is abundantly evident. Mrs. Prentiss was ailing, lonesome and experiencing hard times financially. Most of all she wanted her husband to come home. And husband Charlie was feeling the pressure. After more than one attempt to explain his military obligation, Prentiss underscored his words in emphasizing his situation. *Dear wife I want to go home once more* but no not yet, I am bound to shoot some rebs first we don't think no more of shooting a reb than to shoot a skunk'.6 Apparently Millie Prentiss finally understood that her husband was not coming home except honorably. She must have given him some reassurance for Private Prentiss proudly responded: " . . . I glory in your spunk not wanting me to desirt, it would be a disgrace to us both, we have had three desirt with the last 2 weeks." 7 For all soldiers, letters from home were usually a source of great strength. During this particular time, Prentiss instructed his wife to write the "19" very clearly in addressing envelopes mailed to him in order to avoid any mistakes. 8

Throughout the military, desertion was a serious problem, particularly during late 1862 and the first months of 1863. The 19th Michigan was no exception. During January and February, 1863, 18 men deserted, more than in any other two successive months. Considering that 23 men deserted during the entire year, the frequency during this two month period was exceptionally great. Only during September, 1862 when the regiment was being organized, did the monthly total of desertions exceed the twelve who quit the regiment in January, 1863. 9 Among those who took "French leave" in February, 1863, were two of Judson Austin's friends from Cheshire. "Elder and Mat", presumably Eldridge Morey and Martin Jones, disguised their identity by donning slave's apparel and made it home safely. Austin assumed they would be treated harshly if captured. "I expect they feel as though they had got out of prison but they will have to keep their eye open or they will have to come back & wear the marks of the hot iron on the side of their face with their heads shaved in the bargain. ". . If I should run away I never would be taken as long as I could fight." 10 In many cases deserters were dealt with severely including execution. One can imagine given the epidemic, that officers were threatening wicked punishment, sure to deter most. But like others, "Elder and Mat" returned on their own free will and went unpunished.

Seemingly all of the sources of irritation surface when morale is low. For certain, men found plenty to complain about. The regiment's inactivity and the failure to prosecute the war became a sore spot with many. In rather apologetic fashion, the First Sergeant of Company E wrote to the editor of his hometown newspaper stating: "It has been a long time since I have written you, but the fact is I have been almost ashamed to write of our long inactivity during the past three months. . ." Then almost with tongue in cheek he continued: "we have never met the foe in battle and are yet the happy possessors of bloodless bayonets and full cartridge boxes." 11 Consistently, Private Austin groused about being misled as to war aims and engaging the Rebels. "When I enlisted to come down here thought I was going to count on towards puting this thing to a cease. I mean the war, but the way things have been working & ar working & likely to work I am only helping keep the war along & keep it going . . . I was fooled when I enlisted as well as a great many others . . .Why Sarah who can tell what we are fitting for. Some say The Negro & others say for our country & the Union. But I think they are all mistaken." 12 Austin believed they were fighting a war encouraged by politicans who stood to gain personally by willfully obstructing the termination of the conflict. Hager was sputtering about pressing the enemy and "ending this horrible war." 13

Yet that was not all that was bothering the sergeant. He was most upset about the army's practice of retaining afflicted men in hospitals for months regardles of their physical condition and then eventually releasing them from the servie because of disability. Hager also believed that a government hospital was the wrong place to regain health. Angrily he told his wife that: "It seems to be the policy to discharge no one until they are sure to die." This practice had grated on Hager for some time and now in February, one of his men and a comrade from Allegan County, was being considered for discharge after a five month stay in a Cincinnati hospital. "It is outrageous to kill men in camp when they are wanted in the field. It seems a bad policy to keep so many men in hospitals; it would be much better to given them furloughs, until they are able to enter the field. It was just as certain last October, that Mr. Knapp would be worth nothing in the army for a long time, as it is now, so with others. They would have been fit for service by this time." [14]

Negligence was another symptom of the time. Charlie Prentiss admitted to his wife that he had skipped drill and that he was unconcerned about what might happen to him. Several months earlier, soldiers were awed by the assemblage of troops all in a line. Prentiss was now telling his wife that he was sick of seeing these formations. [15] Sergeant Hager related another man's approach to avoiding duty. Anticipating that the regiment was about to change location, he secured a pass to go to Murfreesboro. Hager delighted in noting: "He will be disappointed when he finds that the Regt. is here." (Murfreesboro). [16] A rash of suspected self-inflicted wounds, with soldiers even desperately shooting off fingers, represented yet another overt version of despondency. [17]

Like everything else, adversity is relative. How bad one's situation is depends on what it is compared with. After receiving a letter from home which conveyed the potential of marriage to a certain lady, Sergeant Griffis concluded that his lot in the military was not so bad after all. He retorted. "Now if I had to Serve another term in the army or bee married to Miss penitent I would Say here is for Unkle Sam." [18]

The mood of discontent, anti-war and despair which gripped the nation caused many soldiers to express their feelings and attitudes toward slavery and the continuance of the war.

Sergeant Hager knew where his company commander stood on these vital issues and made no attempt to hide his disappointment:

> Our Capt. is not what I wish he was. He would rather see every negro in Slavery, and an assurance given to the south that they should always remain so, than to have the Democratic party destroyed. I have but little faith in his patroitism. He is a good officer and I have no doubt, would do well on the battle field; but has not much faith in the *Right*. I am glad to say that our Col although a Democrat, is not so much in favor of slavery as the Capt. Bassett did the same as tell me that he came into the army because the public would despise him if he did not come; and he would not disgrace himself and family by staying at home. 19

Lieutenant George Shaffer, second in command of Company A, devoted a goodly portion of letters to his wife explaining the depressed condition of the regiment. He considered sickness, hardships, and the lack of military success the major reasons for low troop morale. He also shared his personal views:

> This however is not the case with me. I am in favor of peace of course; but not such a compromise as we could make at present. These men in the North who have said so much about peace have encouraged the rebels and caused them to think that we all were very tired of the war, and that if they can hold out a few months longer we will give them their independence. We could not settle with them now in any other way. In the first place I would have been in favor of letting them go rather than have a sivil war, but since it has gone thus far, I am in favor of fighting them untill we conquer let that take long or short time. 20

In the absence of campaigning which might have served to occupy men's minds and relieve some of their discouragement, it appears that commanders at several levels decided to talk it up and raise spirits with praise and inspiration. "I will tell you what our Gen Baird tells us. he says that this Regt. is the largest and best in the south & behave better & says that we stand No 1 & also says that we keep the cleanest & the cleanest camp ground etc. we are frequently visited by the Generals & Maj. Gen & all of the big Gen & they call us No. 1"[21] Baird may have been a West Point graduate but he was still a politician. Pumping up spirits was not the only thing that needed remedy; men also needed to be shaped up for low morale often bred despondency. One can surmise that Colonel Gilbert killed two birds with one stone in his handling of recently promoted Corporal Lewis Labadie. Obviously pleased with the Colonel's evaluation, Labadie wrote:

> I am well and the Colonel say I am the toughest little devil in the regiment our living would not be extra if it was not for our having plenty of powder and Balls and By god as long as we are well sesech chickens Shep Hogs any thing entable has to suffer I had old Snooks arrested the other day and he had to walk ten rods and Back for 6 hours with a Big napsack on his Back for using insulting language to me goddam them they musnet undertake to shit on this chicken if they do they will smell hell. [22]

Commanders seized the opportunity to capitalize on the anniversary of George Washington's birthday to hold a patriotic rally; this also offered another opportunity to bolster esprit de corps. The 19th Michigan was present and in all likelihood General Rosecrans attended too and probably made a speech. "Our big rosea" was popular with the men, making a big impression on Private Prentiss. "I tell you what it is I fell proud of our leader Gen Rosecrans (don't know how to spell him) I & we all have confidence in him, No traitor about him. If I go into battle I want to go under him, he is my choice. . ."[23] Hager described the occasion as ". . . a sort of political meeting of the brigade. . .There were several good speeches made, and our Col. made as good a one as any of them. He is sound on the war, and down on the copperheads, and so are all our principal officers. Capt. Bassett is a little shakey on the war, but I hope when he gets out of it personally, he will be all sound. Hubbard keeps up good courage. . .'' [24]

The 19th Michigan broke camp at Danville, January 26, 1863 and marched north enroute to Louisville. Rumor had it they were being sent to Vicksburg. An 85 mile march was a formidable distance for these men and in preparation, some sought to lighten their load by sending home extra items of clothing and gear.[25]Actually all of General Gordon Granger's command was being concentrated at Louisville before moving to Nashville to support Rosecrans. [26] The march was pursued with vigor. On the third day, the 22nd Wisconsin was the lead regiment and deliberately set a fast pace. But ''tomorrow our Reg, take the lead'' wrote Sergeant Hager ''and I presume we shall pay them off.'' [27] There had always been rivalry among troops; one of the most common seemed to exist naturally between eastern and western soldiers with eastern units being held in low regard by western troops and commanders. Somehow the 19th Michigan and 22nd Wisconsin had developed a competitive relationship and on this march were having it out. As described by Delos Lake, the 22nd Wisconsin's determination to get even resulted from an earlier march in December, 1963:

> when we went from Nicholsville to Camp Dick Robinson we led the 22 Wisconsin Regt they said that we was the d——dest fellows to walk that they ever see and they said that if they ever got the lead on us (the 19) they would show us that they would leave us fare in the rear well yesterday they lead the whol of the division our Regt next. they dident distantee us ten rods in all day . . we traveled 23 miles. at night we went into camp hooting and yelling the 22 had nothing to offer. today it was our turn to lead the 22 we marched 15 miles in just a half a day. the 22 was no where to be seen when they came in they were pretty mute, and when there Col

halted them the nearly all droped to the ground. [28]

The march was calculated to take six days but its fast pace got them to Louisville on October 30 in just four and a half days. On the way, a 22nd Wisconsin soldier wrote to his sister emphasizing the difference between a civilian's walk and a soldier's march.[29]Members of the 19th Michigan were proud of their march; it is remarkable how a little exercise could change attitudes. Their stay in this river city was short. For the next day the regiment marched to Portland across the river from New Albany, Indiana and boarded a steamer unimaginatively christened *"Ohio No. 3"*. They laid over until the second of February, when as part of a fleet of more than 60 vessels including a half dozen gunboats, they began the journey down the Ohio. [30] Traveling all night, they made Evansville by mid day on the 3rd. There, supplies were procured and the sick were taken ashore to the hospital. Company B left Sherman Stephens and James Martin at Evansville to convalesce. The convoy reached the mouth of the Cumberland late that night and began taking on fuel. While the fleet refueled, orders were received to hurry up the river to Dover where the Confederates had begun an attack that afternoon. Recognizing the urgency, Colonel Gilbert instructed some of his own men to help shovel coal and soon the fleet was steaming up the Cumberland. [31] The fight was over when they reached Dover as ". . . forunate or unfortionate we were ten hours behind time they were burying the dead when we landed they dug a trench and throughed them in like hogs that is the rebels ded our ded was all put in boxes and buryed Separate."[32]

Unlike the earlier battle at Fort Donelson, this engagement was fought at Dover, a couple of miles above the fort. The Rebels under General Nathan B. Forrest had struck hard with overwhelming numbers on the 3rd. Yet the 83rd Illinois resisted stubbornly. Fortunately another fleet had preceded that carrying the 19th Michigan, and its gunboats arrived in time to contribute decisively in the Union's successful defense. Casualties were heavy on both sides. Colonel Gilbert authorized his men to go ashore and inspect the field. Their correspondence carried spirited descriptions of the stout defense of the 83rd Illinois.[33] This was the closest the regiment had come to a real live battle and the dead made an impression. "I tell you it would almost make your hair stand up on your head to see the dead men and horses laying in the field."[34]

After a brief stop of two days at Fort Donelson, the fleet resumed its journey toward Nashville. Gunboats were deployed ahead of the transports, as the convoy proceeded cautiously up the river half anticipating an ambush. None came and the fleet arrived safely in Nashville on February 7, 1863. The men were busy assembling wagons which had been taken apart for transporting and then engaged in the task of unloading the vessels. On the ninth they went ashore and marched three miles south of Nashville to establish camp. [35]

Maintaining both physical and mental health was a continuing battle for most. Private Henry Noble recognized an interdependence. In his mind the sequence included losing one's appetite, becoming ill, complications in the form of homesickness occurring, and soon there was no will to survive. To his girlfriend he vividly described the process:

A man here gets sick and unless he has a strong constitution he sinks rapidly to the grave. He loses his appetite there is nothing he can eat no dainty morsel such as he would get were he at home and his mind naturally wanders back to his home and the luxuries he enjoyed while there and he becomes disheartened and homesick. No loving wife mother sister or *sweetheart* is near to cheer his drooping spirits and administer to his wants and he gradually falls away and eventually dies Homesickness here is a fatal disease and seldom fails in bringing its victim to the grave. While we were at Nicholsville a man died in the hospital who (they said) died with nothing else but pure homesickness. But I guess there was a little something else mixed with it. [36]

Others attributed the voyage on the river as a major cause of sickness. The men lived for several days in close cramped quarters denied the usual opportunities to exercise and their meals were irregular. [37] Once ashore, rainy cold weather compounded their problems. Since the men were housed in tents, it was difficult to avoid sleeping in a damp bed. Lieutenant Shaffer estimated that 10 per cent of the regiment was sick. "Our diet it hard bred fat pork and coffee. A man that can stand all this and keep well must have an iron constitution sure."[38] Considering Sergeant Hager's previous experience as a farmer, his choice of words used to describe the health of his squad at this time sounded like the care and feeding of livestock. After detailing the general state of health of several afflicted men, he summed up the condition of the remainder by stating: "The rest of the Otsego boys can eat their rations."[39]

Spiritual health represented yet another dimension of men's lives that needed nourishment, and Chaplain Cogshall was depressed over the lack of religious observation and increasing amount of card playing. He reprimanded the officers for setting a poor example. The repentance of one soldier only served to reinforce his anxiety. "This evening wrote a letter for Benj Green to his wife & afterwards read a chapter from the Bible and prayed with him he seems to be very penitant & earnestly desires to be a Christian & I feel happy while I prayed for him & was able to ask pardon for him with much confidence Oh for a revival of piety among these so many of whom are to find a tomb among Strangers."[40]

Although the tendency always seemed toward detailing more and more men away from the regiment, the 19th had a few returned while at Nashville due to the disbandment of the mounted howitzers. At least one who came back to Company A was not particularly welcomed. Since many of them were acquaintances prior to the war as were the wives, their correspondence often contained rather personal observations. "The boys Say they are Sorry that Lailyn came back he is So Sascy . . . very much like May." [41]

On February 14, the regiment exchanged their Austrian Rifle Muskets Caliber .54 and .55 for Enfield Rifle Muskets, Caliber

.577 and .58. The reaction was universally positive, with the men expressing great confidence in the Enfield. [42]

Despite a bright spot of enthusiasm caused by the delivery of new guns, the troops continued to complain. One can imagine that Charlie Prentiss believed that even the birds had forsaken him or at least for everybody else they sang. Half way through a letter, his thoughts were broken by an indiscreet bird which: ". . . marked my ltter above a small yellow spot near the middle of the page." [43] Escalating prices were also a common source of irritation. Potatoes were reportedly selling for $9.00 a bushel and other provisions at similarly high prices. [44] Each new location brought another episode in the regiment's foraging history with soaring prices encouraging the activity despite the military's efforts to limit it. In the absence of guards some of the men left camp:

> . . . and went to an old barn which was well filled with tobacco and as they have to pay a high price for the weed here in Tenn they though it no harm just to confiscate a little and their being several fat hogs near by and meet being scarce in camp they thought they would lay in a supply of pork also About a dozen hogs had been killed and large armfulls of the coveted tobacco were moving toward camp when an officer accompanied with some guards made his appearance. The Tobacco was dropped and the fresh meat abandoned and the men scattered in all directions. The officer only succeeded in capturing a few of them among whom was quite a number of our company They were brought before the Col and sentenced to stand guard four hours with their knapsacks on But as they managed to secure a large quantity of tobacco under their overcoats they considered it cheaper then to pay $1.50 per pound for it. [45]

Although his request had been denied once, Captain Elisha Bassett renewed his efforts to resign from the enemy. Strangely enough attitudes toward his resignation had changed during the interim. Now instead of begrudging his desire to leave, some of his men felt little regret. "Capt. Bassett is bound to resine & leave us & that is not all I nor we dont care, he dont prove to be the man we thought he would be, he is a hard harted & little feeling man, has no feeling for the sic, & if he does go home & leave us, he will never here the last of it if we ever come home, what a fool a man can make of him self if he sets out. Our company is down on him & he can *go* double quick, any thing but a coward, thats whats the matter, when I come home I can tell you all about it. . ." [46] Hager's feelings were much the same. The Captain ". . . is about sick and bound to go home. I don't care much how soon. He has lost his interest in the company in a measure; but I am afraid we shall have a slim set of officers when he leaves." [47] That possibility concerned Sergeant Hager greatly. It also affected him personally as he was potentially in line for a second promotion which quite naturally he desired. Again, with Bassett's resignation pending, both the captain and Lieutenant Hubbard encouraged his expectations. First Lieutenant Darrow's resignation earlier had precipitated three promotions including Hager becoming first sergeant. [48] This time, however; Hager was less than confident of his chances of receiving an advancement. Somehow he learned that the colonel had other plans. "But from what I can learn, such is not the Col programme. He intends to promote hubbard and Lilly, and make the sergeant major our second Lient. The Capt says if he goes home he will prevent the sergeant major from being a Lieut. in our company if possible; for he is a miserable little lowlined fellow. The whole regiment dislikes him; but he is the major's brother, and must have a commission. We can't help it ourselves, except through Gov Blair . . .We have got forty men in our company more fit for Lient. than the sergeant major." [49]

On February 21, 1863, the 19th Michigan edged closer to the front, moving 10 miles farther south of Nashville to the vicinity of Brentwood. Active guerillas and Rebel cavalry kept units located there in a constant state of readiness. Men were ordered to sleep fully clothed with loaded guns at their side. [50] Certain the Rebels were attacking one evening, Company E deployed as skirmishers and hurried south of camp, yet no Rebels were found. That little scare caused another when the 19th's ". . . Major came back, his sword rattling along. The guards of one of the other regiments took it to be rebel cavalry and raised the alarm which spread through the whole brigade before the mistake was discovered." [51]   The regiment was sensing its closeness to the war. As Henry Noble wrote a letter to his special girl back in Michigan, several men slept nearby in the tent. The stillness was broken by the outburst of a sleeping comrade: "Pitch in boys here they are." [52]

Captain Charles A. Thompson, Jr. of Kalamazoo entered the service as commander of Company F. [Michigan History Division].

Officers of the Nineteenth Michigan. The photograph presumably was made shortly after the war since Lt. Colonel Anderson is the ranking officer. Capt. Elisha Bassett, dismissed in 1863 is included in the group. Identified in the front row are Frank D. Baldwin, David Anderson, and David Easton. In back row, L to R: Frank Stewart, Unknown, William E. Clarke, Henry Olds, LeRoy Cahill, Lucius Wing. Others unknown except Bassett, second from right. [Michigan History Division]

Captain Lucius Phetteplace, Coldwater, enlisted as First Sergeant of Company H, later became commanding officer of Company K. [Michigan History Division]

First Sergeant Thomas Horton, Arlington, had enlisted as a private in Company G. [Michigan History Division]

Captain Charles P. Lincoln, Coldwater, began as first
sergeant of Company C. [Michigan Historical Collections]

6

ENGAGEMENT AT
THOMPSON'S STATION

The new year began quietly in the western theatre following the Union victory at Stone's River at the close of 1862. Major General William Rosecrans, in command of the Army of the Cumberland, had halted his pursuit of the Confederates when his army occupied Murfreesboro.

As was often the case during the Civil War, Rosecrans' army was as exhausted and disorganized in victory as was the enemy in defeat. The Army of the Cumberland needed recruits to replace heavy casualties suffered at Stone's River, its supply lines had been seriously disrupted, and Rosecrans determinedly sought cavalry strength to match the Confederates. Amidst refitting, foraging and healing, Rosecrans was being pressed by the General in Chief Henry Halleck to begin an offensive. In early March, several Union armies began probing General Braxton Bragg's lines to determine his strength. The Confederates were launching similar tests.[1]

Rosecrans ordered Brigadier General Charles C. Gilbert, commanding General Gordon Granger's second division at Franklin, to reconnoiter the Columbia Pike as far south as Spring Hill. His advance was also to serve as a foraging expedition.[2] Gilbert selected Colonel John Coburn's brigade to execute his mission. Coburn's brigade moved some 18 miles from Brentwood to Franklin on March 2.[3]

Coburn's force, as organized at Franklin, included his own

brigade, the 124th Ohio Infantry Regiment, the 18th Ohio Battery and cavalry detachments from the 9th Pennsylvania, 4th Kentucky, and 2nd Michigan. He reported his strength at 2,837. [4] Coburn's own brigade made up the core of his forces numbering 1,845 infantrymen. The 33rd Indiana with 606 and the 19th Michigan with 531 present for duty were easily the largest units. The 22nd Wisconsin had 378 effectives while the 85th Indiana mustered just 330 for the march. His mounted troops totalled some 600 and the 124th Ohio added about 400 additional foot soldiers.[5] Attrition caused by sickness, death, and resignations left the 18th Ohio Battery at less than minimum strength. On the 27th of February, 1863, 39 infantrymen from Coburn's brigade joined the battery in order that it would have the necessary manpower to function. The reinforcements included several members of the 19th Michigan. [6]   These replacements must have accounted for twenty-five percent of the battery's manpower and most certainly these 39 men were ill-prepared for battle. The battery they joined was also short on experience having never engaged the enemy. Their subsequent conduct at Thompson's Station reflected their inexperience. Commanded by Captain Charles Aleshire, the battery consisted of six three-inch rifled Rodmans. [7]   Its caissons carried 1200 rounds of ammunition.[8]

Early on the morning of the fourth, Coburn's force marched out of Franklin with the 2nd Michigan Cavalry leading, followed by the 33rd Indiana, Colonel Coburn, staff and body guard, three guns of the 18th Ohio Battery, the 22nd Wisconsin, 19th Michigan, 85th Indiana, the remainder of the battery, the wagon train and the 124th Ohio bringing up the rear. [9]

Just prior to noon, Coburn's command met its first resistance as skirmishers clashed with Confederate cavalry four miles out of Franklin. The Rebel forces were those of General Earl Van Dorn's army then assembling at Spring Hill. Van Dorn's advance guard was also performing a reconnaissance mission. Coburn's task force began to deploy with infantry units as skirmishers and the 18th Ohio, getting into position. The 33rd Indiana and the 22nd Wisconsin fled off to the right of the pike, while the 124th Ohio and the 19th Michigan came abreast of the west side of the road. [10] The artillery answered the Rebel fire and the second round ". . . from our piece sent one rebel and his horse to the hogs (for in fact the hungry beasts eat them both up that afternoon where they fell) . . ." Still another missile made a direct hit smashing a gun carriage. [11] After a brief exchange of 15 minutes, the Confederates broke contact and pulled back to the next ridgeline.

Coburn acted promptly to apprise General Gilbert of his situation while the brigade remained in position awaiting further instructions. The enemy driven by Coburn's command was estimated as being from 2,000 to 3,000 strong. Although Coburn believed he could advance, he expressed concern that if he did, Rebel cavalry would flank him and be between him and Franklin. Explicitly he asked, "What shall we do?" It is probable that a second message was carried to General Gilbert at the same time. In it, Coburn attempted to apprise his commander of the Confederate artillery strength and how burdensome the long string of wagons had become. On the tough decision of whether or not to advance, Gilbert ducked his responsibility and passed the buck to his subordinate, simply telling Coburn he had considerable discretion. Gilbert did, however, authorize him to detach his forage elements. Colonel Coburn took advantage of the opportunity and released half of his wagons to the rear. [12] What seems incomprehensible, however, is that General Gilbert could leave Coburn the option to proceed, knowing that if he did, the enemy would soon be in his rear and have him cut off from Franklin.

Coburn's force resumed the march, pushing Confederate pickets for an additional two miles. Informed that a sizeable cavalry force was threatening his left flank on the Lewisburg Road, Coburn ordered his command to halt, then to fall back in order to secure his flanks. The Union forces camped on ground previously held by Van Dorn's advance.

Further information of the supposed threat ahead became more apparent at daybreak when two Negro youths entered the Union lines and reported that Van Dorn's entire command was

93

massed just south of Thompson's Station. Coburn dispatched the informants back to Franklin, accompanied by a mounted escort, to advise General Gilbert. In response, headquarters was silent. Gilbert may have believed that Coburn had considerable latitude in the execution of his orders and in a very general sense that may well have been the case; yet, for certain, one option which Coburn did not feel at liberty to exercise was to retreat. [13] Coburn had filled 39 wagons with forage, made contact with a force he could not handle, and kept on going.

The battle tally for the first day of the engagement showed the Federals getting the best of it inflicting some 10 Rebel casualties while suffering only three wounded among its ranks; two members of the 9th Pennsylvania cavalry and a corporal in Company F, 19th Michigan Infantry. Joseph Coshun became the 19th's first combat casualty. In addition, the Union artillery would be short one gun. One of the Rodman's was down with a broken axle, accidentally disabled while changing positions. [14] Pickets posted, half-asleep Yankees waited for tomorrow.

The morning of March 5 broke cold and "Nary reb was seen." [15] With the 124th Ohio guarding the ammunition train, Coburn's force marched south in search of the enemy. The anticipation was short for after marching about four miles the Rebels were met in force. With a Confederate battery laid in on the pike, Coburn's lead infantry regiment, the 22nd Wisconsin, drew fire as the first round sent them digging for cover. "It was no near that the whole regiment involuntarily crouched to the earth, the command was immediately 'over the fence and lie down!' and that command was obeyed as quickly as any command ever was." [16]

Coburn ordered his brigade into action with the 19th Michigan sent to the east side of the pike to anchor the left flank, the 22nd Wisconsin abreast and also on the left, the 33rd Indiana deployed across the road from the Badger regiment and the 85th Indiana in line holding the extreme right. [17]

Coburn's infantry occupied a range of hills overlooking Thompson's Station from the north with the village nestled midway in the valley floor below separating the two armies.

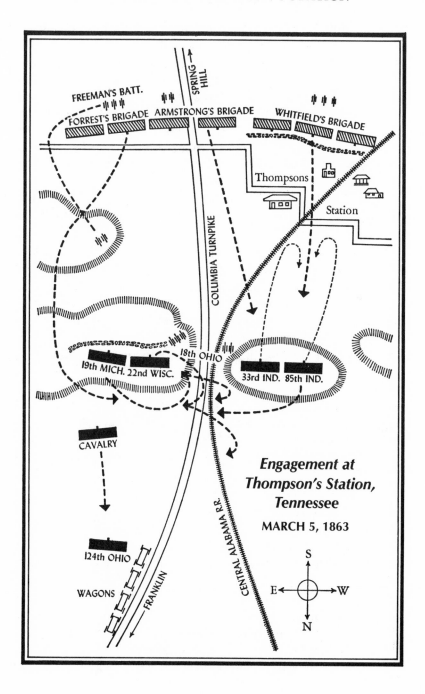

FREEMAN'S BATT.

FORREST'S BRIGADE   ARMSTRONG'S BRIGADE   WHITFIELD'S BRIGADE

SPRING HILL

Thompsons

Station

COLUMBIA TURNPIKE

18th OHIO

19th MICH.   22nd WISC.

33rd IND.   85th IND.

CAVALRY

124th OHIO

WAGONS

FRANKLIN

CENTRAL ALABAMA R.R.

Engagement at Thompson's Station, Tennessee

MARCH 5, 1863

S
E ← ⊕ → W
N

Coburn had seized the high ground flanking either side of a narrow gap through which passed the Central Alabama Railroad and Columbia Turnpike before descending to the valley below. The Union commander positioned two guns of Captain Aleshire's 18th Ohio Battery right of the pike and alongside the 33rd Indiana while the other section got into action just off the roadbed to the left occupying a slight rise. The Union cavalry were drawn up in the rear of the 19th Michigan and less than a half mile back on the pike, Coburn had located his trains under guard of the 124th Ohio Infantry.[18]

Although Coburn's information about the disposition of Conferate troops was incomplete, he was aware that the Rebels held the commanding terrain on the south side of the valley to his front and that their artillery located along the pike and in the rear of Thompson's Station had found the range. Coburn unknowingly was cooperating with Van Dorn's plan. More importantly, he was badly outnumbered. When the engagement began around 10:00 a.m., the Confederates had approximately 5,300 men present. Later in the morning, Brigadier General William T. Martin's First Brigade arrived adding 700 fresh troops to the already disproportionate numbers. There was a sharp difference in mobility as all Confederate units were mounted. Comparing artillery made the odds ever worse. In Captain S.L. Freeman's Tennessee Battery and Captain Houston King's Second Missouri Battery, Van Dorn had slightly more than twice as many big guns. [19]

The union commander first sent three companies of the 33rd Indiana forward to drive out Rebel sharpshooters who had occupied Thompson's Station. The Hoosiers succeeded and Coburn next sought to remove a much greater threat by silencing the battery to his right front. Coburn again looked to his fellow Indianians as he ordered forward the rest of the 33rd and the 85th Indiana. The Federals filed off their hill, formed into separate columns and went for the guns. While opposing batteries exchanged fire, the Union offensive pushed forward through "an iron hail." The Hoosiers advanced to within a short distance of the depot when they were suddenly met with

Colonel J.W. Whitfield's brigade which had remained conceal-ed behind the wall until the advancing forces were at close range. The advance of the Indiana regiments was stopped and thrown back. [20]

The retreating Yankees fell back toward their first position with Whitfield's brigade and the 3rd Arkansas from Brigadier General Frank Armstrong's brigade applying the pressure of a determined counterattack. Reaching the crest of the hill, they rallied to defend.

Excitement and adrenalin ran high. In an unusual act of heroics and recklessness, Major William R. Shafter left the 19th Michigan and rode hard across the pike arriving just in time to help consolidate the Indiana troops rallying to make a stand. Shafter stayed long enough to participate in a charge which drove the Confederates back down the hill. [21]

On the east side of the pike, too, the Union position was being seriously tested. The 19th Michigan and 22nd Wisconsin had first gone into position on the reverse slope of a cedar crowned hill. There they had sought shelter from Confederate artillery fire as both regiments assembled behind a stone fence. During the early hours of the engagement, Coburn had assigned these regiments a reserve role. The Rebels acted promptly to threaten the Union left as Brigadier General Nathan B. Forrest, commanding the Confederate right, sent two guns of Freeman's Battery to occupy a hill about a half mile southeast and flanking the Union left. [22] Company C of the 19th Michigan was order to send four ot its best marksmen forward as sharpshooters. They crept down into the valley using a cornfield to camouflage their approach on several unidentified horsemen. Their presence was soon detected and Freeman sent a artillery shell crashing down through the row of cornshocks. The foursome raced to the rear ''accelerando double-quick'' easily scaling the stone fence behind their regiment position. [23]

With his flank exposed, Colonel Gilbert ordered his regiment to march to the right and rear and occupy a position under the guns of the 18th Ohio Battery. To meet this new artillery threat, the Union battery turned its guns to face the foe and the duel continued. Thus situated, both infantry regiments were immediately under the path of the artillery projectiles and the guns were ". . . sending their demoniac sounding missiles. . . so close to our ears that all those unaccustomed to such sounds would dodge their heads and unvoluntarily shrink closer to the stone wall as they went by."[24]

A first battle would bring out both the best and worst in a volunteer regiment. In almost remarkable fashion, the 19th Michigan Infantry consistently demonstrated its willingness to fight. There were just a few exceptions. Captain Elisha Bassett's conduct was undoubtedly the most disgraceful. During the engagement, he took cover behind a tree and refused to command his company; finally he deserted, riding back to Franklin unable to face responsibility or fear. Following the battle, Colonel Gilbert recounted the incident while proceeding to press charges:

> As soon as my regiment became engaged he abandoned his Company and took shelter behind a large tree 15 or 20 yards in the rear of our line. I found him there & in asking what he was doing there & why he was not with his company he replied that he could not take any part in the fight, that I must not depend upon him for anything, that the Lieut could command the Company & begged me to excuse him. I repeatedly ordered him to his post but he refused to obey. We soon had occasion to change our position when he ran off down the Rail Road track where he lay for some time. He at length ran off again further to the rear & crumpled a horse belonging to one of the Cavalry & rode back to Franklin - I have never seen a man exhibit so much cowardice & fear as Capt Bassett did on this occasion - His Company was ably commanded by Lieut Hubbard & did well. Capt. Bassett admits all the facts & only excuses himself in the pretense that he was sick. He was sick before the action commenced & it would have required no more physical ability for him to have re- mained & done his duty than it did to run away. . .

He also claims that he had tendered his resignation a short time previous & he ought not to be required to risk his life when he was expecting to leave soon. I respectfully ask that he may be dismissed the service.[25]

At this critical time, Aleshire's gun section which supported the Union left, stopped firing and withdrew to the pike. With the Union artillery gone, Forrest now made his move to get to the enemy's rear. The regiments commanded by Colonels J.H. Edmundson and James Starnes moved forward determined to flank the cedar hill.[26] Union commanders tried to adjust to meet this new threat. The 19th Michigan was in an exposed position following the departure of the gun section. It was also in a column by division formation meaning that companies were in columns two abreast, a formation which lent itself to movement but could mass only a two company front if the regiment were attacked in either the front or rear. Gilbert marched his regiment around the hill previously defended by the artillery and took up a new position near the road. They he left them in the same formation facing the railroad![27] The 22nd Wisconsin followed suit shifting its position toward the pike forming a new line near the brow of the hill and to the left of the 19th Michigan.[28]

The ranks of the infantry were filled with untried volunteer soldiers and there is little doubt that the 22nd Wisconsin, including its commander, Colonel Utley, was tense. They now held the Union left, they were pinned down by artillery fire and they had just been alerted that the Rebs were flanking them with a large force. They waited, searching the cedars at the top of the hill and suddenly: ". . . smoke . . . betrayed the enemy and a volley from almost every gun in the regiment greeted them."[29] Dismounted Confederate cavalrymen pushed forward attacking both Union regiments in the left and rear:

We were compelled to face this attacking force by the

99

rear rank, and as a consequence, only two or three companies of the 19th Michigan on the left were able to effectively return the fire, as the 22nd Wisconsin was now in our front and nearer the crest of the ridge. The enemy's fire along the whole line of the Wisconsin troops was terrific, and although they were also exposed to an enfilade fire from their batteries, the Wisconsin boys, with such assistance as could be rendered by their Michigan comrades, bravely repelled the attack and compelled their foes to retire. The command given by the cool and courageous Colonel Utley, of the 22nd Wisconsin, a moment before this attack upon our lines, became a pet byword or expression throughout the brigade for months afterwards. It was: "Look out, boys; get ready to shoot; the damned rebels are coming." And they were ready. [30]

Staying the Rebel advance was short lived for they came again pushing toward the turnpike and now, if not denied, would soon divide Coburn's command.

Again, the 22nd would move or at least part of it and here the chain of command would break down. Utley was at the left of his regiment; Lieutenant Colonel Bloodgood, second in command, rode with the right. It is apparent that up until this point during the battle, Utley had issued orders through Bloodgood rather than assuming personal direction. Now in crisis, Bloodgood ordered the regiment up onto the pike supposedly under brigade orders to extend the Union left; Utley interpreted the movement as a rout. With the enemy in their midst and unable to hear above the roar of battle, the regiment responded to two commanders; Company A and the larger part of D left the field while the remainder heard Utley's command to halt. [31]

Yet this was only the beginning. Bloodgood and his part of the 22nd got out onto the road in time to meet the rest of the artillery also pulling back. Soon all of the cavalry were withdrawing and along with the 124th Ohio which escorted the ammunition, began an independent retreat toward Franklin.

Within minutes, Coburn's effective strength was reduced by more than a 1,000 men and his ability to withdraw had been forfeited. [32]

Under heavy pressure the 19th Michigan stumbled across the road just in time to support the repulse of another Confederate attack on the Union right. It arrived on the hill the Indiana regiments were defending at the critical moment when the full thrust of the Confederate assault was being felt. "They charged right in among us but our company had fixed bayonets and was determined to hold the hill. . ."[33] The Rebel charge was met with a "murderous fire."[34] Orders were immediately given to charge; the 19th Michigan struck with a fury engaging Armstrong's Brigade in a fierce counterattack. Confederate John Wyeth would later write that "Armstrong was badly handled in his affray . . ."[35] The lines met head-on:

> With bayonets fixed, we charged them to the stone fence at the foot of the hill . . . At this fence Whitfield's brigade was in line, and with desparate courage sought to stay our advance. In this unequal contest of one regiment against a whole brigade, the fighting was more than hand-to-hand, and the acts of individual daring and courage were many. A sergeant of your companion's company (Company C) sprang upon the stone wall, seized the Texan's brigade colors, bayoneted its bearer, and we retain possession of the flag until the close of the contest. [36]

Only cold steel discouraged these Texans forcing them back toward the depot. The 19th Michigan also came away with both the battle flag of the 4th Mississippi Cavalry Regiment and Armstrong's brigade colors. [37] They also brought off a number of prisoners. Sergeant John Griffis captured a Confederate and his lieutenant, Reuben Larzelere took custody of the prisoner, obligingly escorting him to the rear. And Lieutenant Larzelere stayed in the rear. [38] In the first charge, Company A alone lost five killed and seven wounded. "We made four charges down the hill and drove them every time. We killed a great many of them in the third charge. I got another prisoner and told him to go to the rear. As soon as Orlin Laylin saw him he said he would watch him so he up and shot him."[39] In one of these charges, a Confederate soldier fired at Sergeant John Coblentz and missed. He ". . . then threw down his gun and up with his hands; but Coblentz said it was too late, and he bayonetted him."[40] In a similar act of passion, Private Tim Deggett killed another Confederate. A fellow soldier later recalled the incident. "Tim is a rough wicked boy but has a heart like an ox, makes a good soldier. He is the one that shot the Reb at Springhill after we had surrendered."[41] These incidents dramatize the fierce struggle that ensued. The violent actions of Coblentz and others, also illustrated an unusual employment of the bayonet. Certainly fixing bayonets and charging the enemy was common throughout the Civil War; using the bayonet to kill an enemy was not.[42]

The Union troops held their ground, but now the greatest threat was being concentrated on the left flank and Coburn began reorganizing his defense. The 85th Indiana was ordered to change front facing the east as Coburn began organizing his new line parallel to the railroad. He brought the 19th Michigan alongside and to the right of the 85th. The 33rd Indiana remained the only regiment facing south as its left joined the 19th Michigan on the right at a 45 degree angle to the main line. The 22nd Wisconsin was drawn up on the extreme left next to the 85th Indiana.[43]

But the Confederates kept coming back, again and again. Two guns of King's battery were strategically positioned on the hill east of the pike which had previously been defended and would soon zero in on their target. Van Dorn then sent the brigades of Forrest, Armstrong and Whitfield to drive the Yankees from their hill. This time, their attack was too much; resistance broke and Coburn's brigade retreated, hoping to organize a stronger position on the higher ground to the west. King's Battery was relocated on the hill just abandoned and again directed effective fire on Coburn's retreating forces. A new line was quickly thrown together as battle weary Yankees awaited what would be the last Confederate assault. Forrest was ready for the clincher - having swept around behind the Union position he had effectively sealed off any possibility of retreat. With the fresh regiments of N.N. Cox and Jacob Biffle, he ordered his brigade to charge. Union ammunition nearly exhausted, resistance was hopeless. After firing a volley at the approaching Rebels, Coburn's command threw down their weapons and surrendered. [45]

In this last Confederate rush, a captain in Biffle's regiment captured the colors of the 19th Michigan. [46]

The casualties suffered at Thompson's Station attest to the fierce struggle that had been waged. Coburn's losses included 48 killed, 247 wounded and 1,151 captured or missing. The 19th Michigan and 33rd Indiana shared the dubious honor of recording the highest number of unit casualties. Those killed and wounded in these two regiments totaled 213. For the Confederates, Van Dorn reported casualties of 357. They suffered an astounding total of 38 casualties among officers including 14 who were killed in action, grim testimony of the price paid by officers who led by example. [47] Although victorious, the Rebels knew they had been in a real fight. Shortly after surrendering, a Confederate soldier approached the ranks of Company E stating: "For God's sake give me one of youan's guns, for youn's killed weans before weans had thought of firing at youans." [48]

Following Thompson's Station, there was a sustained effort to fix the blame for defeat. Among infantry officers and privates, the concensus was clear; the fault lay with the supporting cavalry, the artillery, and Bloodgood's portion of the 22nd Wisconsin for cowardly retreating in the face of the enemy. No doubt, Coburn seriously missed these elements during the critical point of the battle; however, the die was cast by others many hours earlier. Naturally the cavalry, artillery and that portion of the 22nd Wisconsin involved saw it differently. It was the infantry who stayed and fought in an impossible situation, ignoring the opportunity to retreat. Alibis and excuses were abundant. Considering the contradiction, everyone could not possible be telling the truth. To suggest that the facts about command decisions at Thompson's Station are elusive, is a gross understatement. Those who escaped had real reason to defend their actions or to provide excuses; there may even have been some collaboration. Those who were captured were surely looking for someone to blame. And, they had plenty of time to brood while in prison. They too, may have gotten their stories together. Naturally their reports were written after they were released and following the opportunity for considerable reflection.

For Colonel Thomas J. Jordan, commanding the Union cavalry, the explanation for what happened at Thompson's Station was fairly simple. First, Coburn made a serious tactical error in attempting to seize the Confederate battery west of the pike. That fateful decision was the beginning of the end. "Seeing that all was lost, I was ordered by Colonel Coburn to call in my cavalry and form it in such position as to cover his retreat." Jordan then acted promptly to withdraw the Union artillery just as it was in his estimation about to be gobbled up by the unrushing Rebels. After a 15-minute wait and deciding that Coburn was not coming, he started back toward Franklin in order to save his own neck. According to Jordan, his retreat was seriously contested by Rebels numbering more than three times his own strength. And to top it all off, Jordan claimed to be unaware of the very existence of the 124th Ohio. If only they had not left the field without orders, he could "have safely covered the retreat."[49]   Finally, Jordan arrogantly and ridiculously claimed that had this Ohio infantry regiment not retreated or had it sought his instructions, he could " . . . have given the enemy such a chastisement as would have made him more cautious in the future."[50]

Despite the facts, everyone had a plausible explanation for his actions. Captain Charles Aleshire reported that he withdrew his battery upon Colonel Jordan's orders. His report suggests that advancing Confederates threatened his gun positions and, therefore, prompted the decision, with the section west of the pike being last to leave. Aleshire implies that he did not immediately respond to Jordan's command, staying as long as he could pouring canister into the charging Confederate ranks. Two other observations cause even more reason to wonder. "I did not withdraw these guns until the infantry had all left." [51] Earlier in the fight, he reportedly warned Coburn that he was running out of ammunition.

According to Lieutenant Colonel Bloodgood, he too left the field under orders. In his recollection, the 22nd Wisconsin had just crossed over the road to the west side when it became evident the Rebels were flanking their position. To counter this threat, one of Coburn's aides ordered Bloodgood to move his regiment and thus extend the Union flank. Bloodgood said that in the process, part of the regiment got cut off and ultimately his portion which shifted toward the pike was "compelled to retire." [52]

There is much about these three versions which demands close examination. The notion that the cavalry and artillery retreated only after a hard fight in which their safety was threatened and their ultimate escape seriously challenged is an exaggeration. For one thing, the Confederates obviously did not think they put up much of a fight. Van Dorn in his report, dismissed the role of the Union cavalry and artillery very casually. "The Federal cavalry, with one regiment of infantry, after offering some resistance to General Forrest, taking battery and baggage train with them, precipitately left the field." [53] Both Van Dorn and Forrest make it clear that the latter began his sweep around the Union left flank after the artillery had been withdrawn. [54] Casualties are another indication of how heavily a unit is engaged. Reading the accounts of Jordan, Aleshire and others, leaves the impression that the artillery and cavalry were in the thick of the fight. [55] Yet the 18th Ohio Battery did not suffer a single casualty and the entire cavalry force numbering some 600, had a total of 18 casualties; certainly not very heavy losses compared to the 19 dead and wounded suffered by a single infantry company of the 19th Michigan. [56]

A number of other aspects concerning Jordan's actions and his accounts of the retreat must also be questioned. His statement that he was heavily pressured as he tried to cover the retreat of the artillery and supply train is difficult to accept. It seems significant that Forrest makes no mention of a pursuit, probably because his brigade was busy on the west side of the pike helping assault the Union position there. [57]   After being ordered by Coburn to prepare for a retreat, Jordan made no further attempt to communicate with his commander. The only initiative that he demonstrated was to get to the rear. Then too, for a unit whose primary assignment is to act as the commander's "eyes and ears," it seems inexcusable that Jordan would not know which units were attached to Coburn's brigade. Finally, in assessing Jordan's leadership, one has to suspect that he was especially anxious to avoid capture on this occasion for the colonel was fresh out of a Confederate prison in Richmond. He had been captured during a retreat near Tompkinsville, Kentucky and had just rejoined the 9th Pennsylvania Cavalry and assumed command in January, 1863. [58]

After examining the apparent facts, it is difficult to conclude that Aleshire was eager to engage the enemy. Colonel Gilbert issued a stinging indictment of the Captain's conduct when he reported that:

> . . . early in the day, March 5 before any firing commenced on either side, Captain Aleshire attempted to retreat with his battery. He met Colonel Baird of the Eighty-fifth Indiana, and myself on the turnpike, as we were advancing. We halted him, and ascertained from him that he was going back with his battery without orders. We protested against it, telling him he would create a panic among the men; but he persisted, and would have done so had we permitted it; but just at this juncture he received your order to take position and reluctantly turned about. [59]

Aleshire's claim that he was nearly out of ammunition is also questionable. According to Coburn and his two aides, Lieutenants Edwin I. Bachman and H. B. Adams, the latter was sent to verify Aleshire's concern. Surprisingly, Adams reported that there were 230 rounds of shell and 70 rounds of canister left. [60] It is also hard to believe that the Confederates were about to overrun his gun positions. Generally, artillery becomes vulnerable to foot soldiers or dismounted cavalry when it is unprotected by its own infantry. Aleshire's statement that he was left to his own defenses is utter nonsense. He pulled his section on the left long before either the 19th Michigan or 22nd Wisconsin crossed over to the west hill. Furthermore, he abandoned that position prior to the time the infantry regiments engaged the attacking Confederates. [61] His action precipitated the move to envelope the Union left. [62] On the right side of the pike, it took three Confederate attacks combatted with numerous counterattacks and hours of hard fighting before Coburn's brigade was finally dislodged. Long before the infantry withdrew to another position, the 18th Ohio Battery had departed the scene and was making its way back toward Franklin. Additionally, it appears that Captain Aleshire was confused when he wrote his report. Aside from Jordan's ignorance of the 124th Ohio, he seems to be the only officer who did not know the disposition of Coburn's brigade. Even more puzzling is his statement that he talked to General Gilbert shortly after leaving the field but before starting toward Franklin. [63]

Lieutenant Colonel Bloodgood's claim that he was ordered by one of Coburn's aides to extend his flank is unsupported. The only substantiation comes from a private in Company A, 22nd Wisconsin who stated that ". . . one of Coburn's staff officers rode up and gave the order to Lieutenant Colonel Bloodgood to file his regiment out on the pike and check the flanking movement." [64] Throughout the engagement, Coburn employed only two aides, Lieutenants Adams and Bachman to deliver messages. The reports of both deny any knowledge of such an order being given to Bloodgood. [65] The recollection of Brigade Quartermaster Sergeant John Wilkins also weakens Bloodgood's statement. In his position, Sergeant Wilkins was able to observe the action as he moved about directing the resupply of ammunition and movement of wounded to the rear. He apparently had some conversation with Bloodgood for he wrote, "I believe the Lt. Col. said that there was no use of fighting." [66] Even more convincing is a significant discrepancy revealed by the fact that Lieutenant Colonel Bloodgood wrote two versions of his retreat from the battlefield at Thompson's Station. His official report dated March 8, 1863 in which he claims to have acted upon orders, turns out to be a second edition. His first account was written to his brother on March 5, 1863 and describes a substantially different set of circumstances which led to his exit from the battlefield. Just hours after the battle, Bloodgood wrote: "In the confusion we got no orders; each regiment had to look out for themselves . . I sent word down the line to the Colonel to move the regiment in that direction by the flank . . . I gave the order as there was no time to hesitate." [67]

Coburn, himself drew sharp criticism from several sources. Caustically, Chief of Staff James A. Garfield referred to him as a fool. [68] Colonel Emerson Opdycke, stationed at Franklin, shared Garfield's opinion and speculated ". . . that Coburn desired the honors of a victory for the sake of the 'stars'."[69] Major General Granger found the brigade commander most responsible stating: "If anyone is to blame, it is Colonel Coburn, in not keeping General Gilbert advised, and in not approaching the enemy with sufficient caution. . ."[70] It is upon Granger's last point that Coburn's leadership is most vulnerable to criticism. Coburn clearly went beyond what he must have understood was the prerogative of a reconnaissance mission. His greatest error was allowing his command to become engaged in a pitched battle. Yet, criticism of Coburn must be tempered somewhat by considering the failures of his commander, General Gilbert. Gilbert must be faulted for indecisiveness which set the stage for Coburn's dilemma. Seemingly, he had two alternatives: either clearly remind Coburn of his mission or support him. Both of which he failed to execute. Ironically, Gilbert had been under investigation for failure to support General Alexander McCook's corps at the Battle of Perryville. His commission having expired in March, he was not reappointed. [71]

As might be expected, there were many evaluations of the outcome of Thompson's Station and not all came from high places. One unusual account if left by a member of the 19th

Michigan Infantry who spent March 4 and 5 helping man the guns of the 18th Ohio Battery. Carlos Baker's assessment is certainly unique from the standpoint of his potential for objectivity. He praised Colonel Coburn explaining that insufficient numbers accounted for the difference between victory and defeat.

> General Coburn was in the thickest of the fight, he gave his orders with a clearness and precision that was charming to see and hear at such a time, riding from one Battery to the other and to every part of the field encouraging the men, and showing clearly that he did not fear to go where he would order his men to. He rode up to our Battery not more than ten minutes before we fell back and sung out to us: "Give it to 'em, boys! fight the devils!" And we did give it to 'em with canister until they were almost upon us and then 'we fell back in good order,' and so the day was lost just because we did not have men enough; if we only had twenty thousand of the men that were lying idle at Nashville to have went with us into the fight and fifty pieces of good artillery as the 18th Ohio Battery and all the men as good and true as they are and plenty of ammunition, etc, we would have captured the rebels en masse, instead of having them take us up between their thumb and finger and just blowing the life out of us; but if and if don't fight battles nor gain victories, they required good management and hard work. [72]

Unless history destines that one surrender as Benjamin Prentiss did at Shiloh, regiments rarely distinguish themselves by being captured. Quite the opposite, being captured can be the worst kind of defeat. It often labels a regiment and almost casts shame on its members. It leaves a kind of reputation which causes a unit to seek an opportunity to redeem itself despite the fact that it may have put up a good fight. There is little question that the fact of being captured marred the reputation of the 19th Michigan and blighted its exceptional conduct at Thompson's Station. Following parole from prison and subsequent reorganization, the 19th Michigan was relegated to a long period of inactivity and "safe" duty in Tennessee. The memory of Thompson's Station would linger for a long, long time.

If one can look beyond capture and defeat, the 19th Michigan Infantry performed in exemplary fashion at Thompson's Station. In its first engagement the regiment's ability to resist stubbornly attack after attack while consistently maintaining its composure was truly remarkable. It fought with a vengeance, aggressively engaging the Rebels in hand-to-hand combat and head-on counterattacks. And it paid the price. The regiment went into the fight with an effective strength of 531; 21% became casualties. The 19th Michigan lost 20 killed and another 92 wounded, greater casualties than any other regiment, Confederates included. [73] Some of those who were wounded and survived the day were taken to Confederate hospitals in Columbia, Tennessee. Their wounds were severe and crippling. James Polite, arm broken and shot in the breast; William Depue, wounded in the arm so severely that it was amputated; Aaron McConnell, wounded in the hip; Martin Sammueller, shot in the ankle and his foot amputated; and Darius Ackerly, one eye shot away and wounded in the left thigh; vivid examples of the agony of war. [74] For others hospitalization meant only prolonging their inevitable death. The horrors of March 5 struck hard at the bodies and minds of these men from southwestern Michigan. "This has been a sad day for us I feel crushed & stunned" wrote Chaplain Israel Cogshall. [75] Despair characterized the letters of some. Judson Austin mustered all of his strength to write to his family and describe their personal tragedy. "This is the most dreadful letter I ever tried to write in my life. I tell you it comes hard for me to send the news home. But is must be done by someone and while you read this, thank God from the bottom of your heart that there is someone left to tell the sad fate of the others. Sad, sad, indeed that men should meet to shoot and kill each other in this kind of style." [76] Austin went on to account for the wounded and missing and the death of two Company B comrades. "One was Henry Blakesly, a fine young man, but this could not stop the fatal ball . . The other is my brother, your brother, and our friend. He was shot while loading his gun. The ball struck him in the front part of the head and life ceased almost instantly. This was a trying time for me." [77] Another more fortunate 19th Michigan soldier lay convalescing in a Nashville hospital. He had counted three bullet holes in his coat, a fourth ball had struck him in the hand. His aspiration was to even a score. "I hope it will get well for I owe a grudge to one of Van Dorn's 'butternuts.' If he wears the same clothes I will know him." [78]

Commendation for the regiment's conduct on the battlefield came from a variety of sources. It was generally observed that they had fought well. Colonel Utley recalled seeing them ". . . repulse several charges, where the enemy outnumbered them three to one." [79]   General Baird's Assistant Adjutant General, Captain B. H. Polk, provided the following assessment: "It may be said in general terms that the 19th Mich. behaved splendidly and fought with an unflinching resolution and bravery rarely if ever excelled." [80]   The Confederates were impressed too. Van Dorn showed his respect by allowing brigade commander Coburn and Colonel Gilbert and Major Shafter of the 19th to keep their sidearms and horses after surrendering. [81] Confederate soldier turned author John Wyeth, would later record that the 19th Michigan " . . . had greatly distinguished itself. . ." at Thompson's Station. [82] And there was pride within the unit too, illustrated by a soldier's admiration for this company commander. "Our officers behaved nobly, and here let me say that no other man will company 'E' have to lead them but the noble and brave Capt. Baker." [83]

The outcome of this engagement at Thompson's Station had little impact on later military operations in the western theatre. It did, however, supply Rosecrans with information regarding the enemy's strength although the price for obtaining it was high. Significantly, from Rosecrans' perspective, it served to confirm his grave concern over the superiority of Concederate cavalry. And for Coburn and his brigade, it meant their induction into the realities of war.

7

PRISONERS OF WAR

Hurried off the battlefield, the 19th Michigan Infantry began a difficult and miserable 17-day trek to prison. The first part of their journey was covered on foot, when they were forced to march some 75 miles from Thompson's Station to Tullahoma, passing through Columbia, Lewisburg and Shelbyville enroute. The first night they made Columbia, a hard march of 20 miles, as the Rebels obviously tried to get a lead on any potential pursuer. They were confined at the courthouse in an area described as a "nasty place". The next day, rations were issued for three days - a half pound of pork and a handful of crackers.[1] These meager provisions were soon consumed, long before another issuance was forthcoming. One famished soldier scrounged corn from the horses to eat, while another stole an ear off a Negroe's wagon as it passed by.[2]

Their march to Tullahoma was arduous because they were traveling over rough roads and enduring the cold misery of incessant rain. Aside from the rain, they all experienced several good soakings as they forded creeks sometimes waist deep, causing them to be wet for days.[3] An enterprising noncom in Company I avoided one stream by paying a Rebel cavalryman a dollar to transport him across.[4]

From Lewisburg, the column moved northeast toward Shelbyville in what seemed like a roundabout way. First Sergeant George Livingston concluded that the detour was probably just part of the punishment being inflicted. The Confederates, however; were trying to avoid the Union cavalry. Just in case they were unsuccessful and the Federals rescued their captive comrades, the prisoners were immediately directed to sign parole oaths.[5] The column trudged on eluding Union cavalry, passing through Shelbyville, and arriving at Tullahoma on March 11. At Shelbyville, pro-Union citizens befriended the prisoners bringing them food until their supportive deeds were detected by Rebel army officers and stopped.[6] Those who left accounts of the regiment's agonizing journey to Libby Prison concurred in describing their brief stay at Tullahoma as the worst part. The men arrived at dusk, rain-soaked, and weary, and were left standing in an open field in front of Bragg's breastworks. They spent the night on their feet, standing in mud over their ankles while cold penetrated their tired bodies. [7] In the morning the Confederates made it even tougher by taking away their blankets, overcoats and canteens.[8] Despite stringency and privation, some members of the regiment believed their guards, members of the 4th Mississippi Cavalry, treated them considerately and humanely. At least once during the march, Rebel guards shared their own rations of corn meal with prisoners. In general, the enlisted men appeared anxious to aid their captives but the officers quickly intervened at the first evidence of leniency. A surprising bond of respect prevailed among these combatants, which was revealed when the prisoners departed Tullahoma aboard railroad cars, their guards gave three rousing cheers and the prison-bound, returned an equally hearty farewell.

The 19th Michigan rode the rest of the way to Libby, although their suffering was hardly lessened by the convenience of travel. All prisoners were herded into open cattle cars with as many as 70 packed into a single car. It took ten more days on the rails to reach Richmond with only occasional stops along the way. At Lynchburg, Virginia, the prisoners were paraded down a main street and subjected to the taunts of children. On March 22, the 19th Michigan Infantry Regiment began its confinement in Libby Prison, Richmond, Virginia. [10]

Quite naturally, feelings of bewilderment and anxiety followed the capture of the 19th Michigan. The weeks that followed were times of uncertainty. Since mail to and from prison was difficult and infrequent, soldiers were generally cut off from any correspondence with their families. Undoubtedly in some cases, families were unsure if their sons, husbands, or fathers had even survived the battle or the horrors of prison. There was even speculation that Colonel Gilbert was dead.[11] Rumors could be especially damaging given the circumstances. Charley Prentiss was concerned about the grief rumors could cause and he wrote to his wife cautioning:

> . . . I dont want you to believe anything you here in
> the newspapers. We have had quite a number of papers
> & every one has lied about the battle of Tompson station
> . . . You have undoubtedly heard some awful stories
> about that battle & what you here different from that I
> tell you is false, one of the boys of Co. I came in the day
> of the battle in great excitement & says he saw 6 men
> fall from on his right hand & swore by all that was good
> & great that he saw one half of the regiment fall, when
> he was not in the fight atall . . . now if he is a good
> righter or composer & send it to some editor & have it
> published, many a poor womans heart will be broken.[12]

Countering the negative potential Prentiss feared, the newspapers' practice of printing soldiers' letters provided invaluable information concerning the whereabouts of other soldiers. Ira Carpenter, himself confined to a hospital, provided such a report concerning the condition of several members of the regiment convalescing in various Nashville hospitals. Certainly his letter also reassured concerned readers that he and others were being well cared for. "I have been happily disappointed in regard to the hospitals. . ."[13] His hospital experience was far better than most expected.

The remainder of the regiment, included Company D, those who escaped the field, and others who had been left behind in camp due to sickness, were destined to enjoy only a short reprieve. The day after the battle, a contingent rode out toward Thompson's Station under a flag of truce hoping to bury the dead and care for the wounded. They were met by Confederate pickets who conveyed their request to General Van Dorn and after waiting five hours, were told to leave. Allegedly the dead had been buried and the wounded ministered to, but Rebel surgeons questioned the adequacy of care given to the wounded due to the shortage of bandages, ether and choloroform. [14]

The Rebels had infested Middle Tennessee, posing a serious threat to the area in and around Franklin. On Sunday morning, March 8, Chaplain Cogshall set out to find a church to attend. His search illustrates well the war torn conditions in the Franklin vicinity. He ". . . found Methodist riddle with Bullets and deserted. Episcopalian used as a hospital." Finally Cogshall went inside a Presbyterian church but the booming of cannon caused him such concern that he rode back to camp where he discovered that the remnants of his regiment had orders to move.[15] This small force was sent to join Company D of the 19th Michigan which had been guarding a railroad bridge over the Little Harpeth River two miles south of Brentwood. Those companies of the 22nd Wisconsin which survived Thompson's Station were ordered to Brentwood to guard the railroad station. Lieutenant Colonel Bloodgood commanded the 22nd Wisconsin Companies, and Captain Bassett exercised authority over the 19th Michigan detachment since he was the senior officer present.[16] Apparently Bassett's leadership was as sadly lacking here as it had been earlier on the battlefield. Chaplain Cogshall's journal includes frequent entries bemoaning the lack of discipline and the casual attitude of the men and their commander. The day following their arrival at the bridge, Cogshall recorded an angry rebuke:

> To day is bright & clear tried to get a detail put up
> tent but Capt Bassett is either utterly incompetent to
> perform the duties of commander or has deliberately
> made up his mind that he will do nothing he has deter-
> mined that he will leave the service at all hazzards & so

will do nothing in it He has tendered his resignation 3 times already failing in all attempts to get help I took off my coat called to my help our cook & the man who takes care of Q.M. & my horse & went to work & before noon had up the 5 tents we occupy inclusive of cook tent. We are in a most deplorable condition There is no authority no Subordination men go where they please & when they please Have been strongly tempted to resign my Chaplaincy to day if the Rebels desire us to accompany our commands they have only to come & take us.[17]

Near the end of the week, Captain Bassett called the men out for a formation. Many ignored the order and of those who stood the formation, many carelessly reported without their arms. In general, men disregarded orders, firing their rifles at will and foolhardily riding the mules about camp.[18] Cogshall's mood turned from anger to sadness as he lamented: "If matters do not change we shall become a laughing Stock When I look at things as they are & remember what this fine Regt once was I am Sick."[19]

Once again a detachment was sent back to the battlefield at Thompson's Station. This time in an attempt to identify the dead buried there. Two mass graves were opened but only one body was identified as a 19th Michigan soldier. The bodies were reburied and personal affects sent home to family and friends.[20]

The "free" portion of the 19th Michigan enjoyed a pleasant situation although located at a place frequented by marauding guerrillas. Their defense of the railroad bridge was strengthened considerably by the availability of a stockade located near the crossing. Charley Prentiss wrote confidently to his wife that the regiment occupied a practically impregnable fortress:

They cant get in upon us before we know it & have time to get in the stockade. With 200 men we could hold back & fight & whip 4,000 of infantry or cavelry or mounted cavelry. This is the ground plan of the stockade this about 100 ft. squir built of logs set up end warp 12 ft high above the ground & a good trench on the out side 3½ ft dept. we have amnition enough to fight a week, there is a small port hole in each log, just large enough to stick the mussle of the gun through so you can see how safe we are situated. [21]

In the early morning of March 25, a Negro slipped into camp warning the 19th Michigan that the Rebels were tearing up the tracks south of the stockade. By daylight, the Confederates were visible on all sides. [22] Earlier that morning, Forrest had surprised the Union outpost at Brentwood, forcing it to surrender after a very brief exchange. Leaving part of his command to finish the task of looting and burning, Forrest personally led the 4th Mississippi and 10th Tennessee Cavalry Regiments to attack the stockade and its garrison. [23] After getting into position, Forrest sent in a demand for surrender. While Bassett hesitated momentarily, Forrest encouraged his decision by ordering one of S.L. Freeman's guns to fire. "... they shot one shell amungst us which struck a tree in the rear of my tent & burst ... it came so clost to me that I coued feel his breath." [24] The gesture convincingly prompted Bassett to surrender. In all, Forrest captured 230 at the bridge and 521 more in Brentwood. When the news reached Major General Gordon Granger, he angrily blistered the two outposts, calling them "milk and water soldiers." [25] While angry because Bloodgood and Bassett had given up without a fight, General Granger maintained he could have relieved the garrisons if they had only resisted for a short while:

> From all I can ascertain, Lieutenant Colonel Blood-good surrendered Brentwood, and Captain (E.B.) Bassett the stockade, unnecessarily, after firing but very few shots, and without harming a man killed or wounded. Had they fought for one hour, our cavalry and infantry would have arrived on the spot and cut the rebels to pieces. I visited the stockade in person, and found it very strong - capable of holding 200 men and it

could easily have been defended for a long time, but not a mark of a bullet could be discovered on it. [26]

Like their comrades before them, this 19th Michigan garrison captured near Brentwood was immediately marched south toward confinement in Richmond. These captives followed a similar route and despite being prisoners of war anxiously anticipated reunion with their fellow Wolverines. "We have not found the other boys yet, but find their names writen in the prisons when we stop."[27]

Owing to the absence of correspondence and very sketchy descriptions recorded in diaries and journals, very little is known regarding the imprisonment of the 19th Michigan Infantry Regiment at Richmond. The enlisted men and officers were separated and confined in a tobacco warehouse named Libby Prison. Confinement for those captured at Thompson's Station began on March 22 while the remainder of the regiment entered Libby on April 9. The enlisted men in the first group, spent a total of 31 days in captivity although only 9 as inmates at Libby. They were released March 31. Their officers, however, were not exchanged until May 6. Those captured at Brentwood were POW's for 18 days which included just 2 days of confinement at Richmond. These men were shipped north on April 11. [28]

Aside from these basic facts, the sparse accounts left afford only a glimpse of prison life. It seems certain that the men experienced hunger, cold and a crowded existence. Meager rations were provided twice daily. The prison staple was mule meat. "The beef they gave us, was tainted so bad you could smell it one-fourth of an hour before we got it and a week after."[29] Occasionally "rice soup" was substituted for mule on the menu; judged to be ". . . the water the mule meat was cooked in, with a little rice in it."[30] Blankets were in short supply, requiring at least some sharing while others went without. The lack of fires and window glass added to the cold misery. The men slept on bare floors in double rows with feet practically meeting in the center. Twice each day the men were formed in ranks and "counted by a little saucy rebel

119

sergeant."[31] Since they had been exposed to smallpox, a Negro frequented their quarters carrying a bucket of burning leather intended as both a cure and preventive. And it was "nothing to see 10 or 15 men with shirts off hunting lice."[32] Near the end of their confinement, it was reasoned that someone had irritated the prison authorities causing the water to be shut off for 48 hours. Yet enterprising guards made the precious commodity available at $1.00 a pail.[33]

The regiment regained its freedom at Annapolis, Maryland and after a brief stay, was shipped west to Ohio. The men rendezvoused at Camp Chase in what was termed a parole camp but their future was unclear. Disorganization and aimless waiting characterized the weeks that followed. Men longed to return home to Michigan yet furloughs were not granted. Large numbers ignored that small technicality and took "French leave". In many instances, it appears that officers out of sympathy looked the other way. Of course, they too "deserted." Private Rice's account of his decision to go home is illustrative of the permissive control being exercised. Supposedly he requested a leave from the commanding officer. Although denied on the basis that he lacked such authority, the officer rhetorically asked "Don't you know the way home?" That was sufficient encouragement and "we started off in small squads as if for a walk; and so a large share of the 19th Michigan went home."[34] Those who remained in Camp Chase were in some cases motivated by a strong sense of duty; others stayed because they feared reprisals from commanders who enforced army regulations. Ed and Les Baird and their buddy Vern Rose, just were not as lucky as some. They "skedaddled" only to be caught and returned to camp and confinement in the bullpen.[35] Sergeant John Griffis was one who felt a strong obligation to duty. He made it clear to his sister that ". . . unless I can come home honorable I shall never come." [36] and he made his conviction stick. Never privileged to have a leave, Griffis was killed at Resaca, May 15, 1864.[37]

8

"ON OUR ROAD BACK TO DIXIE"

Shortly after noon on June 8, 1863, a reorganized 19th Michigan Infantry marched toward Columbus, Ohio and began its return journey to the South. At Columbus the men drew four months back pay and in typical army fashion, many soldiers became very drunk. Near dusk they departed by train for Cincinnati, a noisy and generally intoxicated regiment. Their train arrives very early in the morning, and the men were immediately marched onboard the steamer *Shenanago*. After a short layover, they were soon proceeding down the Ohio. [1] In remarkable fashion, history was recurring for this Wolverine regiment. Certainly the coincidence did not escape the thoughts of these men as they recalled a similar trip which started near Columbus and advanced to Louisville, Nashville and finally on to Franklin. Memories were recalled as they floated past Camp Hooker and Fort Jones. The irony of practically reliving so recent an experience and the second time knowing generally what was in store for them, must have evoked reflection. It was Henry Noble's impression that the officers were anxious to get back in the field. That was how one made rank, an ambition that obsessed many officers. William R. Shafter had just made lieutenant colonel and the occasion called for a special formation at which Gilbert announced the promotion. His remarks brought cheers and the expected request for the new lieutenant colonel to speak. Shafter said

121

"he never made a speech in his life but he would be with them in a fight." Still smarting from the disgraceful conduct of his commander at Thompson's Station, Private Austin instructed his wife to "Tell Cap. Bassett these are the kind of men we want here. fiting men not talking men."[2] It is not surprising that Private Noble was less enthusiastic than Shafter and others about starting another campaign, yet he was a soldier with dedication and braced himself for whatever the future might hold. "But we enlisted to fight and must take what comes and leave the result in the hands of God. I am in hopes that I shall live to see this Rebellion crushed and be permitted to return home safe and sound. Many a young man has left as good a home and as many friends as I have who never will return but has laid down his life upon the battle field or within some gloomy hospital. And will this be my fate?"[3]

The trip aboard the *Shenanago* was pleasant and serene. The enchantment of the river and picturesque shoreline soon captured a young man's thoughts, displacing anxiety and concern with lust for life and new adventure:

> I think I never saw such spendid landscape scenes as are presented to the eye all along on both sides of the River and were I a landscape painter I should want no better studio than the hurricane deck of some Steamer on the Ohio R. Here is the advantage that we have of you folks at home. Although we are deprived of some of the luxuries that you have there and are exposed to many dangers and hardships yet we have opportunities to view portions of the country that we never would see were we out of the service of Uncle Sam. [4]

The 19th Michigan had spent less than 24 hours in Louisville when it boarded a freight train bound for the Tennessee state capital. The ride was less than pleasurable as they jolted along in cattle cars without any seating. The 185-mile trip finally ended with their arrival in Nashville around midafternoon on June 11. The men were billeted on the fifth floor of a large unfurnished building. Consistent with the privilege of military rank, the officers stayed in hotels. Some took up residence at the Commerical Hotel which according to the chaplain, was "First Class in nothing but its charges."5While in the city, the whole regiment went to the theatre. It was the kind of evening that an articulate soldier like Henry Noble would enjoy. "Ill assure the performance was splendid being composed of two acts the first was called the Farce of the Robers and was quite exciting after which a young fellow that acted the Irishman to perfection came out and sang some comic Irish songs. The performance ended with Paddy Miles or the Limeric boy which kept the audience in a roar of laughter."6 Apparently Noble laughed until he hurt and became so worked up that his sleep was filled with exhilarating dreams. Despite the fun, it upset him so, he vowed to forego any more theatrical productions. 7

The day after their arrival, the regiment moved a short distance out of the city where it established camp near the state prison. Here it drew new weapons, accoutrements and tents to replace those lost to the Confederates back at Thompson's Station. The 19th was again issued the Enfield rifled musket, a weapon appreciated by the men. Yet it was the new tent more than anything else that drew the most attention. Previously the regiment had been sheltered in Sibley tents, a tepee shaped structure capable of accomodating 16 to 18 men. The new shelter called a dog tent, was designed to hold two men. Each carried half of the structure in his knapsack. The two halves each about five feet square, were buttoned together to form the skin. Poles and sometimes even muskets were used to hold the tent erect. Nearly every soldier's letter commented on his new living quarters. Sergeant Hager described the shelter in detail. Prentiss welcomed the new tent expecting it to provide more privacy and fresher air to breathe. The concensus, however, did not support his opinion. Most were unhappy with the switch and probably for the reverse of what Prentiss saw as an advantage. The two-man tent destroyed a coveted sense of community and some immediately found ways to button several shelter halves together forming a larger tent in which several men could reside. 8 Others doubted the serviceability of the new equipment. "They are a very nice thing in fair weather but should we have any rain (which we undoubtedly shall) we might as well be outside as in They are made of course linen and will shed rain about as much as so much paper." [9]

When off duty, soldiers were free to roam about. The scars of war reminded one soldier of how thankful the folks back home should be that war was being fought in Tennessee instead of in Michigan. One day while out nosing around, Private Cyrus Wheeler visited what had been a beautiful brick house. Now deserted, ". . . the window casings are torn out and the walls are otherwise mutilated. The garden wall is torn down the rose bushes and flower beds together with the other ornaments and shade trees are all broken down and destroyed. . ." [10] Aside from the expected ravages of war, this once lovely southern home had been singled out for condemnation; an inscription on a post stated: "this is a Secesh house." [11]

On Thursday, the 18th, the regiment was on the move again pointing toward a new base at Franklin. Henry Noble reiterated an earlier conclusion that the officers were itching for a fight. To his girlfriend he explained: "We could have staid here if our Col had been willing but the old hero is to ambitious for that accordingly he telegraphed to Rosecrans to be permitted to go to the front. Of course his request has been granted and we are going where the famous 19th will have a chance to exhibit their fiting propensities to the best advantage." [12]

Stopping briefly at Brentwood along the way, the regiment was again reminded of its recent past. Not only the place but the reported presence of menancing Rebels certainly convinced Colonel Gilbert that he wanted no part of being captured again. Gilbert ". . . was afraid that we might possibly meet with more than our numbers in which case if taken we might have the pleasure of another trip through dixie which would not terminate so favorable to our interest as it did before as there is no more exchanging of prisoners and a few of us might get initiated into the misteries of pulling hemp." [13] Despite the heat, he pushed his command, reaching Franklin the same day. There were few troops stationed in the village and the possibility of an attack caused great anxiety. For several days the 19th Michigan was called out at 3:00 A.M. in the morning and remained in line of battle until daybreak. [14]

The 22nd Wisconsin arrived in camp at Franklin on June 22, rejoining the old brigade for the first time since Thompson's Station. It received an official welcome complete with military honors as the 19th Michigan, 33rd Indiana and 85th Indiana all lined up, and the Wisconsin boys, led by a band, marched past at present arms. [15]

Earlier Noble had blamed Colonel Gilbert's eagerness for causing the regiment's relocation to Franklin. However, the decision to move on June 23, 1863, was made for bigger reasons and by bigger officers. General Rosecrans was being pressured by both Washington authorities and Grant to launch an advance upon Bragg aimed at keeping his forces occupied and in Tennessee. Bragg had prepared a strong defense, anchored at Shelbyville and Wartrace with his flanks extended by cavalry to Columbia and McMinnville. The terrain formed a natural barrier as all roads leading to his position passed through a series of defiles each heavily defended. The Nashville and Chattanooga Railroad provided a lifeline to both armies connecting critical points of Nashville, Murfreesboro, Wartrace, Tullahoma and Chattanooga. Nashville and Chattanooga were the supply bases for the opposing armies. About 45 miles of track separated Rosecrans' headquarters at Murfreesboro and Bragg's at Tullahoma. [16]

Rosecrans planned a brilliant offensive strategy which worked to near perfection. Using Granger's corps and the bulk of his cavalry to fake a thrust at Bragg's left, Rosecrans intended to hold General Leonidas Polk at Shelbyville, while his remaining three corps struck General William Hardee, hoping ultimately to outflank him. [17] Henry Noble did not know the details of the plan but his confidence in Old Rosey flourished. Jokingly, he informed his girl of his own plans for the Fourth of July. "Gen Rosecrans an I talk of having a celebration down near Tullahoma and expect to have a grand old time he has not handed me the programe yet therefore I can't say what the performance will be. But I presume there will be quite a display of fireworks and perhaps a sumptuous dinner of hard bread and bacon." [18]

The Tullahoma Campaign was largely a lot of hard marching through mud and driving rain for the 19th Michigan. Orders came on the 23rd for the 5th and 6th Kentucky Cavalry, 78th Illinois Infantry, 33rd Indiana and the 19th Michigan to march to Truine. Starting in the early afternoon, they covered the stretch of 14 miles by dusk. [19] Though a part of Granger's Reserve Corps, the regiment was not deployed idly while awaiting a call to reinforce the attacking columns. The men were busy providing security for supply trains and prisoners and part of the time, rebuilding railroads. At Truine, the 19th along with other units, drew the assignment of escorting a caravan of several hundred supply wagons bound for Murfreesboro with provisions for Rosecrans' army. The going was tough over roads in the worst conceivable condition. Men and beasts combined strength to haul wagons through clutching mud and mire. The train halted at dark; six hours of straining and pulling had netted a mere three miles. "We could not travel the pike on account of the bridge being destroyed, and it was rumored that there was danger of the rebels attacking us there, consequently we were obligbed to go the dirt road, and in many places were compelled to go through plowed fields where the soil was saturated with water. Imagine what good roads were left for us to march over after 300 wagons with 6 mules attached to each, and two regiments of cavalry had preceeded us, the rain all the while pouring down in torrents." [20] A drenched and fatigued supply train reached Murfreesboro on the 26th, however, there was little time to rest. The following day, Rosecrans drove the Confederates out of the gaps and maneuvered around Hardee's flank to seize Mancester. [21] Up at 4:00 A.M. and rolling within an hour, the 19th Michigan and others guarded an ammunition train through to the front. By the 29th they had reached Guy's Gap and waited. [22] The next day Bragg withdrew south of the Elk River; Rosecrans had successfully prevented his sending troops to reinforce Vicksburg and the Tullahoma Campaign was over. The last time the 19th Michigan traveled through Middle Tennessee the circumstances were different and the ranks had not forgotten

In fact, Sergeant Hager felt cheated being in the rear of attacking forces. "I understand that our men are in possession of Tullahoma. I wanted to help take that place, for it was there I suffered most. . ."[23]Shelbyville had special memories for Noble recalling that he had ". . . bought five dollars worth of provisions and ate them at one meal when in the hands of the rebs."[24]

For the first time in several weeks, the regiment enjoyed a break from almost constant marching. Encamped near the Murfreesboro and Shelbyville Pike, the 19th Michigan remained at Guy's Gap until mid July. The basic fare amounted to defending the Gap and its signal post while others were busy getting out ties and repairing the railroad toward Shelbyville.

Although the day passed without celebration, July 4th would have been a big holiday for many of the men had they been home in Michigan. Undoubtedly, many recalled fonder occasions. Perhaps the day and its normally festive spirit encouraged the carefree attitude of two men who were fooling around at regimental headquarters staging a mock duel. Naturally, both assumed their weapons were empty. The Enfield rifled musket was equipped with a cap intended to be placed over the muzzle when the gun was not loaded. As the two soldiers took respective positions, these caps were properly seated but in one musket there was also a full charge. The muskets were raised, and the command to fire was given. In a shocked horror the onlookers saw the loaded weapon drive both cap and round through Private Charles Adairs' skull, striking at the same time a citizen observer in the arm. A twenty-year-old soldier who had distinguished himself at Thompson's Station with unusual valor, was dead within hours. The guilt had to be terrible for the soldier who carelessly snapped his gun only to kill a friend. Despite numerous accounts of the accident, no one identified the man who fired that fatal ball, only relating that he was the Colonel's orderly and "felt very, very bad about it." Surely the burden of his grief was surpassed only by that of a poor widow back home in Schoolcraft who had lost her only son, a terrible waste.[25]

The accident was the second in as many days. While on

127

guard duty the night before Adairs' tragic death, William Snooks discharged his musket, tearing away the trigger finger on his right hand. It was suspected that the wound was self-inflicted for purposes of an early discharge. Whatever his intentions, Snooks, who was 51, succeeded only in dismembering himself. He remained in the army, survived the war, and died a natural death in 1873.[26]

Controlling the conduct of soldiers was a constant problem for military authorities. Certainly the behavior of regiments varied greatly depending on many factors, not the least of which was the leadership of the commanding officer. Yet it seems almost impossible to make comparisons of good and bad regiments because there are no generally accepted models of conduct in either extreme. Despite these qualifications, it does not appear that the 19th Michigan Infantry had serious discipline problems. During the summer and early fall of 1863, the regiment had a very limited number of incidents involving misconduct. The typical infractions of leaving without a pass, falling asleep while on guard and unauthorized foraging occurred occasionally. Some of the boys in Company B, including playful Lester Baird, got into a row upsetting old strait-laced Sergeant Hager. "I get all out of patience to see what fools men will make of themselves." [27] Gilbert believed in making an example of offenders; consequently, the punishment was sometimes a little unusual but probably an effective deterrent. Prentiss recorded that a man was required to stand fully apparelled on a barrel for eight hours because he had gone swimming while on picket duty. Another offender had a ball and chain fastened to his leg while he walked six hours a day for ten days. [28]

More serious was the similar misconduct of two lieutenants, strangely within the span of little more than a week in July. Both Augustus Lilly and Aaron Brewer were guilty of being negligent as officers of the picket guard. Lieutenant Lilly was the first offender and his conduct was ludicrous if not sad:

It was a dark rainy night. About midnight the pickets on the right became alarmed and several guns were

128

fired to which Lient. Lilly paid no attention. The Col commanding the Brigade having heard the firing and learned that the pickets had retreated, sent the officer of the day to Lient. Lilly with instructions to reestablish the posts. The gallant Lient replied in substance that he thought it was dangerous for him to leave his quarters, he might get shot and did not in fact leave his position or visit his posts until morning. The camp so far as Lient. Lilly had anything to do with it was entirely undefended. It is the duty of every officer in charge of a picket guard to visit his posts at least once during every night and always to ascertain immediately the cause of the alarm when there is one Lient Lilly did neither. He was more anxious for his personal safety than for the command. Such conduct in an officer is a disgrace to him and so far as his influence and example can have any effect will disgrace the 19th Regt. . .The more such officers we have the worse off we shall be. [29]

At the time, Colonel Gilbert commanded the brigade. He placed Lilly under arrest and the punishment he imposed was both novel and amusing:

Lient. Lilly is released from arrest and will report for such duty as the commanding officer of the Regt. can put him to without making it dangerous for himself or the command. He will take especial charge of the four men of his guard who were driven in and if a gun is fired or an alarm given will conduct them and retire himself to some safe position and only come out when the supposed danger is all over. The men with Lient. Lilly in command will form the Nucleus of a new Co. to be designated Co. Q and all found shirking their duty or guilty of any unsoldierlike conduct will be transferred to it. Other officers will be detailed to assist in the command as soon as they prove themselves worthy of this distinction. [30]

Gilbert came down much harder on Lieutenant Brewer. Arrested for "gross and unexcusable neglect of duty" as officer of the guard, Brewer was dismissed from service, probably paying for his mistake and Lilly's too.[31]

For some reason, foraging activity seemed to have slackened during this time, perhaps reflecting the provision of better rations by the army. Though according to Charlie Prentiss, any reference to the consumption of fresh meat was a misrepresentation of the truth. Tongue in cheek, Prentiss boasted of having fresh meat three meals a day:

> The fresh that we have is what some folks call *maggets* about ¾ inch long when we take the cover off the box they jump out, we take the hides off those that we have caught by chargeing bayonet them & make a lassoo, so when they jump above the box we let one of the best & expert men of the company through the lassoo over his head, then all get hold of the end of the roap & start for some good stout tree, he will pull so hard that he will soon choke to death, one or two will make us a good meal if we are not hogish, sometimes we are in a hurry & cant wate for them to choke to death so we go at them & stone them to death with our hard bread. That is what makes me so healthy & tuff. [32]

Camp was broken early on July 18 as the 19th Michigan made a short four mile move, to occupy the village of Fosterville, a pestilent hellhole wracked by war:

> Fosterville is a perfect sean of desolation & destruction, There was once some five or six stores & now we use them for stables, hospitals & prison or guard house. We pass by the dwellings, look in & see the occupants of the house a hard sight to behold. I cant describe their looks & feelings, But it is awful, Some of the children perfectly *naked* & the mother not much better, hardly cloths enough to cover her person, hardly a chair in the house, an old bed in one corner of the

room, not fit for a human being to sleep on, no
provisions to live on, the very features of these poor
objects denotes distress & poverty, These persons that I
describe to you are the poor class of Union people &
their husbands pressed in the Confederate army . . . The
Depot is almost all torn to peaces, the watering tank torn
down & miles of the track torn up to get the rail used for
horse shoe iron. [33]

The war around Fosterville was an ugly affair since the area
was crawling with bushwhackers and guerrillas. The night
before the regiment's arrival, a captain and a private, members
of the 33rd Indiana had been killed a short distance from town.
Determined to avenge the crime, Union authorities sent out
scouting parties to scour the area. For several days, the 19th
Michigan was involved in the search.

Fearing for the safety of a work detail which had been
repairing tracks a few miles out from Fosterville, Colonel
Gilbert ordered the men back to camp. Among those returning
was Private Noble of Company B. Naturally one of his first
concerns was to get his tent set up and for that, he needed
some straw for a mattress. Noble set out to scrounge the
ingredients for a soft bed:

I was in an oat field belonging to a sesech lady when I
was astonished to see one of our company approaching
with the intention of arresting me. I could not see the
reason of such an act but *kinder* thought that it was
something about the shock of oats that I had pulled
down - preparitory to taking them to camp for bedding. I
was marched a prisoner down to the house where there
was a dozen of our com and two Lients and a Capt and
was placed between two Guards. The old lady came out
and I was shown to her as the man that was stealing her
oats she gave me a lecture that would have done very
well for a culprit but as I did not feel very guilty I could
hardly keep from laughing in her face but I controlled
my mirth as well as I could and when she had got

131

through I was marched to camp. But long before this I was told the reason of my arrest There has been a Capt and a private killed or taken prisoner near here a few days since and they are trying to ferrett out the guilty party and the inhabitants of this house are suspected of knowing something about it They made a show of coming there to guard her property and seeing me there, they arrested me to draw suspicion. [34]

According to one account, five suspects in the murder of Captain Israil Dilee and Private Lothario Jones, including a woman, were apprehended. Colonel Gilbert hung one of the men three times in attempting to wring a confession out of him; the last time he almost waited too long for the man had stopped kicking when they cut him down and it took several minutesto revive him. In this vulnerable state, officers got him to admit knowledge of the murders but when he fully recovered, he denied having any information. The five prisoners were escorted to Murfreesboro for further investigation, but the murders remained a mystery.[35]

Relieved by the 10th Illinois, the regiment was ordered to Murfreesboro. They made the 14-mile hot and dust choking march on July 23, 1863. In all probability, Private Noble referred to that miserable trek when he finally got around to writing a friend at home in Martin. "If you want to know how any one feels after marching all day in the hot sun and dust just go out into the road and kick up a dust and stand in it with your mouth and eyes open for the space of half an hour. . "[36]

Considering Gilbert's backround and his style of leadership and management, it seems as appropriate to refer to Henry C. Gilbert as a political colonel as it has been to call John McClernand a political general. Perhaps a commander had to be a politician to succeed with a volunteer regiment full of self-determination and independence. Pettiness, jealousy and back biting were characteristic of relationships. The 19th Michigan had its share of ambitious officers and noncoms; both Shafters, Hubbard, Labadie, and Shaffer all eagerly sought advancement. Not surprising then, Gilbert managed pro-

132

motions and personnel matters much like a patronage system. The departure of a single officer set off a lot of jockeying for position and a chain reaction of advancement.

In all likihood, Elisha Bassett never rejoined the regiment after its capture. In June, 1863, he became the second company commander to be cashiered, dismissed from the service for cowardice at Thompson's Station. Prentiss tells an incredible story regarding Bassett's dismissal:

> You want me to tell you where Bassett is. We supposed that he was at home, if he is not at home you may find him hiding himself in some rockey cavern unnone to us all & it is well for him that he is not here, Bassett has a dishonerable discharge from Rosecrans & it is to be published in one of the most influential in you state, This order was on dress paraid to select one of the soldiers from the regiment place them in front of the regiment & he (the soldier) was to cut all of the buttons off his coat, cut off his sholder straps slit his coat all in strips, brake his swourd then drum him out of camp, that is what would been the matter if he had been here, He is a lucky man. [37]

Hubbard was then promoted to captain, Sergeant Major John Shafter jumped to first lieutenant, Sergeant Lilly made second lieutenant, and there was a shuffle among Company B's non-commissioned officers. These changes did not suit Sergeant Hager at all. He was principally upset with the promotion of John Shafter. Because of illness, Hager did not join the regiment when it was reorganized at Camp Chase. He resumed his duties as orderly sergeant on June 25 at Murfreesboro and immediately had a bad experience with the new lieutenant. "Our celebrated 1st Lient. took our morning report book the next morning after I joined the Regt. and wrote among the remarks." Phinehas A. Hager, returned from desertion "Don't you think I was mad? I will bet I was. I told Capt. what was done, and he took the book and scratched out desertion and wrote convalescent camp. Shafter is a nummy.

The boys all hate him.'' [38] It seems reasonable to speculate that the younger Shafter's promotion was politically right. Aside from his prominent family connections, Shafter's brother being lieutenant colonel made him someone to be reckoned with, and it was to Gilbert's advantage to placate him; however, it can be assumed that Gilbert respected both Shafters. John Shafter's subsequent actions indicate that he personally believed his position was privileged. Hubbard, the new company commander, was ailing and there was talk that he might resign. Although Hager's feelings toward Hubbard were mixed, he much preferred him to Shafter. Referring to Hubbard's illness, Hager wrote: "We all pray that he may get well, for we know who would command the company then.'' [39]

Although Bassett had disgraced himself and was gone, Hager knew that the former captain had some political clout too, which might have discouraged Colonel Gilbert's promotions. "The Col. seems to owe our company a spite. I wish we had Bassett for a Capt. still, then the Col. would not dare to run over the company. Somehow I don't feel safe with Hubbard; He is not reliable in every respect. He had no business to make D.O. Brown Sergeant instead of David; you must not let what I said about Hubbard get out, for it would get him down on me. Hubbard is not malicious, but he is confounded odd, as well as egotistic.'' [40]

Another of Gilbert's personnel transactions caused amost as much ill will. When Hazen Brown resigned his commission, Colonel Gilbert promoted Lieutenant Henry Adams to captain and appointed him commander of Company D. Some members of the company were disappointed with the choice and that Lieutenant Frank Baldwin was passed over. [41] No doubt, Henry Adams was a favorite. Hailing from Coldwater, he and the colonel were intimate friends. When the colonel served as acting brigade commander, he immediately summoned his new captain to serve as adjutant general on his staff. Prior to the war, several of Gilbert's relatives resided in the Adams household. [43]

Now rumor had it that William Shafter was campaigning for

the colonelcy of a black regiment. And Hager was pulling for him too - and to take his brother with him. [44]

Being on the good side of Colonel Gilbert was worthwhile even for relatives. While at Fosterville, a sutler was selected with the unanimous choice being John R. Champion of Coldwater. Before marriage, Gilbert's wife was a Champion and presumable John was her brother. [45]

The progress of the war was always a topic of interest which soldiers shared in their letters. Newspapers were a great source of information as was word of mouth, though frequently unreliable. Until Union victories were achieved at Gettysburg and Vicksburg, anti-war sentiment continued to gain momentum. Copperhead activities grated on soldiers like Francis Thompson; he vowed a personal war of extermination upon his return home. "I think this thing will soon close, and what is left of us will get home to see our families and friends, and have the privilige of cleaning out some of the Northern traitors, or what we call Copperheads. I think if there is anyone on earth that needs punishment, it is a Northern Traitor. I would shoot one of them quicker than I would Jefferson Davis himself. I dare not think of them often, for I cannot think of any punishment that is severe enough for me to inflict on them." [46]

Prentiss was more concerned with an old nemesis named John Hunt Morgan. Although Morgan did not surrender until July 26, Prentiss liked the news he was hearing. "Old John Morgan & all his forces is captured, I hope that this may be true, if it is we will not be troubled with him anymore, He has been a perfect eye sore to us for a long time, I was well satisfied that when I hured that he had gone into Ind. that he was a goner." [47]

While most men found the routine of garrison duty boring, the man who made it all function was the orderly sergeant. Chief among his responsibilities was the development of a duty roster, assigning men to perform a variety of mundane yet necessary tasks. Sergeant Hager gave his wife an unusually descriptive picture of his role and assorted problems:

We drill one hour before breakfast, and about two

hours in the evening. I am usually busy with guard mounting and morning report, for something like one hour, then I usually spend a half hour on my gun, and accouterments; then sometimes I have to make three or four details during the afternoon; the Sergt Major will come around and say "Orderly Hager I want two men to report to the Col. immediately." Well I get my list of names and see whose turn it is, and then go to hunt up the men, perhaps I find them and perhaps not; if not I must take the first men I can find and then remember the absentees for the next detail. Then perhaps the men who are detailed will slide out, and the first I know the old Col. will come around and want to know where the men I detailed are? and order me to hunt them up. Another time, some man who is detailed on guard, will be the last one to get ready, and when he does come out you find he has got citizens pants on, or is without a coats, and you, being in a great hurry, think perhaps it will not be noticed, and let him go out, and as a result get ordered up to the Cols. quarters and taking a scolding for taking a man on guard, not properly dressed, or equipped, but I can stand it all, for all orderlies get served alike. . . [48]

Hager explained too, that Colonel Gilbert's temperament often depended on how late he had been up the night before. "The Col. drinks and gambles; and as a consequence, is not alike at all times. After being up until 2 o'clock in the A.M. drinking and gambling, it is natural that he should require every poor soldier to be very prompt in the execution of his duties and very exemplary in his deportment." [49] Yet Hager's problems as orderly were not confined to satisfying the colonel for there were the men assigned duty that had to be dealt with as well as company officers. The relationship among Hager, Prentiss and Hubbard illustrates the delicacy. Prentiss was never easy for Hager to handle and at this time, Charley was favoring a wrist injured in a fall. Hubbard's close friendship with Prentiss and Hager's puritanical attitude compounded the problem. "Mr. Prentiss has a lame wrist, which bothers him about holding his gun. I dont excuse him from duty because he wont go to the Dr. and be excused; indeed I have no right to Sometimes Hubbard excuses him and then when I go to him (Hubbard) for instructions in the matter, he tells me Prentiss must be excused by the surgeon, or do duty. Prentiss thinks I am rather hard." [50] All three were caught in the middle. One of the jobs that enlisted men were called upon to perform at this time was "riding shotgun" for wagon trains carrying supplies to Nashville and Tullahoma. Henry Noble and his buddy Cyrus Wheeler drew that assignment for a wagon train bearing provisions enroute to Nashville. In describing the ride to his girlfriend, Noble amusingly compared the comforts of an army wagon with that of a shiny red buggy owned by a young lawyer in Martin who was vying for his sweetheart's attention:

> Did you ever see a government waggon if you never have you cannot form but a small idea of its magnitude. They are a large heavy concern without any springs and on a rough stone road like the ones they have to travel over here it is enough to jolt the top of a poor fellows head off or perhaps shake his teeth loose. You can judge then how we felt on our arrival at Nashville after a ride of thirty miles in one of these instruments of torture. Perhaps you will be delighted to learn that I intend bringing one of these vehicles home with me to use on all occasions of pleasure rides and the like of that wont it be nice? I think that it will outshine *Billy's buggy* at anyrate. [51]

With a hot sun blistering down, the regiment suffered greatly from the summer heat. In order to provide shade, one company constructed a canopy of poles and cedar bows to cover their streets. Hot weather coupled with the lack of fresh meat and vegetables contributed to the generally poor health of the regiment. Quite a number of men were sick and hospitalized with dysentery and diarrhea. [52] Every generation of military and every situation produces its own vernacular, the Civil War being no exception. Being the most common ailment, diarrhea was frequently called the Tennessee quickstep. Private Austin was even more original in describing this common health problem. Darius "Marble has the back door trots. I have got so use to it that I don't know as I could get along without it." [53] Several deaths occurred; one attributable to sun stroke. Death also took its toll on the morale of those who survived:

> I have just returned from the burial of one of our comrades. He belonged to Co. K. I also attended one last Sunday from Co. H Our Chaplain preached the funeral service of them both and O Mary what a solemn sight it is to follow the corpse with the fife and muffled drum playing the Dead March or some other solemn tune. After arriving at the ground of deposit the corpse is taking from the ambulance and lowered into the grave and then a platoon of soldiers called pall bearers is ordered to march by the flank with there arms reversed. They then are commanded by the Sergeant to load which they do and then shoulder arms, aim, fire. They fire three voleys and this ends the burial of the brave boy. But O how sad it makes me to march by so many. [54]

Civil War soldiers were capable of doing some very foolish things. In Private Martin Jones' case, he may not have been thinking though he was a very carefree soldier. Anyway, while Daniel Knapp's funeral was in progress, he played his violin. Gilbert took prompt action to restore Jones' sense of morality requiring him to stand on a stump in front of headquarters and read a chapter from the *New Testament.* Following his reading of the scripture, Gilbert gave Jones the Testament apparently feeling that he needed it. Far from reformed, Jones remarked that he would not take a dollar for the book. [55]

Being a chaplain provided few joyous occasions; ministering to the sick and dying was a more common task. Chaplain Cogshall did perform a marriage while the regiment was stationed at Murfreesboro. The groom was thirty-nine-year-old Colonel John Parkhurst, commanding officer of the 9th

Michigan Infantry. Parkhurst from Coldwater, married a twenty-year-old Murfreesboro lass. Colonel Gilbert and Captain Adams stood up with the couple. [56]

Israel Cogshall was sick, weary and tired. Probably tired of the war, tired of being so close to death, and tired of some men's apathy. Like so many of the men he had cared for, Cogshall himself suffered from fever and diarrhea. He had enjoyed the friendship and favor of Colonel Gilbert, yet, in July he submitted his resignation. But resigning was not all that easy. First, the surgeon had to certify that men were disabled or physically unfit to perform military service. That document accompanied the resignation papers through a maze of military channels all of which meant delay. Cogshall was then notified that his request was being held up until he cleared his ordinance accounts. To this notice he jeeringly recorded: "A brilliant order Truly" Impatiently Cogshall was then notified for a leave of absence while his resignation was being processed. Granger promptly turned that request down which did not improve Cogshall's opinion of the General. "I think he lacks many of the qualities of a Gentleman." [57] Charley Prentiss thought Cogshall was a poor excuse for a chaplain and Prentiss was a "church going" soldier. Others agreed with his criticism of Cogshall's performance. Prentiss credited muchof the heathenish conduct he observed to Cogshall's ineffective ministry. According to Prentiss, there was nothing holy about Sunday. "To day is sunday & I dont suppose that one half of the regiment knows it, while I set here & write I can see gambling, card playing here swairing of the worst kind & would be drinking if the boys coued get it." [58] Prentiss' indictment included laziness, failure to preach, and simply not developing a relationship where men would seek his consultation. Along with others, Prentiss initiated prayer meetings and then invited the chaplain. [59] Regardless of Prentiss' judgement, Israel Cogshall was the best chaplain the regiment ever had. His resignation was accepted on September 9, 1863, and he was not replaced.

One of the unexpected jobs given to the chaplain was that of postmaster. When Cogshall left, Sergeant John Duel of

Company B was given that assignment. Almost more important than eating, receiving a letter had an immense impact on morale. The 19th sent out about 160 letters a day. Hager wad Duel's tentmate and he aptly remarked "I live at the P.O." [60]

In one very obvious way, the 19th Michigan was not the same regiment that left Dowagiac a year earlier for its ranks had been appreciably reduced. At a brigade drill in early August, Company B could muster only 28 men for the formation. [61] To build that strength back up, a recruiting team of two officers and six sergeants was dispatched to Michigan. Captain Joel Smith was placed in charge and instructed to complete his work in 60 days. Lieutenant James Shoecraft and Sergeants Paschal Pullman, William Bryan, Eugene Bacon, John Coblentz, Charles Pursel and George Livingston accompanied Smith to Michigan. Only Companies G and K were not represented. [62]

At about the same time, Colonel Gilbert also returned to Michigan after notification that his 18 year-old daughter Lucy was seriously ill. [63] During his absence, Lieutenant Colonel Shafter commanded the regiment. Summoning all of the non-commissioned officers to headquarters, Shafter ordered a halt to the practice of discharging firearms in camp; violators he warned would be arrested. An unconcerned private guessed that the lieutenant colonel was just trying to impress Mrs. Shafter who was visiting camp. [64]

Late summer was a comfortable time for the 19th Michigan; it had secure easy duty and was spared from the horrors of Chickamauga Creek. Most of the Granger's Reserve Corps was at scene with several units getting into the fight during the waning stages. Within the regiment, there was a special concern over the fate of the 13th Michigan for many old friends were members. The wounded from Chickamauga were loaded in railroad cars and shipped through Murfreesboro enroute to hospitals in Nashville. At the depot, members of the 19th witnessed the casualties, ". . . covered with blood and dust . . they look almost frightful." [65] The regiment fed a whole train of wounded soldiers. Run over by the cars, one poor soldier, a train guard, required the amputation of both legs, the operation being performed by the surgeon of the 19th

Michigan. [66]

Although Rosecrans lost the fight, he did retain possession of Chattanooga. General Braxton Bragg delayed his pursuit missing a crucial opportunity to deliver a crippling blow, settling instead, for the less decisive strategy of siege. Once again, the Nashville and Chattanooga Railroad became immensely important, serving as Rosecrans' unbilical cord. [67] Coburn's brigade helped maintain that vital supply line. Early in September, brigade headquarters was shifted south to Tullahoma; companies and detachments were distributed at key points along the route. While most of the 19th remained at Murfreesboro, Company D occupied a stockade three miles south defending an important railroad bridge and Companies A and E were dispatched to the Duck River in defense of another bridge. [68]

Hoping to put the cork in the bottle, Bragg unleashed Major General Joseph Wheeler to cut and slash the only remaining line supplying the Army of the Cumberland. On the last day of September, Wheeler crossed the Tennessee River at Cottonport splitting his raiders into two elements. Three days later his forces intercepted a large mule drawn supply train, destroying both cargo and train. Wheeler then proceeded on to McMinnville in time to receive the garrison commander's sword as Major Michael Patterson surrendered a force of nearly 600 soldiers. [69] As anticipated, he turned next toward Murfreesboro. Right up to the moment of his arrival, preparation continued on the fortifications, with breastworks being constructed about three quarters of a mile from town. Around 10:00 P.M. and after most soldiers had turned in for the night, word of Wheeler's approach was received. The men were awakened and directed to occupy the fortifications. Townspeople were also alerted, and they too sought protection within the earthworks. The civilians were encouraged to bring their possessions with them for post commander Utley planned to use his big guns on the town if he could lure Wheeler into the trap. [70] Occupancy of the fortification was completed around 1:00 A.M. "We were then allowed to lie down on the ground until day light. We were then under arms all day expecting every minute to hear a shell come hurtling among us. About eleven o'clock A.M. we heard a much more welcomed sound; it being the whistle of a locomotive coming from Nashville. On the train which was attached, were about six hundred soldiers. . ." [71] Wheeler made an appearance before the defense of Murfreesboro, long enough to hold those forces in place while his main body isolated Company D at the railroad bridge stockade. Supposedly a worried Colonel Gilbert had appealed the night before to withdraw the arrison in light of Wheeler's anticipated approach. Colonel Utley refused the request. [72]

News of Wheeler's raid reached First Lieutenant Frank D. Baldwin, commanding the detachment of 50 late Sunday afternoon, October 4. Pickets were strengthened and the long anxious wait began. Monday morning early, Wheeler cunningly conducted his reconnasisance of the stockade by disguising his troops as Union cavalry. Not surprisingly, Baldwin could not tell the difference; assuming the mounted horsemen were U.S. cavalry, he allowed them to inspect his fortification unmolested. By 9:00 A.M. he realized his mistake, Wheeler had arrived and was preparing to encircle his position. Soon it was time for decision, and a flag of truce was hoisted demanding his surrender. As duty and courage dictated, Baldwin challenged Wheeler to a fight. Yet only quick relief could save the lieutenant and his men from the inevitable, because gumption and minic balls were no match for cannon and cavalry.

Against stockades, artillery was a great equalizer and the Confederates commenced firing. The first round snapped the flag staff in two, sending Old Glory crashing to the ground undoubtedly causing considerable shock effect. Strangely, though, most of the rounds were too high, either passing over the stockade or exploding overhead.[73] It seems impossible, that at 500 yards, the Confederates could not hit the broadside of a stockade unless their inaccuracy was a deliberate attempt to frighten the garrison into submission and avoid unnecessary casualties or, perhaps, Wheeler felt compassion for this display of courage. Allegedly, when Baldwin turned down the demand for surrender, Wheeler remarked that "if fifty or sixty

Captain Frank D. Baldwin of Constantine, an original member of the officer cadre, photographed in later years. He began service as a first Lieutenant in Company D. [Author's Collection]

men were going to fight a whole division, it was time they went back home." 75 Private Darwin Carpenter was dispatched to bring help. He slipped out of the stockade unnoticed but soon ran into Confederate pickets which ended his mission. Fearing for his own safety, he successfully hid until the Confederates had captured the garrison and left. His message was unnecessary, for the roar of the cannon was clearly heard in Murfreesboro. The cannonading continued for an hour and a half, Baldwin estimating about 40 rounds were fired at his fortification. Those that did find the mark, hammered gaping holes in the walls, spliting logs, showering the air with wooden "shrapnel." Most of Baldwin's casualties were inflicted by these splinters. One perfectly timed fuze exploded a shell inside the stockade striking Sergeant Jim Harris in the face. Harris was left hideously disfigured, because a sizeable portion of his nose and jaw was torn away. Even the most determined lieutenant would be influenced by this terrible wound. There had been plenty of time for help to come from Murfreesboro; in its absence, Baldwin called it quits.[76]

Facts concerning casualties, the size of Wheeler's command, and the amount of artillery present, are unclear due to several conflicting opinions. Although recognizing these disparities, the reports of those who were at the stockade must be given the most credibility. Baldwin reported that he suffered six casualties, all were wounds, only two of which were considered serious. He stated that his troops killed two Confederates and wounded another eight. According to one source, Wheeler had 14,000 men, a whopping exaggeration, of course. More realistically, Wheeler probably had around 1,500 when he began his raid. He said nothing about the number of artillery he commanded or the casualties suffered at the stockade. Baldwin recalled that the Confederates had a dozen pieces. [77]

The captured Yankees were ordered to pile their knapsacks on the bridge as kindling to help fire the structure. This failing, Baldwin's men were forced to chop the posts and supports causing the bridge to collapse. [78] A demoralized Company D was then started south down the Shelbyville Pike. Incredibly, this company had been captured for the second time in the sort space of eight months and each time while defending a stockade on the Nashville and Chattanooga Railroad. After marching about 20 miles and nearing Guy's Gap, the Prisoners were marched off the pike into a wooded area, searched and relieved of most worldly possessions of value. Wheeler then offered a deal; he would release them providing they stayed in place until sundown. Baldwin gladly consented, kept his word and by 9:00 A.M. on October 5, he and his command were back

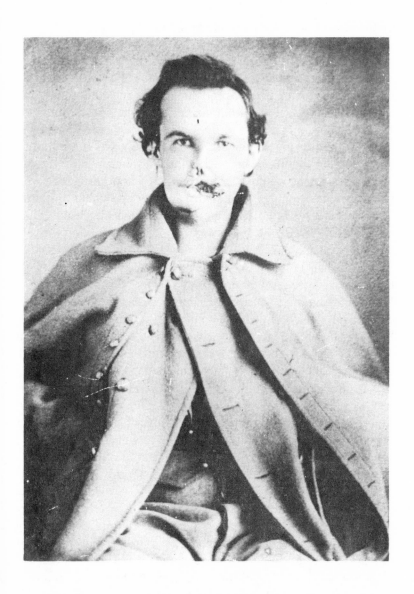

Sergeant James Harris of Constantine showing disfigurement from a wound received when a shell struck a stockade three miles south of Murfreesboro, Tennessee, on October 5, 1863. [Michigan History Division].

in the stockade. The next morning they reported to Colonel Gilbert at Murfreesboro.[79]

Back at Murfreesboro, Wheeler had things stirred up. Members of Company B nervously and reluctantly assumed their picket posts. First Sergeant Hager recalled their wary attitude. "I was sent with fourteen men to one of the most exposed posts on the whole line, and our boys knew it was so and it was amusing to ehar the excuses some of them had for not standing sentinel at particular outposts. One had the diarrhea until he could hardly stand up, another's feet were lame from wearing new boots; and another knew that it was not his place; but we lived through the night; and bugbears vanish at daylight." [80]   If the truth were known, the soldier with the loose bowels may not have been faking. When it was all over, Sergeant Hager could tell his wife: "My health is good Excitement agrees with me." [81]

Wheeler hurried south with Union cavalry pressing hard at his heels. At Shelbyville he split his command giving the Federals two forces to chase. By October 9 he had returned to Alabama having concerned many Yankees and temporarily disrupting a very important railroad. [82]

With Rosecrans bottle up, General Joe Hooker with his 11th and 12th Corps from the Army of the Potomac was sent to Chattanooga to help relieve the Army of the Cumberland. Wheeler's activities greatly impeded Hooker's advance as he sought to move by rail. Major General Daniel Butterfield, Chief of Staff and temporarily in command, was unhappy about the lack of resistance to Wheeler's raid. [83]   Part of the Reserve Corps was very much involved and Granger clearly considered the Duck River Bridge the most important to hold. [84] After the Confederates had gone, Butterfield set out to expose negligent officers. He ordered an investigation of Baldwin's conduct and recommended the dismissal of Coburn for failing to defend a bridge just south of Wartrace. The lieutenant who gathered the facts concerning Baldwin's surrender, based much of report on an interview with a civilian, who thought he saw 14,000 cavalrymen accompanying Wheeler. [85] The investigation failed to convict anyone. Since a court of inquiry exonerated Major

Michael Patterson commanding a garrison of several hundred at McMinnville, it would have been difficult to fault Baldwin with a force 50 for surrendering too easily. [86] Hooker did initiate charges against the two officers. Hooker also thought he learned something abut defending bridges, recommending that earthworks replace stockades thus ". . . if the enemy should make use of artillery in his attack, no apprehensions will be felt by the occupants from the splintering and flying timbers." [87] Perhaps Company D's experience was not totally in vain.

THEY DIED TO MAKE MEN FREE

9

DUTY AT McMINNVILLE

Unable to prevent another devastating Confederate foray, the Army of the Cumberland was forced into a defensive posture of reestablishing what the Rebels had destroyed and waiting for the next raid. The 19th Michigan was directly involved in both attempts. Earlier Company D had failed to hold a bridge at Stone's River; now on the 25th of October, the regiment arrived at McMinnville in the wake of Wheeler's destructive visit just three weeks earlier. McMinnville was an outpost protecting an important gap through the Cumberland Mountains; it was also a supply base and the terminus of a railroad linked to the main line between Nashville and the front. Gilbert found it in ". . . a most deplorable condition. The rebels robbed the citizens of pretty much all they had. And after they left the First Tennessee Cavalry was sent here, and from what I learn were a nuisance hardly inferior to the rebels. They stabled their horses in public buildings and quartered in the houses. The town is filthy beyond description."[1] Naturally, the Colonel's first concern was to make the place secure against Rebel attacks which were certain to come. Gilbert apprised his commander at Tullahoma of the situation and sought his guidance concerning logistical support:

I have got soldiers and contrabands at work cleaning up. I have posted a company on each of the main roads leading into town and am throwing up breastworks for their protection. The place is very defensible and I think we can hold it against any force that will be likely to attack it. It is commanded however, by mountains about it, and artillery might after awhile do us much damage. The Cavalry all left yesterday. There is a small company of home guards that are worth but little, and about 70 or 80 men in hospital. Supplies are needed for them immediately. We ought to draw our rations in bulk and have a post comissary. I shall want a small supply for contrabands that I have set to work and for some families that I find literally starving. How are we to get rations? Having had no instructions on the subject, I sent a small train to Murfresboro this morning. We shall be out before they get back. [2]

The distance to Murfreesboro was about 50 miles, a two or three day round trip for a mule train. During his raid, Wheeler had burned the railroad bridge spanning Hickory Creek three miles out of town, torn up tracks, damaged a locomotive, and captured the Union garrison, an East Tennessee cavalry outfit. [3] Being rather isolated made any Union command occupying McMinnville very vulnerable and the ranks of the 19th Michigan were already veterans at the business of surrendering. The potential of being "gobbledup" made for uneasiness particularly since some of the men understood they were to hold the post at all costs.[4] Aside from its risky location, the chief concern within the ranks was whether their mail would be delivered regularly. Pleasant weather was a plus, and those who could envision McMinnville without its war scars, recognized how attractive the community had been nestled beneath the majestic Cumberland Mountains:

This place is an has been at one time quite a flourishing little town. It is pleasantly located and contained at one time 1500 inhabitants. But now is nearly in ruins The stores some eighteen in number have been plundered of everything of any value and the

Union people have emigrated to some of the northern states and those that remain although the most of them claim to be Union are little less than rebels Their reason for claiming to be Union being to protect ther property.[5]

A sergeant in Company A reached the same conclusion regarding the loyalty of local people stating: ". . . the majority of the people are Union while they see our bayonets."[6] Still another soldier understood that ". . . only 13 men in this county. . . voted the Union ticket at the time Lincoln was elected."[7]

Being in the rear for six months by no means spared the 19th Michigan from the war. The area was infested with guerrillas, bushwhackers and other unauthorized belligerents all waging their own Civil War against East Tennesseans who supported the Union and their Yankee protectors. These partisans engaged in guerrilla warfare - robbing, pillaging, and murdering; concentrating their depredations on those caught in defenseless situations. Their forte was raiding and bushwacking and sniping at sentinels and bridge builders. Their menace was a continuing cause for concern, and few' letters written to folks back in Michigan left out mention of their activities. Colonel Gilbert took the situation seriously putting his men to work immediately to build fortifications and construct a strong perimeter defense. Work continued on the forts during much of their stay; the Colonel was never really satisfied that they were completely ready and perhaps they were not. Those who threatened the post at McMinnville were at best Confederate cavalry or mounted infantry minus the usual supporting artillery. Surely the outpost would have been easy prey for Rebel regulars such as Morgan, Forrest and Wheeler but for once these Michigan infantrymen were at the right place at the right time while the first string Confederates were off in another part of the war.

Vigilance soon became a way of life. The constant threat of attack with a little rumor, imagination and exaggeration thrown in, made for a fairly tense situation. Although the guerrillas never elected to attack the garrison at McMinnville, the 19th Michigan was always aware of their immediate presence. "Last night 3 bushwackers came sneaking up to our pickett but our boys now have to play them cusses a trick with a Hole in it and shot one of them and the rest skedadled they shot him throught the hips and today our boys went out and got him. . about every night we can see their camp fires up on the mountains but they are to cowardly to attack us open day light."[8] Exchanging fire, generally at considerable distance, was a fairly regular occurrence. On several occasions bands of guerrillas appeared, yet each time, after sizing up the garrison, moved on without offering to fight. The hit and run nature of the enemy was aptly demonstrated in an incident described by Private Austin:

This morning just before daylight we was routed out of our nests by the sound of muskets fireing not far off. All hands were soon on their taps with cartrage box slung over our shoulders & gun in hand. The shooting only continued for a few minutes & then stoped. We heard some one sing out, come back here you damd cowardly suns of bitches & that was the last of it. When it come to light enough some of our scouts were sent to see what was up. Our pickets go clear to the river at several places & one place where thare is a picket post on the river there is a ford or shallow flat bottom so teams can wade the stream. This is called THE BLIND FORD. Her is whare the shooting began. Three rebs rode up on the opposit side & fired over at our picket & the picket fired in return. It was not long before the rest of the picket were thare from head quarters when they all fired their guns at random toward the skulking rebs. I dont think it anything but fun although I had my gun with a good lead in it and if I had got a chance to use it I think I should squinted as clost as I used to when I was shooting at a heghog in Mich.[9]

Their appearance, however, always caused plenty of anxiety

The band of the Nineteenth Michigan Infantry at Minnville, Tennessee in 1862. Jimmy Gilbert, Jr., the colonel's nephew, is the boy standing in front. [Michigan History Division]

as troops were quickly assembled anticipating attack.[10] While soldiers learned to disregard the potential of personal injury, amazingly they were more annoyed by other ways that the bushwackers could interfere with their lives. Since mail was slow and irregular, a private speculated that it was probably risky to allow letters to accumulate at headquarters awaiting pick up lest the Rebels be given a chance to read their correspondence.[11'] Following a Confederate attack on a 19th Michigan supply train, another enlisted man considered himself lucky that his package of food from home made it safely to its destination.[12]

Shortly after its arrival, the regiment retaliated by sending out a detachment on foot some 26 miles toward Sparta. It boldly attacked a band of mounted guerrillas, surprisingly capturing seven while dispersing them.[13] The next day rumor had it that the Rebels were coming in after their captured compatriots.[14] The threat did not materialize and another scare passed. Surely everyone felt a little more at ease after the arrival of the 23rd Missouri Cavalry in early November.[15] The general absence of comments about guerrilla activity in soldiers' correspondence for the remainder of the year, probably indicated that everyone was settling down and that the marauders had taken a good enough look to decide temporarily that the place was no pushover. Moreover, the introduction of 800 Union cavalrymen changed the complexion greatly.

Late in the year, the regiment received a new officer, supposedly a replacement for Lieutenant Colonel Shafter who was leaving to raise a black regiment, the 17th U.S. Colored Infantry. Eli A. Griffin was just 30 years old when he joined the 19th Michigan as a field officer in November 1863. He had seen prior service as a company commander in the 6th Michigan Infantry and suffered a wound while participating in an unsuccessful assault on the Confederate works at Port Hudson earlier in the year. Griffin was clerking in his father's store in Niles, Michigan when the war began.[16]

The new year brought a resumption of guerrilla warfare with an attack on a 19th Michigan supply train near Woodbury, half-way between Murfreesboro and McMinnville, naturally at

Lt. Colonel Eli Griffin of Niles joined the regiment in November, 1863 as its major. [Michigan Historical Collections]

a vulnerable point. Train guards fought off the ambush losing only a few mules to the attackers.[17] A detail sent to cut logs for bridge construction was the next target, but miraculously no one was hit.[18] Sniping at defenseless men angered recently assigned Major Eli Griffin as he vehemently promised reprisals should it happen a second time. "The guerillas have fired upon my bridge workmen once and should the firing occur again down goes the houses of some of the sesech in that vicinity. They fail to give us information concerning the whereabouts of the sneaking villians and I am determined to put a stop to it."[19] The intensity of guerrilla activity increased until skirmishes nearly became a daily occurrence. Late in February, a band of irregulars raided a community near McMinnville and robbed the residents of their personal possessions; at one residence, upon finding a Tennessee Union soldier at home visiting his family, they dragged him from the house and shot him in cold blood. The same raiding party visited a nearby cotton factory "playing smash generally." Colonel Gilbert sent a detachment from Company B to the rescue but they arrived too late, after the raiders had skedaddled. About ten soldiers managed to commandeer mounts and rode off in hot pursuit but to no avail; losing the trail, they gave up the chase. "They would not have brought in any prisoners, had they caught them. They would have shot every rascal of them on the spot, after they found that poor fellow, lying dead, but still warm."[20] The war around McMinnville was taking on an ugly complexion: "no quarter" was rapidly becoming the bitter attitude within the ranks of the 19th Michigan.

The 19th Michigan's enemy more closely resembled an outlaw than a soldier. The regiment's task was greatly compounded because it assumed the role of a police force, not as an assignment, but out of human decency for poor helpless people left to the mercy of lawless men. Colonel Gilbert described the plight of local people in a detailed account to his commanding officer:

> There are two military organizations operating in the country south & East of this place under authority

156

country south & East of this place under authority
derived as I suppose from Gov Johnson that have become an intolerable nuisance . . They are mounted and
wear the Federal uniforms and are constantly engaged
in plundering and pillaging the inhabitants. I have
heard of their depredations all winter. Today a party of
citizens living in the Sequatchia Valley somewhere
about Pikeville and known to be true loyal men captured and brought in to their post a Lieut and 2 men . . I
have had very numerous calls from citizens all over the
country on this subject of these two commands and all
concern is saying that they are just as much of a nuisance as Carter and his gang of guerrillas. They rob,
plunder and pillage union men and rebels indescrimin-
ately and are charged with gathering up horses and
selling them for their own profit. The men brought in today are charged with robbing a store. The lient with
threatening the lives of the citizens who arrested the
men. I shall detain them for the present. As I have no
mounted men here I can afford citizens at a distance no
redress for their grievances and at the urgent request of
many I submit their complaints to the Commdg. Genl.''[21]

Although a soldier's wife was at times perilous, these poor
non-combatants living in East Tennessee experienced a Civil
War of brutal dimension, certain of being victimized. The War
Department's first concern was defeating the main Confederate armies but Sergeant Hager recognized that eventually
the countryside would have to be scoured in a concentrated
effort to eliminate these partisan forces if peace was truly going
to be restored:

After the regular rebel armies are dispersed; our
government will have to hunt out these bushwackers,
like any other band of robbers, and hang them on the
first tree. No person is safe outside our lines. The men
living at the factory have not slept at their homes for the
last three weeks. A terrible state of things exists in the

vicinity of the two armies. No man can call anything his own. If any man has been an active rebel our forage trains take pretty much everything he has and if he has not been a rebel, the bushwackers take everything. Between the upper and nether mill stone, the people are ground to powder. God grant the war may every reach the homes of those we love.[22]

Remarkably the guerrillas inflicted almost no military casualties among those who garrisoned McMinnville. No evidence exists of any soldier being killed or wounded by small arms fire. The only loss among the 19th Michigan resulted when a soldier ventured outside the lines alone and was never heard from again.[23] No doubt three members of Company H received a good scare when they went beyond the lines and were overtaken by bushwackers who relieved them of their outer apparel, boots, and guns, and then unexpectedly turned them loose.[24] One can imagine that these men gladly accepted the embarrassment of returning to camp in a very unmilitary bearing in lieu of the fate usually dealt victims of these ruthless bandits.

In December, Gilbert issued strict orders outlining his expectation for constructing fortifications. Except for one company, presumably assigned to provide security, every other unit was instructed to detail all able bodied men to work on the fortifications, six hours a day, six days a week, regardless of weather.[25] Given the experiences of the 19th Michigan and the constant threat from guerrillas, it was only natural that Colonel Gilbert gave special attention to preparing defenses. For over three months, except when the ground froze hard in January, work on the fortifications was as regular as any other daily routine. Defensive preparations were thorough including the construction of redoubts rimming the perimeter of the post each backed up with a blockhouse Even the old courthouse was fortified as an added strongpoint. Gilbert also had installed abatis in front of his earthen works to discourage cavalry charges. Storing wood, provisions and water within each blockhouse was yet another precaution taken.[26]

Judging from the appearance of McMinnville when the regiment arrived, the 19th Michigan in six months time restored the community to more normal conditions. Aside from constructing a defensive network, the bridge over Hickory Creek and damaged sections of track were rebuilt thus reopening the road to Tullahoma.

Even the disabled locomotive was again put back in running order. Their presence and influence caused 11 stores to reopen where there had not been a single business operating back in October.[27] Much has been written about the ingenuity and the variety of skills represented in practically every regiment. An examination of regimental rolls reveals that the 19th Michigan was typical of other units as its ranks were filled with men capable of performing most crafts and trades. Their transformation of McMinnville demonstrated the talents and industry of Civil War soldiers. A cursory look at special duties assigned indicates the variety of capabilities and their significance to the military's mission: enlisted men were detailed to butcher cattle, break mules and repair wagons. Gilbert was so confident of the carpenters in his command that he enthusiastically volunteered to reconstruct the Hickory Creek Bridge claiming they could complete it in six weeks.[28] Like the executive officer of a modern military unit, the lieutenant colonel or major of a Civil War regiment was often in charge of the multifarious work details organized in a garrison situation. Griffin's letter to a friend provides a good description of a busy regiment putting the Post of McMinnville into a state of readiness. "I am building a Rail Road bridge 160 feet long which has the labor of 120 men every day. I have one Saw Mill running which has one sawyer and 10 timber cutters and two teams to haul logs everyday. I have 5 Redoubts building with from 100 to 300 men at work daily on them. I have 15 men cutting timber to use in fortifying Court House and use in forts. Have 13 mule (6 mules) teams at work daily."[29]

In 1861, when politicians and statesmen in Washington failed to avert a crisis, the great issues of the day were turned over to the soldiers for resolution on the battlefields of history's greatest Civil War. The first resolve was to save the Union; the response was overwhelming, volunteers swarming to recruiting stations, shouldering the musket with enthusiasm and conviction. Early battles such as Bull Run and Shiloh helped to awaken a badly disillusioned people. The fantasy of a short war soon became the reality of a long terrible conflict with dreadfully heavy casualties increasing the need for more and more volunteers. Resorting to conscription became still another reality. In 1863, Lincoln added a second resolve, freedom for the black man. The realities of warfare, a new cause, pacifism, and slackening enlistments all played heavily on the mind of the soldier. Now veterans, members of the 19th Michigan began to express their views on most of these matters with increasing frequency and concern. Being in garrison allowed plenty of time for the men to think and write, and for attitudes to surface.

Three hundred thousand more - so went out the call for additional troops in October, 1863. The press back home foolishly or perhaps cunningly headlined: "The Last Call of the War."[30] A week later, fact replaced fiction and a draft became effective in Michigan. Theoretically, conscription and enlistments were supposed to work in concert with the threat of being drafted with its unpatriotic connotation spurring voluntary enrollments. Then too, the government upped the ante, offering a bounty and premium of $402. There were other provisions, namely an allowance for substitutes and commutation which seriously tainted the process and angered those already in the field.[31] The regiment's recruiting team of Captain Smith and six NCO's had already been at work for several months and the first recruits were beginning to reach McMinnville in December. According to Gilbert's orders, the recruiters were supposed to finish their work in 60 days, but they ended up taking 6 months.[32] Naturally it was necessary to recruit if a regiment's strength was to be increased; however, for many officers, minimum strength was important for selfish reasons: it qualified a company or the regiment for higher grade officers.[33] In a letter to the Governor, Colonel Gilbert made the relationship between recruits and promotions very clear and appealed for Blair's assistance in assigning draftees

160

to the 19th Michigan. "I wish to make a special and earnest application for recruits. We now have 3 men . . .who cannot be mustered into the service as Lieuts unless the co can be filled up to minimum. It will take about 60 men to fill up the companies to the minimum - of course you cannot make recruits but I thought perhaps you could have some of the drafted men assigned to us. If you can we shall consider it a great favor."[34] The first recruits arrived without the proper documentation making it impossible to muster them. Gilbert fired off a terse letter to Captain Smith directing him to get with the bungling officer who was holding up the process.[35] He soon learned that troops without enlistment papers were far better than no troops at all. When the arrival of new enlistees lagged, Gilbert determined that many of his new soldiers were being held in Louisville to pull guard. Corresponding with the Adjutant General in Nashville, he urged that his troops be sent forward pointing out that ". . . raw recruits detained in a place like Louisville are apt to get sick & deseased & acquire bad habits. They ought to be with the regiment to get started right."[36]   For whatever the reason, it ultimately became necessary for the regiment to send a detail back to Michigan to escort new recruits to the front and this at the direction of the Secretary of War.[37]

One has to sympathize with a regimental commander's problem - if he did not keep a close eye on the situation, his unit strength could quickly dwindle. Among the most subtle causes was the gradual siphoning off of men through special details that never seemed to end. Four infantrymen assigned to the 18th Ohio Battery just before the engagement at Thompson's Station were still absent in December, 1863 despite Gilbert's appeals.[38]   Colonel Gilbert's correspondence with higher headquarters in March, 1864 provides a very typical illustration of the problem. Because the army relied heavily on regular soldiers to provide nursing and orderly services, physicians and hospital administrators were notorious for "requisitioning" men for their purposes. Once a patient overcame his ailment, he often stayed on as a hospital staff member. While at McMinnville, Gilbert was determined to retrieve a number

161

of men being detained at hospitals in Murfreesboro. Contact with the medical director failed to secure their release. He was told that his men would be returned as soon as they were able to perform duty, generally a convenient excuse. Particularly difficult to accept was the case of Private Nelson Parish since he hadbeensent to accompany a wounded man to the hospital five months before. In another situation, Gilbert was aware that a man who had been sick was being used as a hospital cook in spite of the doctor's claim that he was still ailing. Sometimes it was the soldier who wanted to remain away from his unit and, in those situations, medical authorities gladly obliged them. Corporal William Slipper had been confined to a Murfreesboro hospital and when he did not return, Gilbert learned he was clerking in the office of the Sanitary Commission. Comically, Colonel Gilbert made the adjutant general aware of the Corporal's limited abilities although he still wanted him back. Slipper ". . . is not a very handy man but is not sick and ought to be with the Regt. he only complains (to me) that he is too old to do field duty but is only a year and a half older than when he enlisted and recd. the bounty we need just such men for light duty here."[39] The net effect of Gilbert's tenacity was the reduction of his absent sick list from 132 in August, 1863 to 62 eight months later.[40]

Veterans gladly welcomed the arrival of recruits and as one enlisted man observed some seemed like mere boys.[41] The war did have a way of aging a man. It was also incredible how quickly the war or just being in the military could waste a life. Newly recruited John Anderson was a native of Fawn River, a little place of less than 600 residents in St. Joseph County. Just 19 years old, he had enlisted in December but did not reach the regiment until February 1, 1864. Tragically, he died six days later, officially the victim of disease; unofficially, he died after falling down a flight of stairs.[42] Despite their warm reception, the assimilation of new soldiers probably caused some adjustments. Alonzo West, also a new recruit, was assigned to Company E. Shortly after his arrival, he and Oliver Hanks, one of the old hands, got into a scuffle. The fracas resulted in a broken leg for Hanks; one can imagine that what started out to be a little initiation had backfired. [43]

Among the new enlistees were at least nine blacks, all mustered in as cooks for three years of service.[44] Until this time, it was common practice for officers to utilize ex-slaves as personal servants on a gratis basis. In a letter to his wife, Sergeant Hager explained the new rules stating: "The black men all have to be regularly enlisted; and then they draw ten dollars a month, and rations the same as any soldier. Government is just forcing them right into the service. I see the Capt. and Lieut. are bound not to hire a servant. They will enlist this man they have as company cook, and then take him for their own cook. It aint quite right, but the officers all do it, and so it passes."[45] Many blacks were accustomed to performing servant's duties and these men were especially well suited to be cooks. But just as surely, many ex-slaves had experienced other work unrelated to food preparation. Colonel Gilbert and Major Griffin may have been breaking in a cook or perhaps the problem was one of communication; anyway, the Major related an amusing incident involving the preparation of pork where clean meant something more than the removal of dirt. "We had Pork and Beans. Col Gilbert asked him (the cook) if the Pork was clean. Oh yes says Pat - I washed it with *Soap Suds* before I cooked it What says Col G common bar soap! Yes says Pat. He wont wash any more food with soap I will bet."[46] At least one of these cooks did not particularly like his new form of bondage for Dennis Woody slipped away during the Atlanta Campaign and was never heard from again. [47]

Rank has always had its privilege, an unwritten maxim as old as the military or war or soldiers. Beyond the use of servants, regimental and company officers enjoyed many other privileges; probably the most significant was being unrestricted by military regulations. Officers were not required to secure passes and were free to come and go most of the time. While enlisted men were hard at work constructing fortifications, many officers found it convenient to delegate supervision to their noncoms while they pursued other more pleasurable activities. At McMinnville in particular, commissioned officers spent a great deal of time fraternizing with the natives. With most of the young male population off fighting a war, the situation was particularly favorable for making new acquaintances. It was also commonplace for officers to occupy private dwellings described by one sergeant, as being better than he ever hoped to live in as a private citizen.[48] Then too, the rules regulating vices like gambling and drinking were loosely applied to officers. Officers, of course, were not furnished rations but their acquisition of food was unrestricted. Griffin was practically a farmer maintaining a cow and 16 chickens.[49]

Assuming Major Griffin's account is correct, the 19th Michigan paradoxically entrusted its recruiting efforts to an officer who had serious misgivings about fighting a war of emancipation. Griffin recalled: "Capt. Smith is a conservative officer. Has declared since he has been in the Reg that had the Presidents Proclamation been promulgated previous to the war he would have *never* entered the army to fight for the this d-d abolition war. This in the presence of officers of the 19th"[50] Yet Griffin himself was no saint when it came to his feelings about blacks, if language can be considered a fair reflection of attitude.[51]

By far the worst racist sentiments were expressed by George Shaffer. Shaffer was a frustrated officer whose ambitions far exceeded a lieutenancy. His lack of speedy promotion left him with a generally bitter attitude. Having lived at Calvin in southwestern Michigan, presumably he had frequent contact with runaway slaves as that part of the State was a well-traveled portion of the underground railroad. Shaffer's feelings about blacks were deep seated and dramatically opposed to Lincoln's proclamation. Yet one sure way to make rank fast was through a commission in a black regiment. Shaffer was seriously considering that prospect despite his wife's objections and his own hatred. "I have about come to the conclusion that the negroes will make as good Soldiers as white if not better in some respects. A soldier is driven around just like negro and white men do not like to be driven so I think that a negro is just the animal we want. The authorities are setting them all free so there must something be done with them so I am in favor of putting them into the ranks and save that many white men and may be get the nigs killed off out of the way."[52]

The court-martial of a private charged with disobeying an order and using abusive language, left an inescapable message regarding race relations. The board which decided the sentence was composed of members of the regiment and it ordered Darwin Carpenter to be treated just like a black man; five days hard labor ". . . on fortifications with the negroes. . working the same hours of the negroes."[53]

It should be understood that these expressions are isolated and extreme examples of prejudice. Based on the correspondence and an examination of diaries, most persons did not expose their attitudes, one way or the other, perhaps indicating a lack of concern. Shaffer's prejudice is balanced by the abolitionist attitude of Phinehas Hager. Sergeant Hager's opinion is not at all surprising for he was consistently a moralistic, principle minded and God fearing man:

The more I learn of the cursed institution of Slavery, the more I feel willing to endure for its final destruction; and this war will - nay has given salvery its death blow. We have only to bury its ugly carcass, and our beloved country prospers as never before. Think of four millions of human beings relieved from the vilest system of human bondage, the sun ever shone upon; and the slaves are hardly as great gainers as the poor whites of the south will be. They are certainly more degraded than the slaves. Those who come in from time to time are the most miserable objects I ever saw. Only yesterday a woman sold our boys some eggs; and she could not count the money. The Provost Marshall asked a man what was the population of the town he lived in; his answer was principally oak - some beech and maple, and other timber. After this war is over, this whole country will undergo a change for the better. Hundreds of thousands of northerners are going to come south to settle; and abolishing slavery will dignify labor; and that fact of itself will revolutionize everything. [54]

Even beyond emancipation and a conscription act which allowed those of means to avoid miliary service, the war had other meanings. For Sergeant Hager, the loss of a second close relative was still another personal tragedy of a cruel war. [55] Lietuenant Shaffer knew the war was being deliberately prolonged by abolitionists with economic interests and by inept decisions of the biggest abolitionist of all, President Lincoln. The earlier removal of his idol, General George B. McClellan, and the current decision to stash General Lovell Rousseau, another "fighting general", was evidence of Washington's misdirected purpose. [56] Even though the South was far from surrendering militarily, a corporal in Company D sensed that attitudes championed at the outset were coming home to roost. "One man of this town said a few days since that the people of this vicinity were the worst whipped people he ever saw. Many of them I think are getting their 'rights' much faster than they anticipated three years ago. Only yesterday we saw a group of them marching into town between two clusters of bayonets borne by the stout arms of Col Shafter's sable invincibles."[57] Quite often soldiers wrote letters resembling essays using newspapers as their public forum. Sergeant Hager felt strongly enough to address a long letter to the Sunday School class which he and his wife attended in Otsego, sharing his views as to the cause of the war. The explanation was very simple - given a basically ignorant citizenery, the aristocracy controlled and manipulated the mind of the South and made the decision to fight:

> The element to which I refer, is the ignorance of the common people. In Michigan it is a rare thing to find a person unable to read and write; but here in Tenn. not more than one half the adults can read, and a large portion of those who *can*, appear to possess but very little general intelligence. They read but little, and think less. They have been accustomed to regard what Esq A and Dr. B say, as law an gospel; and when these leading

men thought it would be for their interest to secede; theytold the people that their rights were being invaded; and unless they threw off the yoke of the Washington government, they would be but little better than slaves. At the same time they misrepresented the position of the government, on the slavery question and every other question particularly affecting the south . . . all manner of misrepresentations were resorted to, in order to excite the hatred of the people towards the yankees. Had they possessed the intelligence of the people of Mich. they could never have been so deceived.[58]

Hager's sensitivity to the lack of education exhibited by many Southerners is not surprising. Being a school teacher, he surely had more education than most and his ability to write far surpassed the capability of most Union soldiers. His vocabulary, spelling, sentence structure and punctuation were uncommon. Not a lack of education but the crude habit of ". . . women chewing Tobacco and eating Snuff. . ." struck another noncom as being characteristic of crude ignorant people.[59]

According to some theorists, all wars are waged for economic reasons. It is fairly easy to assign the cause of war to a clash of economic interests or to accuse manufacturing or other vested interests anxious to capitalize on an economic opportunity. Accounts of contractors who cheated the government during the Civil War with faulty merchandise are numerous and familiar. Nothing seemed to give more credence to the oft repeated charge that the conflict was a rich man's war and a poor man's fight than the government's practice of allowing substitutions and commutations. The same label, however, is pinned on most other wars as well. Beyond Union, freedom and flag, there is self. And initiative, ingenuity and enterprise were already hallmarks of this young nation's greatness. Moreover, the American desire to make a dollar did not cease when a man put on the uniform and those in service were often most aware of the opportunities. Amidst and around Federal regulation, cotton production and trade offered lucrative potential. Apparently the regiment's sutler handled about $200.00 in gold and cotton traffic daily.[60] Major Griffin was also aware that the paymaster at Louisville was putting in a 300 acre cotton crop at Murfreesboro, Tennessee. [61] The spirit of free enterprise manifested itself in a variety of ways. Lee Chapman enlisted in the 19th Michigan back when the regiment was organized. Like other privates he drew a $13.00 monthly salary. A year later he was discharged because of a disability. He was soon back in Tennessee working for the Quartermaster, this time as a civilian and at a salary of one hundred dollars a month.[62] Both Sergeants Hager and John Duel went into business competing with the sutler. Their bonanza was retailing emery paper, writing paper and envelopes to fellow soldiers. Presumably they were motivated by a desire to make a profit and avoid paying the exorbitant prices demanded by the sutler. They laid out $47.75 to purchase their initial inventory hoping to double their money through sales:

> The sutler charges from forty to sixty cents a quire for paper, and thirty to forty cents a package for envelopes. We don't propose to pay twice what an article is worth, if we can help it. John will more than double his money on the emery paper, by peddling it out. We use about a dozen sheets every week in our company. As to paper and envelopes, this company uses twenty sheets of paper, and twenty envelopes on an average - every day. John has been speculating ever since he came out this last time and has cleared more than forty dollars; and has sent home, all his wages until the last pay day.[63]

Seemingly internal strife was as commonplace as any other characteristic of a volunteer regiment's human nature. And certainly when the Confederates did not have the Yankee's attention, each lull precipatated almost every imaginable personnel problem. Enemy pressure kept men straight; safety exposed a less favorable side of many. Here at McMinnville, and for that matter throughout the war, by far the worst personnel problems involved both commissioned and non-commissioned officers. Petty jealousies manifested in widespread bucking for rank far surpassed any other problem among the leadership of the regiment. That many officers believed they were more capable than their superiors was almost an assumed truth. They simply exhibited the kind of behavior so frequently observed among general officers. Given a volunteer regiment, produced by an egalitarian society, one has to wonder it if was not the instinctively American determination to strive toward upward mobility, that lay at the heart of the problem. Again, throw in a very politically minded colonel and a collision was inevitable. Whatever the combination of factors, the internal relations pot was boiling during the regiment's stay at McMinnville. The arrival of the 23rd Missouri and the fact that its commander Colonel William P. Robinson outranked Colonel Gilbert set the tempest in motion. Apparently Gilbert did not appreciate having to surrender command of the post, and his lack of discretion in showing displeasure eventually led to his arrest. That same month, a new major was assigned from outside the regiment, raising the ire of at least one inside aspirant. The transition was further complicated due to Lieutenant Colonel Shafter's testy attitude toward his replacement.

Beginning with Lieutenant Lilly's disgraceful lack of courage back at Guy's Gap, which Gilbert made a mockery of, a string of problems occurred involving line officers. The day Lilly relinquished command of "Company Q," Lieutenant Brewer was arrested.[64] Within a week after the regiment's arrival at McMinnville, Lieutenant Shafter, wrongly assumed he was above the law; disguised as a private he led several enlisted men on a sheep stealing expedition, unfortunately raiding the farm of a loyal Tennessean.[65] About the same time Captain Lincoln, commanding officer of Company C was insubordinate while Colonel Gilbert was administering a reprimand and was subsequently arrested. Gilbert himself could not keep his mouth shut, thus he took his turn being confined to quarters. And before the regiment left McMinnville the next spring, both Lieutenants Charles Fonda and Leonard Gibbon were arrested. Sandwiched between these two misconducts, Lieutenant Alonzo Hale received censure from Gilbert who decided his company was the dirtiest in the regiment. [66]

The arrival of the 23rd Missouri and a new major on the same day was too much to take, especially considering Robinson's date of rank and that young Griffin had just been assigned, without any concern for Colonel Gilbert's preference. Naturally military protocol relegated Gilbert to a subordinate position. The combination was more than the Colonel could stand; after grousing for a couple of weeks, he pushed his new commander too far. Finally Robinson had his fill of grumbling and indiscrete retorts - he arrested the 19th Michigan's commander for abusive and insulting language. [67] Colonel Gilbert was not happy to see the new Major. As with all commissioned officers, the Governor made the apppointment. After the initial organization of a regiment, the majority of appointments were probably based on the commanding officer's recommendation; that obviously did not happen in Griffin's case. Henry Gilbert had strong feelings about controlling the appointment of officers. Presumably Griffin had his own connections to the Governor. At least he, like others, felt at liberty to correspond directly with Blair whenever he needed some special influence. Griffin even claimed to receive letters from the Governor on a fairly regular basis. [68] In a letter to his wife, Major Griffin sized up the Colonel's attitude about his appointment. ''Col Gilbert is a very selfish man and cares very little for anyone besides himself. He wants to have his own way and when he cannot feels sour. . . He treats me very kind of late but when I first arrived was very cool. He said to me that 'He should never forgive Gov B' and that he had felt grateful to Gov Blair but should not any more.'' [69]

Upon his arrival in camp, Griffin had more than Gilbert to contend with. His predecessor, Lieutenant Colonel Shafter, for unexplained reasons, greatly resented his appointment. Griffin reported for duty in mid November, 1863, and Shafter departed to begin his new assignment in Murfreesboro within a couple of days, but Eli Griffin was unemployed at least for pay purposes, until nearly the end of February, 1864. [71] According to Griffin's version, Shafter actively conspired to prevent his being mustered in as second in command. Allegedly, Shafter had told the mustering officer that Griffin had been dismissed from the service and should not be activated. Whatever the influence or reason, his request to be mustered was refused.[72] Griffin made numerous trips to Murfreesboro, all with similar results. One encounter in November illustrates his frustration with and contempt for Colonel Shafter. "I rode to Murfreesboro the other day to get mustered and the mustering officer refused to muster without a permit from Sec of War. But he was a drunken little whelp of a Lieut and Lt. Col Shafter was closeted with him the day before. Lt. Col Shafter is a corrupt villian and has stated that I should never be mustered into the 19th Mich. Reg."[73] Any conclusion as to Shafter's objection to Griffin is speculative; however, sinc ehe and Colonel Gilbert were very close and knowing Gilbert's displeasure with the appointment, Shafter may have been trying to aid his old commander. In recruiting his black regiment in Murfreesboro, he had plenty of access ot those at headquarters where decisions were made.

Generally speaking the officer cadre cordially welcomed the new major, Griffin helped his own cause by making a good first impression. Hager liked his appearance but decided to ask his good friend Henry Stark for an opinion. Captain Stark commanded a company of the 6th Michigan Infantry and knew Griffin when the two served together in that regiment. The captain in response, reinforced Hager's good feelings stating: "Maj Griffin was a very pupular officer in our Regt. . . I would rejoice to hear that he was promoted."[74] Recalling his acquaintance before the war, Sergeant Labadie described Griffin as a "tip top man."[75] Lieutenant Shaffer, himself ambitious for promotion, registered the only other sour reaction. His feelings were personal, being terribly disappointed that someone (George Shaffer) had not been promoted from within. Mrs. Shaffer caught his wrath: "I think this d--m mean in Governor Blair for we have better men in the Regt. for the position than he is."[76] Based on the few opinions expressed, feelings within the ranks were somewhat mixed over Shafter's departure. One private wrote that the men were all sorry to see him leave; another felt he was a good military man but not well liked. [77]   It appears that Shafter and Gilbert were closely identified both in loyalties and perception. Both were clearly commanders, maintained a separation from the men and did not easily back off. Lieutenant Shaffer's observation that "Shafter is a pretty hard nut socially" sounds so much like descriptions of Gilbert. [78]   The new major was remarkably different; impressive looking and likable. The same soldier who expressed regret at Shafter's departure described Griffin as ". . . a good clever looking man." [79] A few months later, an astute Sergeant Hager hit the nail on the head noting: "The Major is a very pleasant man to get along with." [80]

One thing sure, Shafter's leaving demonstrated a relatively easy way to make rank, and several others in the regiment seized the opportunity. [81] And in fairness, some may have been motivated because of admiration for the colonel. It can be sensed that some officers were hoping the new major's presence would improve relations and unless Griffin exaggerated, several men must have taken him into their confidence and talked freely about their displeasure with Colonels Gilbert and Shafter. Like many army wives, Harriet Griffin heard scuttlebutt frequently through her husband's letters. Writing the day after his arrival and feeling complimented by the warm reception of most, Griffin told his wife that Colonel Gilbert and ". . . the Lt Col are disliked very much by the officers." [82]

If one listens to the colonel's chief critics, Henry C. Gilbert was not a popular commander and although each had his own personal axe to grind, their assessment is probably accurate. The three known and most consistent critics were Major Griffin, First Lieutenant Shaffer and First Sergeant Hager. Objective consideration of their opinions is extremely difficult, although the first conclusion is easy; complaining about the commanding officer was stock behavior. For reason already discussed, Major Griffin got off to a very shaky start with the colonel and it would take much doing and a long time before that relationship would improve.

Griffin perceived his commanding officer as surly, old,

selfish, ambitious, cross and anti-social. Yet he grew to like and respect Colonel Gilbert. Like Griffin's feelings, the colonel's personality was paradoxical. "Col. Gilbert has been very kind to me and is very different from what I anticipated. He is a singular man and very much like. . . any old lawyer. Kind but a queer way of showing it."[83]

Enough references within correspondence conclude that Colonel Gilbert was a bad tempered and arrogant man. Gilbert was confident of his abilities and superiority over most men with whom he associated leaving very little need to cultivate relations or "give a damn" what some lieutenant or soldier thought. People should like and respect Henry C. Gilbert for what he was: a strong, intelligent, influential and well-to-do member of society. Yet gilbert was a political being and aside from his indifference to most people, he recognized that a few select individuals had to be manipulated, people with either influence or enough brains to be independent. Politically, Griffin was no pushover but as a person and officer he was an opposite. More than anything else, Eli Griffin wanted to be liked. No doubt he was very popular, very cordial and very social. As a man and officer, being considered a gentleman was the highest possible compliment. Fraternizing with the locals occupied a great deal of his time. He especially enjoyed the company of the ladies. Before his arrival he secured a letter of introduction to some of the more important citizens. He was just as ambitious as Gilbert, had just as big an ego, yet worked at being like while Gilbert expected that kind of treatment for he was already in charge. Not having it made, Griffin's style was "political" in a different sense, illustrated by his conscious efforts to help officers reconstruct clothing records lost during the regiment's captivity and using his influence with a paymaster to get the men paid. All of this he interpreted as earning points: ". . . These things have worked to a charm."[84]

Politically Phinehas Hager was a nobody but he was educated, articulate, about the same age as the "old man" and much like him possessing grit in abundance. Although the two were frequently at odds, Gilbert being aware of Hager's faculties, dealt with him accordingly. The comments of Hager and Griffin imply that Gilbert could blow hot and cold as illustrated in an incident related by Hager in which the colonel shrewdly calculated whom he was confronting.

> The Old Col got on one of his tantrums three days ago; and reduced Q.M. Sergt. Clark to the ranks; and ordered him back to our Co.; but the Q.M. waited till the Col got cooled off a little, and then went to him and got him (Sergt Clark) detailed for a clerk. I never told you how near I came to being reduced to the ranks. It has come to be no disgrace to have the Col. reduce a man to the ranks. He drinks a good deal and is a petish as any old maid. But I have not told my story. We orderly Sergts. had orders from the Col. not to call roll until a commissioned officer was present. It so happened on a certain occasion that the Capt. was gone ot the saw mills and remained over night. The 1st Lient was on picket; and the 2nd Lient was sick. Our men were at that time on picket every other day; and thought I would let them sleep as long as I could; and give them time to get ready for picket; and so did not call them out for roll call, nor get up myself; I think it never occured before that I was not present at roll call, unless on some duty. Neither had I ever failed to call out the company at the proper time. That morning the Col. was watching and saw that our company was not out, and came over and caught me in my bunk; and ordered me to report to his quarters as soon as I had attended roll call. He gave me a very moderate scolding for him; and did not swear at me at all, as he does to most of those he comes in contact with; but I learned afterwards that he commenced to write an order reducing me to the ranks; but changed his mind, alleging as a reason that I was an old man. If he reduces me to the ranks without a regular trial; I will ascertain his right to do so.[85]

And it was no accident that he neglected to tell his wife about the incident; a very dutiful sergeant must have been very embarrassed over being caught in bed during a mandatory formation.

Shaffer's complaint with the colonel centered around a growing conviction that he was not appreciated, tired of doing more than his share, and in general sour on the regiment. "Our Col is an old xxx xx xxx You will excuse me; it would not be military for me to say what-at present, but there is a time coming I hope. The old proverb is; that; every dog has his day." [86] There were other annoyances with Gilbert too. Early in November, while reconnoitering outside McMinnville, Shaffer's detachment engaged a band of guerillas, capturing seven. Among the prizes, Shaffer was given a beautiful black stallion by one of the prisoners. He must have been proud of his achievement, particularly since measurable victories when encountering guerrillas almost never happened. Gilbert took the horse away from him alleging that captured contraband should be turned over to the government. Shaffer was upset and even more so later when he was told by the quartermaster that none of the captured horses were conveyed to the government. For all he cared, the regiment could go to the devil; and in his opinion, most other line officers shared similar attitudes. He wanted to be transferred, where he could be promoted by "old humpy" would not cooperate. [87]

An incident involving Colonel Shafter's brother John, shortly after the regiment's arrival at McMinnville, graphically portrayed the internal affairs of the regiment and its commander's style of leadership. John Shafter was just 23 years old when he enlisted in the 19th Michigan, young considering his appointment as sergeant major. [88] When Captain Bassett's dismissal in June, 1863 left an officer vacancy in Company B, Shafter was commissioned first lieutenant and assigned to that unit. While at McMinnville, he foolishly ". . . took a squad of men (Company B) in the night from a picket station that he was in charge of - took off his own uniform & disguised himself as a private and went to the residence of a Mr. Flanaghan a good loyal man & in his yard killed, dressed, & carried off two sheep - telling the men that if it was found out he would see them safe out of it. While killing the animal he put a guard at Mr. F's door to prevent him from interferring.'' [89] Although arrested, tried, and found guilty, his sentence was never acted upon. From the beginning, the prosecution of his case was tainted with neglect and willful suppression.

As could be expected, Mr. Flanaghan came to camp and complained to the colonel. All those who were not present at roll call the previous evening were required to account for their absence. Several men either confessed or were unable to provide a satisfactory explanation for they were accused of confiscating private property. They were given a choice of either paying three dollars a head for the stolen sheep or standing court-martial; they elected to reimburse the farmer. [90] John Shafter denied any involvement and Colonel Gilbert believed him because of the confidence he had in the lieutenant. [91] Assuming Sergeant Hager was right, the privates were unwilling to take the blame alone and implicated Shafter. Hager was also convinced that Colonel Gilbert was protecting the lieutenant. "The boys got two sheep but had to pay for them; but they did not care for that; for our honorable first Lient. was with them, and was put under arrest for it. That saved the boys from a worse punishment; and would have "cashiered" the Lient, but for his brother. The Col. has exposed himself in not reporting the young man to our brigade commander. If Hubbard was Capt. Bassett the Col. would 'catch grief'." [92]

Lieutenant Shafter still was not ready to admit his role in the affair and Sergeant Hager continued to wonder whether his company commander, Captain Hubbard, had the courage to press the matter. "Hubbard has the papers made out; and now the only fear is that it may cost him to much trouble with the Col. He is pretty mad at the young man for he tore some leaves out of the Capts private memorandum book on which he had written the testimony of some of the boys, with reference to the matter." [93]

During December, Lieutenant Shafter was court-martialed at McMinnville, presumably found guilty and sentenced to be dismissed. [94] Seemingly an effort then began to have the sentence reduced. On January 11, 1864, Colonel Shafter visited the regiment presumably to gain Colonel Gilbert's support in trying to persuade a mitigation of his brother's sentence. Obligingly Gilbert accompanied Shafter to Nashville a couple of days later. In all probability Colonel Gilbert hand delivered a letter to the Assistant Adjutant General urging more lenient punishment. His letter testified to the character, youthful naivete, and courageous service previously rendered by Lieutenant Shafter. He also asked consideration for Colonel Shafter's excellent service record and the reputation of the family. "The young man's father is a substantial leading citizen of Michigan and the family and friends are all devotedly attached to the cause of the Union." [95] Gilbert advised that: "As his Commanding Officer I am disposed to deal as mildly with the young man as the interests of the service will allow. . ." [96] There is no concrete evidence as to the effect of this persuasion, however, Gilbert may have thought he had done some good. He returned to the regiment on January 20, and his remarkably good mood was evident to at least two observers. Within a couple of days, Sergeant Hager wrote? "I understand our Col. has come back very good natured. . . The Col. is getting quite gracious towards Company B recently. I guess Capt. Hubbard knows some things about him that he would rather not have ventillated, and he has discovered that Hubbard dare have an opinion of his own, and defend it, even at the peril of displeasing Col. Gilbert." [97] The colonel's cordial attitude was also noticed by Private Austin in Company B. "The Col has got back from Nashville but has not told what he went thare for . . The OLD COL has been up here looking-around our quarters this afternoon. He was good as pie. I guess it does him good to go off once in a while." [98] The behavior was terribly reminiscent of the aftermath of Captain George White's dismissal.

The waiting resumed with Shafter remaining under arrest for eight months. Animosity toward him was strong within the company. In their correspondence, many referred to McMinnville as "Fort Mutton." After several months, the court-martial proceedings were reportedly lost. If one can accept his statement at face value, Colonel Gilbert's disgust with the final disposition of Shafter's case helps restore a little honor. Writing to Brigadier General W.D. Whipple, Assistant Adjutant General, Department of the Cumberland, Gilbert stated: "As for the papers, I suppose they are gone past resurrection but I don't believe they have been lost & don't like that way of disposing of such a case. If papers of importance can be spirited away between District & Department Head QRS. there is a screw loose somewhere."[99]   Yet a less kindly assessment would view his statement as an attempt to exonerate his own behavior for after all, Shafter was almost off the hook. That was precisely the conclusion of Captain Hubbard as he continued to push the matter. On August 13 he addressed a confidential letter to 20th Army Corps headquarters hoping to prevent: "A misapprehension of facts. . . disgraceful subversion of the ends of public justice . . (and) to defeat an ingenious device to clear an officer guilty of a gross crime."[100] Justice could still be served if the army wanted to. Hubbard informed headquarters, that Captain Henry Ford, Judge Advocate at Shafter's trial, had retained a copy of the proceedings.[101] The attempt was futile. The "decision" had been made months earlier. On August 13, headquarters issued special orders restoring Shafter to duty because the proceedings of his court-martial were lost.[102] In two months, he was promoted to captain.[103]

Along with political cunning, Henry C. Gilbert possessed intelligence, strength and decisiveness. He had the capacity to focus sharply on problems and when he chose to, he addressed them squarely. Presumably concerned with the laxity of his non-commissioned officers, he issued orders prohibiting card playing during duty hours and to encourage compliance, stated: ". . . if any Sergeant cannot find legitimate duty to occupy their whole time during the day - they will apply at these Head Quarters where business will be furnished them."[104] Early in January, 1864 after receiving a number of new recruits all without the proper paper work required to muster them into active service, Colonel Gilbert vented his disgust in a sharp letter to Captain Smith, the regiment's recruiting officer. "Such a poor way of business cannot be tolerated. Do not understand that I am blaming you. Some shiftless officer who is being paid & doing nothing is to blame & if you know him please forward him this letter." [105] This same characteristic of firmness is exhibited in a response to General William Ward's refusal to approve a furlough request for 30 of Gilbert's men. When appealing to the next higher authority, Gilbert argued: "Our being under his command at all is a kind of military fiction. We have never seen him nor he us & he knows no more about us than he does about other commands. I ask that these furloughs be granted . . ." [106] This side of the man corresponds closely with the leadership he showed during battle. After being without the old colonel for several weeks due to his leave of absence, Sergeant Hager's feelings expressed a keenly perceived judgement of equitable balance. "The Col has not returned yet. We miss the old fellow; and in some things want him back. The post commander is a sort of old Granny. He scares to easy to suit the Mich boys. We had rather be scolded by Gilbert than to have a commander that will handle the rebs with silk gloves." [107]

The dominant themes of the regiment's six months stay at McMinnville were guerrillas and internal politics, yet every time a regiment stopped at any one place for any length of time, another chapter it its "camp life" history was recorded Undeniably this portion of its history is a story of the routine and mundane but it is also a recollection of what soldiers experienced most frequently.

Inactivity, that is after getting used to bushwackers, could be devastating to morale. As always mail from home surpassed food or anything else in keeping up a soldier's spirits. From the field, garrison life afforded more time to write but less to write about. Typically, a soldier expected a letter at every mail call. Writing to his sweetheart, one enlisted man threatened to start up a relationship with some Tennessee girl if he did not soon receive a letter. Two days later (January 20, 1864) he complained of receiving no more than a little note since 1863! [108] Private Judson Austin found it strange that a soldier could travel home in three or four days yet a letter from

179

Michigan could take as much as two weeks to reach the regiment.[109] Part of the continuing problem was the vulnerability of the last leg of the mail run to guerrila attacks, forcing Gilbert to make unannounced trips.[110]

As for Private Austin, the army could stand some improvements in the design of its issued uniform too. Having just finished his laundry, he was reminded of its inadequacies stating: "As women are up to changes in fashion I wish they would change the fashion of army shirts & make them longer on both sides. reminds me of a poem I was reading in an almanac 'Like a man without a Wife, Like a ship without a sail, The oddest thing in life, Is a shirt without a tail.' "[111]

Not unlike civilians, soldiers made constant reference to the weather, with it being the universal topic of conversation. Initially, the pleasant extended fall weather drew many favorable comments. Eli Griffin reported that mid November compared favorably to Michigan weather in May; smugly observing that ". . . we *Southerners* are enjoying our horseback rides and working out in the Eve with only light coats on."[112] But it did not last indefinitely, because the new year saw temperatures drop below zero causing much suffering and even catching winter accustomed Michiganders unprepared. While most complained, young Austin asserted: ". . . six weeks of as cold weather as I have seen in Mich. would bring the rebs to term quicker than fighting."[113]

Notwithstanding their idealogical differences, soldiers became close acquaintances with many local citizens and frequently visited their homes, socializing, dining and in some instances, courting. Singing was a favorite activity whether in camp or while visiting a Southern family. Amusingly, the song selection of their Southern hosts reminded them of differing loyalties. A private in Company B wrote that he had never heard a Union song played or sung.[114] Austin may have been frequenting the same home for he wrote of hearing a tune entitled *"Schedaddle"* explaining that the ". . . song represents our *retreat* at the BULL RUN FIGHT. I goes as far as the BATTLE OF SHILO & than the SHEDADDLE comes on the other foot."[115]

Amidst bitter cold temperatures and very limited provisions, small pox broke out among community residents. Soldiers were vaccinated and again reminded that the enemy in the military can take many forms. Despite immunizations at least 13 men contracted the disease.[116]

Trying to maintain morale and a state of physical and mental readiness were no small command problems. These concerns were surely in mind when Colonel Gilbert announced a mess competition emphasizing improved cooking and cleanliness and offering cash prizes to the winners. His orders appealed to a sense of duty and pride and responsibility for the welfare of men. He also encouraged company preparation and serving of meals. In March, the awards were made with Henry Durand, Company B winning top honors and $15.00. Going beyond his originally announced intention of recognizing only the top three company cooks, Gilbert gave each a mometary reward amounting to a total expenditure of $50.00.[117]

Just keeping men occupied was important, for things could get loose with their being in garrison for such an extended period of time. It was not only noncoms that Gilbert found in need of greater regulation. After becoming aware of the number of officers visiting local citizens, he began requiring that they too secure leave before departing camp.[118] It can be assumed that Gilbert viewed the presence of a nearby distillery as another detriment to troop behavior for he sent Company B out to destroy it. Considering the drinking habits of many soldiers, that assignment must have been painful to carry out. Those who disabled the spirit factory did not let it all run on the ground because most got loaded in achieving their mission.[119] Of course high minded Sergeant Hager welcomed its elimination hoping for ". . . more quiet times. Whiskey is our curse here and every where else."[120]

Another Gilbert readiness exercise was calling an alert to see how fast the men could assemble if a real emergency occurred. The drill was called at midnight and ". . . thare was a hustling among the bones & every man was out with his gun & equipments ready for fight in just two & a half minutes. The officer saied he thought he could report favorable to the Col. for

Col told him it would take 15 minutes to get the men out the best they could do."[121] And they could do even better if really attacked. Prophetically, private Austin concluded: "I reckon if the rebs had been here & fired into our pickets some of us would have been out sooner than two minutes."[122]

These problems uniquely associated with garrison affected all levels of the command structure, but only the nature and magnitude differed. In many respects a first sergeant had the toughest job maintaining morale and coping with lethargy. Sergeant Hager described what appeared to be little day-to-day occurrences yet problems that certainly tested the patience and finesse of a company's top sergeant:

> Having fifty men to provide for tis an object to look after the odds and ends; and so I have been having a long confab with our chief cook about our various rations. We find in investigation that we are not getting our full rations of coffee. Then we have concluded to make a change in the assistant cook; another thing still several of the men have got to be instructed that they must take less liberties in the cooks quarters. We draw peas instead of beans; as beans are not to be had and we find that our rations come short; for the men will not eat the peas, and consequently eat more of other things. An orderly Sergt is a delightful position; the men swear at him all they dare because he designates men for a particular duty. . .there are some reasonable men in the army - some always thing they have more duties to perform that others, and they curse the orderly for it. A man is sure to know every duty that he has performed, but is very apt to know nothing of what other men do.[123]

Surely the ever present bushwacker and the constant need for surveilance helped counter the force of idleness. Even for veterans, there were many false alarms, movements and noises that threatened nothing more than a man's imagination. One vigilant sentry upon hearing the approach of an infiltrator raised his rifle in anticipation only to recognize an ally. "I came within one shooting a mule while I stood on post if the long eared southerner had not been well drilled I should have let him down but when I sayed halt, he stoped & stood still long enough so I could see what it was. dont you think I am a bold soldier to stand with my gun ready to shoot when there is nothing but the father of all rabbets to shoot at."[124]

Perhaps the most heartening influence upon this little isolated outpost was the steady influx of southern deserters interpreted as meaning the Confederates were losing their will to fight and the end was nearing. Beginning with Union victories at Lookout Mountain and Missionary Ridge, voluntary surrendering of individual soldiers was a daily event at McMinnville.[125]   The reports of these Rebel deserters encouraged the idea that the Confederacy was crumbling, however, their state of mind at the point represented an exaggerated extreme compared to those who would determinedly fight on for still another year. The haggard condition of these Johnny Rebs, described by one 19th Michigan soldier as being ". . . as rugged as any beggar you ever saw," further supported the imminency of Southern defeat.[126] Some felt compassion for these men yet at the same time convinced that the South was finally getting its due. No one within the regiment expressed that feeling better than Isaac Edwards. He wrote:

I was on pickett Saturday last and there was 28 came in at headquarters and this was not the half of them that came in that day and this is the way they are coming all the time. I had some of them go into my tent and get some hot coffee and bread and meat. They was almost barefooted and one poor fellow I could not help pity so I sent him down to my quarters and gave him a pair of shoes. I questioned them as to the destitution of the rebel army wether they was a speciman as regards to clothing and they said they was. They said the whole of Braggs army was in a deplorable condition and they fully believed that his army would all desert in less than 3 months. I told them if they kept on six months longer

I thought they would get their southern rights that they have been talking so much about. I could not help taunt them a little for they have acted so mean.[127]

Uniquely characteristic of Civil War regiments was the commonality of their backgrounds, since basically all had been recruited from the same locale, many being blood relatives, friends, and acquaintances. It appears too, that most maintained their same cliques of pre-war friendship throughout their military experience, and close associations seldom expanded to include new persons. The relationship of Lewis Labadie, Bill Whitcomb and Soloman Stevenson illustrates this peculiarity. They all came from White Pigeon and probably made the trip over to Sturgis together to enlist in Company E. No doubt they were already friends for that relationship continued. The exchange of correspondence among these men and their wives indicates that familiarity. "Bill's wife says Sol Stevenson's wife goes by the name of the Pigion Lady I guess she is somewhat of a fancy lady from what we hear."[128]

And surely every regiment had its set of characters, soldiers who were always into some kind of scrape. Reading soldiers' correspondence leaves the definite impression that the Baird boys, Ancil, Edward and George of Otsego were typical "hellraising" enlisted men acting a lot like Martin Jones and Eldridge Morey. On December 6, 1863, the regiment received four months pay and not unexpectedly, the boys did a little celebrating. Hager who was in a position to be aware of men's behavior wrote that he hoped ". . . Lester Baird's (George apparently used his middle name) wife will never know how he conducts himself here. Ancil is comparitively steady. Ed is pretty wild."[129] A couple of months later, the Sergeant's report to his wife on the local boys included another unfavorable comment concerning the Bairds. "The Otsego boys are all well, except Ed Baird and he was singing half the night, so I guess he is not dangerous."[130] A General Order later in the month, carried the news that Corporal George L. Baird was reduced to the ranks for being outside the line without proper authority.[131]

As post commander during a time when his regiment was the only military stationed at McMinnville, Colonel Gilbert exercised some unusual perogatives which resembled quasi martial law or an army of occupation. Due to the ravages of war and the absence of any adult male population, East Tennesseans around McMinnville were desparately in need of food and fuel. Gilbert came to their rescue, detailing squads of men to cut wood. The whole process rankled, many knowing that the husbands were Rebel soldiers and the enemy. Major Griffin estimated that they were feeding 300 to 400 women and children a day. His account of two women asking for provisions must have been fairly typical of the plight of civilians. "A few days since the snow flying two women walked 7 miles and had barely clothes to cover them and asked for rations. Something to eat and carry back to their starving children." [132] Supplying families with food became such an operation that a member of the regiment was designated as "Local Special Agent of the Treasury Department of the United States for the Post of McMinnville" and procedures were formalized to regulate the traffic. [133] The next step was levying a tax upon local residents to offset the cost of Gilbert's food program. The Colonel appointed an officer to collect it and apparently the populace paid accordingly. It appears that Gilbert independently decided to impose the tax. [134]   Still another dimension of Gilbert's administrative responsibility was handling deserters and administering loyalty oaths. With amnesty available, the post received numerous requests. According to Private Austin, even some of the bushwackers were taking advantage of Lincoln's offer for pardon including some of the big ones, namely two of the Carter brothers. [135]

Many hoped that the regiment would stay in McMinnville until the war ended but U.S. Grant was now in charge and a grand offensive would soon begin unfolding. Orders were received directing the regiment to move toward the front. After six months in one place, the fare would soon change: ". . . hard tack will be our bread now & the ground our bed for a while." [136]

THEY DIED TO MAKE MEN FREE

10

THE ATLANTA CAMPAIGN

Typically, the ranks of the 19th Michigan had a very limited perspective of the grand strategy being triggered. They were aware that the 23rd Missouri had arrived at McMinnville to relieve them, they were being ordered to the front, and they sensed their impending participation in an offensive movement. Their correspondence reveals remarkable clues of the mental and physical preparation occurring within the minds of men, re-examining their convictions and psyching up for a big fight and the prospects of death. Several members of Company B boxed up their overcoats (in a sense rolled up their sleeves) and left cumbersome extras behind. Sergeant Hager asked his wife to express a heavy pair of woolen socks to cushion his feet for the long march ahead.[1] Back home, Private Austin's relatives were beginning to contemplate the selection of candidates for the November election as the best way to win or at least end the war. Austin's response to his wife left no doubt as to the result he favored and would defend. Non-combatants could best help by electing strong Union candidates who would not compromise its preservation and "not give the rebs a thing but whip them till they are glad to ask for quareters in stead of demanding them. . ." Austin resounded Lincoln's immortal conviction of refusing to allow fallen soldiers to die in vain. "Who would cast their vote to have things put back in the same shape they were 3 years or more ago, with so many thousand of our boys whose bones are left in the southern state support our soldiers & get as many into the army as are wanted to fight these wicked rebs."[2] Austin's first sergeant similarily reaffirmed faith in the Union for in almost prayer like fashion he wrote: "I shall try and do my duty to God, and my country and then if I fall, 'tis in a glorious cause."[3]

Leaving McMinnville and getting into the thick of a hot war emphasized the possibility of death. These emotions confronted one's loyalty to the cause in a prolonged war where the terrible price being paid for uncertain victory seriously hampered enlistments. Forced to resort to an unpopular conscription law which conceded the erosion of patriotic fervor, military authorities anxiously sought to reenlist battle tested veterans by offering generous bounties and a chance to go home on furlough. Regardless of a soldier's dedication, the government was stacking the deck at a weak moment. A young enlisted man in Company B wrote home to his sweetheart in Martin and asked:

> Ruth shall I reinlist? Now I presume you are well aware of the fact that after a regt has been in the service two years they have the privilege of enlisting for three years more from the time that their first enlistments expire and are entitled to a bounty of $400 and thirty days furlough. Our Col tells us that we can all get home the 4th of July in case we reinlist. Now my dear girl let me see how patriotic you are and how bad you want to see me. Unless I improve the present opportunity of reinlisting and come home I may never see you in this world for the rebs are not very particular who they shoot.[4]

A fellow soldier echoed the same considerations yet with greater determination. "I want to get home one more time before I die."[5]

Others well known to the regiment calculated their decisions in different ways. After being home for six months leading the regiment's recruiting team, Captain Smith decided he was not going to rejoin the 19th Michigan. Aware of his company commander's decision, along with seeing several Dowagiac draft dodgers near Chattonooga, must have hurt Sergeant Griffis' morale as he proceeded to the front.[6]

Being centrally involved in a major campaign represented a new military experience for this Michigan regiment. Their past service had given them considerable combat experience although generally on the periphery or in a supporting role. As always it was risky to place too much confidence on what was heard around camp but according to Private Noble: *"They say that our corps is to march on to Atlanta shortly and take the place at all hazzards But They Say is a notorious liar. . ."*[7] Equally aware of the fallacious nature of most camp rumors, Sergeant Hager sought to prepare his wife for the impending campaign and its inevitable results by cautioning: ". . Don't believe the bugbear stories you may hear, but wait for the facts."[8] Again, a few days later he warned : "You must not believe any stories you may hear about the '19th' being all cut to pieces, or anything of that sort, as you probably will. . .There will doubtless be some fighting . . . Don't borrow any trouble."[9]

There would be fighting alright! Had to be, with Generals like Grant and Sherman commanding. The grand strategy called for General George Meade to go straight at Lee's Army south of the Rapidan and for General Benjamin Butler to launch an offensive from the James River toward Richmond. In concert, Grant directed Sherman ". . .to move against Johnston's army, to break it up and to get into the interior of the enemy's country as far as you can, inflicting all the damage you can against their war resources."[10] Grant's orders to his most trusted subordinate stated with characteristic directness and clarity his intentions for the campaign.

The regiment began its advance south on April 21 and after two days of marching, reached the vicinity of Hillsborough, Tennessee. Continuing on south the next day, they forded the

Elk River, camped for the night, and on the 24th arrived early in the morning, at Cowan Station on the McMinnville and Chattanooga Railroad. Here they linked up with the 20th Connecticut recently assigned to the brigade owing to the absence of the 33rd Indiana which had reenlisted and gone home on leave. The 20th's Colonel, Samuel Ross, served temporarily as brigade commander during Colonel Coburn's absence.[11] After resting in camp for a couple of days, the two regiments departed the Station marching southeastwardly, climbing and descending a portion of the Cumberland Mountains, (both sides representing a very exhilarating and conditioning experience for the 19th Michigan) proceeding across a valley and on to Bridgeport, Alabama. Continuing the march, they crossed the Tennessee River and followed the railroad to their rendezvous destination in Lookout Valley, a few miles south of Chattanooga. Here Sherman was assembling his army. The regiment reached the Valley on April 30, having marched 100 miles.[12]

The 19th Michigan now teamed up with its brigade, the 2nd in General Dan Butterfield's 3rd Division, 20th Army Corps, Army of the Cumberland. The 20th, a brand new corps, had been created by combining two existing units, the 11th and 12th Corps. Called the Star Corps after its emblem, each of its divisions represented the colors of Old Glory. The new organization, insignia and commander were all intended to manifest esprit de corps. Judson Austin liked the blue star of Butterfield's division.[13] What most impressed these men was the reputation of their new corps commander. General Hooker's sobriquet "Fighting Joe" unquestionably assumed aggressive action in the minds of these Michigan soldiers. Remarkably nearly every letter examined makes reference to Hooker's inclination for the offensive and in one instance, carried an expectancy of glory.[14] Hooker's corps was one of three comprising George Thomas' Army of Cumberland; General Oliver Howard commanding the 4th Corps and General John Palmer the 14th being the others. Sherman's forces also included the Army of the Tennessee and the Army of the Ohio. General James B. McPherson commanded the

Army of the Tennessee with corps led by General John A. Logan (15th), General Grenville Dodge (16th), and General Frank P. Blair Jr. (17th). The Army of the Ohio commanded by General John Schofield consisted primarily of the 23rd Corps. Both Thomas's and Schofield's armies included cavalry divisons.[15] The preparation, assemblage of troops, the hubbub, and presence of big name generals all combined to excit a new high of confidence and eagerness in Major Griffin. After serving as brigade Officer of the Day, Griffin proudly related to his father that he had seen Generals Sherman, Thomas, Sickles, McPherson and Hooker all at one time and had pointed out his unit's position to them. He shared his admiration for Thomas and his impression of some of the others concluding that ". . .Gen. Sherman looks like doing something. Hooker's face is too red. Bourbon sticks out plain about it. He is the best looking man in the lot."[16] Earlier he had written "Sherman will make them howl."[17]

With Joe Johnston strongly entrenched at Dalton, Sherman would soon unleash his offensive marching south to encounter his opponent, relying on the Western and Atlantic Railroad as his axis of advance and supply line. It would be a campaign of manuever, with Sherman trying to outflank Johnston and deliver a killing blow. His adversary being keenly aware of the railroad's importance to the Yankees, prepared strong defensive positions along it, using the road as an axis of retreat, always hoping that Sherman might foolishly assault a strong point which could be followed up with a crippling counter attack.

On May 3rd, Coburn's brigade left the Valley heading toward Ringgold and the railroad, covering about half the distance in the first day's march. Perhaps it could not be avoided, however, camping on the Chickamauga battlefield was an unfortunate choice, for these men needed no reminder of the horrors of war, especially on the eve of a major offensive. Several commented on bullet-riddled trees and half-exposed bodies. Allegedly some of the Union dead were left completely uncovered. One soldier composed a solemn eulogy stating: "I send you a bunch of wild flowers that I picked within a step of whare one of our soldiers was pretended to be burried. When I looked at the ugly maid grave & than at those beautiful flowers which surrounded it I felt to thank God that he had not forgotten the spot whare the soldier fell fighting the battles of his country." [18] After marching most of the next day, the regiment camped within a few miles of Ringgold. Here they prepared a campsite in a pleasant wooded area and paused briefly but the whole regiment was ordered out on picket. On the 6th, they moved a little closer, following the ridgeline of Pigeon Mountain and descending into the valley. By nightfall their division was encamped in Nickajack Gap, a pass through Taylor Mountain. [19] Short rations and constant marching emphasized the immediacy of a fight, yet spirits remained high. "We march without wheels. Carry 5 days rations and make them last 7. Go anywhere." [20] For an enlisted man, observing officers using shelter tents, meant they were "soldiering in earnest." [21] The size of the army impressed these men too and at least one soldier understood they were to be secretive about military strength. Others were less discreet, anxious to impress their civilian relatives with descriptions of the Union might. Colorfully, a soldier recounted personally seeing both Generals Thomas and Kilpatrick remarking ". . .so you see I am with some big bugs." [22] May 7 brought "march orders" with the whole corps moving forward, following an eastwardly course to a position judged to be about 8 miles from Dalton. Sherman's army fronted the Confederates in a crescent alignment with the Rebels defending Buzzard's Roost Gap at the center some two and a half miles away. [23] Sherman intended to demonstrate convincingly in front of Johnston at Dalton, while McPherson slipped through Snake Creek Gap getting behind the Confederates and intercepting their railroad supply and communications line near Resaca. Generally during the Civil War, soldiers had little conception of military strategy. On this occasion, however, despite confidentiality, a private in Company B read it all perfectly and for him it was not very complicated. "As near as I can learn this part of the army is to make a show in front of the rebels; keep their attention drawn this way so as to give our right & left wings a chance to swing in from each way; then we have them in rather close quarters."[24] The stategy failed when the usually reliable McPherson became hesitant after reconnoitering the Rebel defense at Resaca and withdrew to the southern entrance of Snake Creek Gap. An aggressive and disappointed commander lamented: "Such an opportunity does not occur twice in a single life, but at the critical moment McPherson seems to have been a little timid."[25]

While facing the Rebels near Buzzard's Roost Gap, the army dug in, the 19th Michigan as well as other units, learning a basic element of modern warfare: how to defend by constructing entrenchments. Without the benefit of picks and shovels which were coming along in wagons somewhere in the rear, the regiment hurriedly prepared its position using whatever was available, bayonets, sticks and tin plates.[26] Before reaching Atlanta, they would be experts.

At 2:00 A.M. on the morning of May 10, the 19th Michigan and 20th Connecticut marched several miles under cover of darkness to seize a mountain pass called Boyd's Trail over Rockey Face Ridge. Colonel Ross' skirmishers surprised the Confederate pickets forcing them to withdraw. By 8:00 A.M., the position was secured and the Federals controlled the trail. In a very limited action, the 19th Michigan suffered the only casualty, Sergeant John Bunbury being severely wounded in the thigh necessitating amputation. A week later, he died.[27] Combat was terrible yet men sought it; perhaps because of its inevitability and there being no honorable way of avoiding it, one might as well pitch in and get it (agony, life, battle or war) over with. Following this minor brush with the enemy, a sergeant in seemingly matter of fact feeling wrote: "We had a little turn" to fight.[28] The next day Ross' task force started for Snake Creek Gap. After missing his first opportunity of gaining an advantage on Johnston, Sherman decided to confront him at Resaca, anticipating correctly that the Rebel commander would abandon Dalton and retreat once he learned of Sherman's movement toward the railroad in his rear. Sherman left only a fragment of his army in front of Dalton pushing the rest through Snake Creek Gap, concentrating his attacking forces in

Sugar Valley preparatory to a general advance directly at Resaca.[29] Eli Griffin, aware of Sherman's propensity for the offensive, observed: "We expect a fight at Resaca a screamer." [30]

As expected, Johnston gave up Dalton and fell back to a strongly extrenched position at Resaca. Aside from the presence of some rugged wooded hills, the key physical features were the Oostanaula River and the railroad; the railroad was Johnston's exit south as it crossed theOostanaula River to his rear. Johnston placed his left flank on the river and extended his entrenchments north primarily behind Camp Creek and bending back east across the railroad tieing into the Connasauga River four miles north of town. As Sherman's army advanced on the 13th, it engaged Johnston's outer lines looking for weaknesses to exploit.[31] At daybreak on the 13th, Coburn's brigade marched forward to a position in the rear of the 15th Corps. Later it was repositioned behind the 14th Corps. Although not engaged, the regiment got in line and waited its call while listening to the ominous roar of battle.[32] Strange how everything including danger is so much a matter of relativity. As Sherman's lines pressed forward the front kept getting closer and so did the war. Three weeks earlier when the 19th Michigan received its orders to proceed to Lookout Valley, the front was over 100 miles away. On May 13, the regiment laid on their arms in readiness, very close but still in the second row - safe and waiting and as Sergeant Hamilin Coe noted, making light of the situation (probably because they were either numb or scared).[33] The next day Sherman renewed his attack as the intensity of the battle increased all along the line of Camp Creek, with McPherson on the right, Schofield on the left and Thomas in the center. North of Resaca, Schofield's 23rd Corps carried a portion of the enemy's line and the Federals succeeded on the other end too as General Logan's 15th Corps fought their way across Camp Creek establishing a foothold on the eastern bank. McPherson continued his penetration gaining control of some high ground from which his artillery commanded bridges crossing theOostanaulaRiver. This advantage posed a serious threat to Johnston's position.

Confederate attempts to dislodge Yankee units east of the creek were unsuccessful. [34]   Coburn's command marched forward to relieve a brigade in Palmer's 14th Corps, that unit having been heavily engaged throughout the day. [35]   Having waited nervously in line all day, expecting any minute to be ordered into action while the ground trembled underfoot, members of the 19th Michigan Infantry were awed by their situation. As his mind flashed back to the regiment's first combat at Thompson's Station, an enlisted man wrote: "This is no Spring Hill excursion." [36]   Private Henry Noble exhibited that same worried anticipation making three separate entries in his diary during the day, the first leaving instructions for the disposition of his personal record should he fall in battle. [37] The hours dragged on, even night failing to bring any cessation of hostilities. A soldier captured the anxiety and the immediacy of a toughening campaign when he wrote: "9 o'clock P.M. and still musketry and artillery keep grumbling like the dying groans of a volcano, and this mingled with the sound of axes and falling trees, which extends along our lines for miles each way adds to the excitement of the situation. The whole line is digging and chopping and nearly everyman desparately working to throw up works for protection." [38]   Rest was secondary, the 19th Michigan worked through the night hurriedly throwing up breastworks.

Early on the morning of May 15, Coburn's brigade marched several miles to the left passing the 14th, 4th and 23rd Corps as Sherman got Hooker's Corps into position on the flank, to make an attack upon Johnston's right.   What happened next lacked any resemblance of a concerted attack despite Sherman's own mistaken recollection of that day. He wrote in his *Memoirs:* "During the 15th, without attempting to assault the fortified works, we pressed at all points, and the sound of cannon and musketry rose all day to the dignity of a battle." [40]   And Sherman was lucky for Hooker's whole advance was a mismanaged, confused and sad affair resulting in a standoff and a hillside strewn with dead soldiers.

The plan called for a simultaneous attack by Hooker's corps with General John Geary's 2nd Division and Butterfield's 3rd leading the way. General Alpheus Williams' 1st Division was held in reserve. While they were forming, orders kept changing dooming the movement to failure before the attack even began. Initially General William Ward's 1st Brigade (3rd Division) received orders to spearhead his division's attack with Coburn's brigade supporting on the right and Colonel James Wood's 3rd Brigade in a corresponding position on the left. Appropriately Butterfield sent an aid to point out the terrain and the enemy's position he wanted seized. Then while awaiting orders to proceed, Butterfield changed his mind, issuing instructions for Colonel Wood to attack independently and without delay. Concerned out his complete ignorance of the topography and the Confederate defenses, Wood rode forward, took a quick look and ordered his command to advance hoping for the best. [41]

In front of Wood's brigade rose a thickly wooded hill defended by a light line of Confederate pickets. Beyond this hill, he could depend on Rebel fire to lead him to their main line solidly dug in on a second parallel ridge with a valley separating these two high points. This fairly open valley provided clear fields of fire for a second line of skirmishers and a four-gun battery dug into a lunette at the hill's crest with a strong line of breastworks to the rear, also on high ground. Additionally, Rebel sharpshooters were positioned in trees. [42] Soon the remaining brigades of Butterfield's Division advanced toward the enemy, Ward's brigade leading. Again last minute changes disrupted organization as Coburn's 2nd Brigade all ready to move, in close column of battalions, was directed to spread out in three lines giving a two regiment front: First line - the 85th Indiana on the right, 19th Michigan on the left; Second line - 20th Connecticut on the right, 22nd Wisconsin on the left; and the 33rd Indiana behind the 22nd Wisconsin in the third line. While switching positions, they were commanded: "Forward March. [43]

It appears that the Wood's brigade, the 3rd Division, and Geary's 2nd Division moved at about the same time driving Rebel skirmishers before them. The Rebel fire increased as they descended the first hill and double timed across the valley charging up toward the battery and breastworks weathering a galling fire of lead and iron. These troops stormed past the battery and reached the Confederate line but were thrown back. After hanging on tenaciously for awhile, most of these units retired back across the valley seeking cover, wherever possible. [44]

Yet these striking columns could not have been far ahead of Ward and Coburn's Brigades for at least a portion of Geary's division became intertwined with them as they advanced up the first ridge causing terrible disorganization. Coburn reported that the 2nd Division ". . . was moving by the left flank in from six to eight lines from right to left through my brigade, breaking and intercepting the lines, and preventing any regimental commander from seeing his own troops, or the possibility, for the time of managing them. The brigade, notwithstanding, moved forward over the hill and onward, carrying some men of the 2nd Division with them, and losing others of its own men, who were swept with the heavier current to the left." [45]

As this attacking column moved forward, Ward's regiments got all strung out leaving big gaps and losing contact. Coburn's brigade fared even worse; his right and left wings became separated and upon reaching the central point of attack, he had only the 19th Michigan and 22nd Wisconsin with him. Realizing they had lost contact, the other three regiments stopped at the first hill and waited. Colonel Ross commanding the 20th Connecticut claimed to be wholly ignorant of the mission and simply followed the regiment to his front; when the 85th Indiana stopped, he followed suit. [46]

Recalling his feelings on that terrible day, Private Noble wrote: "I cannot describe to you how I felt when I saw the battle flag and knew we were about to go into battle . . . it was not a very pleasant sensation that I experienced." [47]   About noon, the 19th Michigan entrusted its knapsacks to an orderly and trudged off with its brigade, Gilbert and Griffin riding on either flank, following up behind Ward's 1st Brigade. As they topped the first ridge, the brigades stopped and laid down taking temporary cover before assaulting the Confederates across the valley.[48] Soon the order to advance rang out, but the units in front of the 19th Michigan did not move so Coburn's brigade (at least part of it) tramped right over those lying on the ground. When they were almost clear of this obstacle ". . . those in the rear came up behind us and without seeing a rebel commenced firing right through our lines we were on the side of a hill and they were a little above us This is all that saved us from being shot down by our own men as it was there was more men in our Corps killed & wounded by this piece of carelessness than by any firing that the rebels done." [49] Without being told, the regiment immediately dropped to the ground yelling at their comrades to stop firing. [50]

This frightening experience of being shot at by their own forces occurred several times, demonstrating again the confusion and lack of control that prevailed at Resaca on May 15. Apparently the 19th Michigan itself fired on the 149th New York (3rd Brigade, 20th Corps) as it went over the crest of the first hill. The 102nd Illinois, a part of Ward's brigade, lost several men hit by friendly fire. Likewise Colonel George Cobham commanding 11th Pennsylvania (3rd Brigade, 20th Corps) reported being "exposed to a murderous fire" by other Union troops as they sought to remove the Rebel battery.[51]

When the fire from the rear ceased, the 19th Michigan and 22nd Wisconsin headed down the hill and broke into a run across the valley toward the battery (probably now unmanned) and the enemy's works on the high ground. Their charge was answered with musketry and cannon fire and impeded by a steep slope densely covered with pines and blinding smoke, probably reducing their combat to individual wars. Surprisingly and with unwarranted confidence, Gilbert and Griffin remained mounted riding right into the teeth of the Rebel fire. But luck could not protect such a conspicuous target indefinitely; a slug ripped through Gilbert's breast as he rallied his men to join Ward in another attempt to storm the Confederate line.[52]

Despite the severity of his wound, Gilbert dismounted his horse and attempted to go forward with his men. But he soon weakened and was carried to the rear. Adjutant Henry Brown,

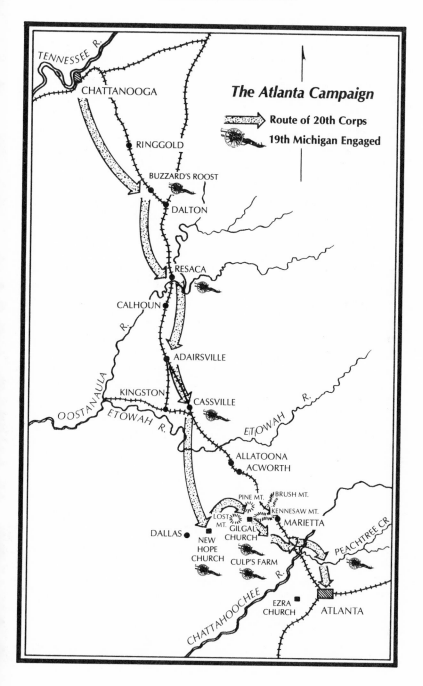

The Atlanta Campaign

Route of 20th Corps
19th Michigan Engaged

was wounded and Captain Charles Calmer was shot through the head as he scaled the Rebel breastworks. The regimental colors changed hands at least four times as noncoms William Tyler, Robert Patterson and Milo Hyde were all wounded before Sergeant Ham Coe brought the bullet riddled flag from the field. [53]

Reminiscent of Thompson's Station, Company B again lost its commanding officer at a critical time; Captain Hubbard who had just returned, sprained his ankle and watched the action from back at the first hill. [54]

Hotly engaged, Coburn sent for his other regiments. His messenger found them but they were unable to respond due to other Union regiments in their front refusing to stop firing long enough for them to advance. [55]

It matters little, pick any brigade in either the 2nd or 3rd Division of Hooker's corps or any of the 30 odd infantry regiments involved, the reports come out the same, a confused disjointed attack. Miraculously it did not end in disaster for Sherman. In capsule account, units became intermigled as they moved forward and separated, losing cohesiveness, direction and command control, causing lines and formations to disintegrate. When units were crossing the valley under heavy fire, where control and mass were essential, men went running forward like stereotpyed untrained militia in a mob. Their wild charge had little lasting impact though some penetrated the Confederate line momentarily but just as quickly were hurled back. Some scattered units remained on their bellies hugging the ground near the fortifications encasing the captured battery but most fell back across the valley seeking whatever protection could be found. Then when the next wave of screaming Yankees came forward, they inevitably ploughed through a tangled mass of soldiers lying in their path. The reports of Colonels James Wood and the Charles Randall (149th New York, 3rd Brigade, 2nd Division) exemplify the situation. According to Wood, the Second and Third Brigade became so entangled that one of his regiments ceased to function as a unit, other regiments were almost as disorganized. The result was mass confusion. With obvious disgust, Colonel Randall wrote: "We were impeded and hindered in all our operations by the great numbers of men of other commands, several times as many as could be of any service, and all totally disorganized and under no command."[56] A close examination of officers' reports reveals that many were as confused after Resaca as they were at the time of the engagement.

It is quite obvious too, that units struck the Confederates in piecemeal fashion each with the same result. General Ward's 1st Brigade was supposed to spearhead his division's assault, but before it ceased, his attack became a pitiful gesture of impotence. Ward had already lost several regiments along the way by the time he made his final rush at the Rebels. Thrown back like the rest, he sought to rally his remaining force of 400 men huddled around the battery fortress. Soon some irresponsible person cried out retreat and an accompanying volley of Confederate fire sent most of his troops hurring to the rear. [57] During the battle, men apparently ran in both directions with equal recklessness for according to a 19th Michigan private "I was run over by some soldiers that were running towards the rear and hurt my back & ankle." [58]

What began as a two brigade assaulting column, withered to less than a respectable regiment, and finally a foolish attempt of 50 to 75 men crawling forward under the leadership of a Brigadier General. Not surprisingly, Ward was hit and Eli Griffin got him to the rear by lending his horse to transport the general.[59]

The big trophy of this ill-fated attempt to turn Johnston's flank north of Resaca was a four-gun battery of 12 pound Napoleons left abandoned between the two lines; possession of the battery became highly contested. At dusk and again around 11:00 P.M., the Confederates tried unsuccessfully to drive the Yankees from the valley in their front. The last foray came with great determination and sacrifice as the 54th Virginia stormed out of their trenches without anticipated support, losing over 100 in 15 minutes. [60]

That night the battery was successfully moved by drag lines into Union possession. Both the 2nd and 3rd Divisions laid heavy claim to the honor. General Geary and Colonel Cobham insisted that the laurels of this victory belonged to the 2nd Division, and they acknowledged no one else's participation. The more convincing account is furnished by Lieutenant Colonel Philo Buckingham, 20th Connecticut. He reported being ordered to lead a detachment representing several 2nd Brigade, 3rd Division regiments to retrieve the enemy guns. When he arrived near the lunette and while inspecting the situation, he confronted Colonel Cobham. According to Buckingham, Cobham told him he was not needed and preferred that his detail get out of the way since he planned to rush in and remove the battery under a heavy cover of supporting fire. Buckingham refused, insisting that such a plan would cost too many lives and that his intention of digging and dragging the guns out had greater potential. Accepting Buckingham's report, his scheme prevailed and worked. He praised Cobham for assisting. [61]

The 19th Michigan had been in its second big fight, the first time, however, that it had attacked well-entrenched foes. Comparatively its losses were heavy; 14 killed and 66 wounded. The regiment lost a company commander, for Captain Chalmer died instantly when he was struck. Colonel Gilbert lingered for a few days but finally succumbed to death in Chattanooga on May 24. [62] It is fair to say that the correspondence and diaries of men lacked an outpouring of sorrow over his death. He was respected, but not loved; he "was brave to a fault." [63] Whatever came his way, Henry C. Gilbert had been a determined soldier.

That night the regiment dug in but morning brought the discovery that Johnston had retreated south, part of his army setting the woods on fire cremating Rebel dead and wounded. The 19th Michigan buried its dead, some within that already famous lunette. [64] Marching with its brigade on the 16th, the regiment crossed the Connasauga River, commandeered a supply of tobacco for all the smokers, and that night around 1:00 A.M., crossed the Coosawatee River on a ferry, Griffin lost one of his horses in the dark and solemnly recorded: "A lonesome day for me." Presumably the impact of Gilbert's

Col. Henry Gilbert, mortally wounded while leading the regiment in a charge on a battery of four guns which he captured at Resaca, Georgia, on May 15, 1864. He died nine days later. [Michigan History Division]

absence was haunting.[65]

After being up much of the night, they marched for eight hours and encamped. On the 19th they pushed hard covering 25 miles before pulling up a few niles north of Cassville. Sherman pressed forward hoping to draw his adversary into battle on the relatively open terrain this side of Etowah. The general's hard pursuit was taking its toll as fatigued soldiers were giving out and straggling increased. Acting as division flankers caused the regiment to march even further. When it reached Cassville one of its companies had only 16 men, losing 24 along the way.[66] The following day, the 19th Michigan and 20th Connecticut were ordered to advance with the division toward Cassville. These two regiments were deployed on the division's right and assigned to support the artillery. Later in the afternoon the 33rd and 85th Indiana Regiments came up to assist. As the sun set, Coburn sent his brigade forward with the 19th Michigan leading and Company B advancing as skirmishers. They engaged Confederate troops in a brief but sharp encounter driving them as they swept through the town. The regiment's losses were one wounded and one killed, Henry Sharp, who died in the action.   Men were pleased with their achievements, winning a little victory, capturing a couple of prisoners and being the first to enter and hoist the nation's colors over the courthouse of this pretty little southern town. "I don't know but you will think the 19th Michigan never was beat but you know we all went through Dixie together & now have to brag while we have a chance."[68]

Johnston, commanding the high ground around Cassville, wanted to engage Sherman there but his dissenting corps commanders talked him out of it, convincing him to fall back. He retreated south of the Etowah River making Marietta his new base of operation. The Confederate commander organized a strong defensive position anchored on the east by the Alatoona Mountains and using the mountain range west toward Dallas to cover all the approaches to Atlanta, Marietta and Ackworth. His outer defenses deployed behind Pumpkin Vine Creek, carefully covering all bridge crossings. With his opponent across the Etowah, Sherman rested his army, collected supplies and reconstructed the railroad in preparation for the next phase of his drive toward Atlanta. Being familiar with the natural bastion the Alatoona range provided Johnston, Sherman wisely chose a less direct route to Marietta and the railroad. He would advance toward Dallas, intending to concentrate there and then approach Marietta from the west forcing the Confederates to abandon Alatoona. [69]

On May 23, it was time to move. Up at 4:00 A.M. and on the road toward the river, they crossed the Etowah during the day on a pontoon bridge. The following day, the regiment continued on toward Dallas, camping near Burnt Hickory. A hard fight with the Confederates awaited them on May 25. Marching with its division, the brigade pushed forward, cavalry skirmishing out in front. By 2:00 P.M., Coburn's men had crossed Pumpkin Vine Creek; each of Hooker's divisions traveled separate roads with Geary's unit some distance ahead. That afternoon Geary's division accidentally collided with a Confederate army also on its way to Dallas near New Hope Church at an important road intersection. [70]   Geary heavily engaged, needed help and both of Hooker's other divisions hurried forward to assist. Judging from the variety of instructions and the rapidity with which they were changed, Hooker had his hands full trying to plug holes in several places simultaneously. Initially ordered to support the 3rd Brigade of his own division, Coburn marched toward the sounds of guns. He was soon diverted toward the front independently deploying the 19th Michigan and 33rd Indiana. As they came under Confederate artillery fire his instructions were changed, directing him to replace a brigade in the 1st Division but before that order could be executed, Hooker sent the 19th Michigan to relieve a hard pressed regiment in the 2nd Division. [71]

The emotions, action and agony within the ranks are descriptively recorded in Private Noble's detailed letter to his future wife:

> We marched on that day until about four o clock P.M. when we came up to where the First Div. of our Corps were buying their dead and they were reported to

be fighting about two miles ahead of us. This was rather startling intelligence for some of us for we had been consoling ourselves with the report that the rebels would not make a stand this side of Atlanta and did not expect to fight that day. We marched on and halted to rest on the opposite side of the road from Gen's Thomas & Shermans Headquarters. Those two worthies were sitting on a log but a few feet from Co. and we had ample opportunity to look at them. . . That night just as it was getting dark our regt went into action our Brigade was marched up under a galling fire of Shell Grape & Canister shot which the rebels poured among us incessantly and our regt and the 33d Ind. were ordered forward to relieve the front line which had exausted their ammunition and forward we went the front lines falling back as we came up it was so dark by that time that we could hardly see the rebel lines but the flash of their guns was a sure guide. There we lay for the space of an hour firing as fast as we could load and then we were ordered to cease firing fix bayonets and lie down. The rebels stopped at the same time and no more fighting was done that night. When we ceased firing Frederick Campbell of our Co. was groaning dreadfully and he proved to be seriously (wounded) with three others I carried him from the field. . . Before we arrived at the Hospital with him the poor fellow breathed his last. I held his hand until we perceived that he was gone and then we left him. He told me to give his love to his father brothers & sisters and then died without a struggle.[72]

The night was terrible, filled with crashing, thunder, lighning streaking across the sky, and the mournful cries of wounded and dying men. Near 1:00 P.M., the 19th Michigan was relieved, again having been heavily engaged and suffering considerably. Its four battlefield deaths represented half of the brigade's killed in action; its total casualties (51) comprised 44 percent of all brigade losses. [73]

Eli Griffin, justifiably proud, extolled their fine performance in a letter to Michigan Governor Austin Blair. "The record of the 19th has been a bloody one since leaving Chattanooga but it has been a reputation that will last and is pointed out even now as being one of the best fighting regiments in the corps." [74]   Beyond his obvious bias, particularly when writing to the Governor, Griffin had reason to laud the 19th Michigan. The regiment had been continuously engaged during the campaign, doing at least its share of the fighting, and losing 175 casualties. Its enlisted strength had been reduced from 717 to 404 in a month's time. Fairly representative of others, Company B could only muster a slim roll call of 28 effectives. New Hope Church had taken another toll on officers: First Lieutenant Charles Manderville, killed in action, Captain Charles Bigelow, died of wounds received, and Captain David Anderson temporarily out of action being wounded by a piece of shrapnel. Only John Baker remained of the original 10 captains and, at this point, the 19th Michigan had only 12 line officers present for duty. [75]

It had been inevitable that somewhere along the line Griffin's luck would run out; that strong possibility surely did not escape his consciousness. Lady Luck had smiled on him as he rode dauntlessly in front of the Rebel guns at Resaca. Following Cassville, Griffin told his father that he had narrowly escaped an exploding shell. At New Hope Church a bullet had grazed his hand. Bravely he wrote: "Tell mother to keep up good courage." [76]

The Atlanta Campaign can be described accurately as a series of battles, yet it was just as much a continuous battle that never seemed to have an end. Combat resembed a prolonged siege with an incessant exchange of artillery and muskertry jarring ground and senses and conditioning men to keep their heads down. After a while, though, a soldier could become careless or numb or just unlucky as stray bullets were always whizzing by and if that did not get him, grape and canister falling within the lines surely would. And if he did not get used to it and keep his wits, then the pressure might drive him crazy. Sergeant Hager was one of those who refused to accept fate and continually practiced precaution while performing his duties. His letter dated June 1, 1864 aptly describes the mental toll this campaign inflicted:

> We are exposed to sharpshooters all through the day; and we have been aroused by heavy fighting every night. . . It is trying to the nerves to be in such circumstances. I presume I do not weight as much . . . as I did last winter. The boys are all very much tired out, and several have gone to the rear I perceive that our men are very much effected by the circumstances under which we are placed. There is not half the levity, and profanity that I have usually seen in camp. Few men can look upon death with indifference; and especially upon death under such appaling circumstances, as we view it here.[77]

Hager urged his wife to place her trust in God and in a kind of special way, asked to be remembered to relatives ". . . all who care for me."[78] But neither bullets nor shot nor fear of death could bend this most patriotic and dutiful old soldiers. "How I would like to see you all; but I want to see the rebellion put down; and I would not go home now if I could; for every man is wanted of present."[79]

In the few days following the clash at New Hope Church, both sides remained satisfied to maintain their respective positions, dug in and facing each other while skirmishers occasionally exchanged fire. Again, a soldier did not brace himself or get ready to repel the enemy's charge, it just came - a minie ball, a piece of shrapnel, and one could be hit at any time. While behind breastworks on the 26th, a sharpshooter from Company G was killed; likewise a colored cook who had enlisted in the regiment. The following day another private was struck down, severely wounded. The next day, May 28, three members of Company H were wounded by an exploding shell, Captain Hubbard received a head wound from an artillery projectile and still another private was hit. The pattern continued on the 29th with a single slug cutting through First Sergeant William Leffler, killing him and striking another soldier. [80]

The terrain and tactics dictated a trench war characteristically involving two principal lines of defense with skirmishers out in front extending for six to ten miles separated from the enemy by only a few hundred yards of buffer. Each move meant building new works with the process becoming fairly sophisticated and efficient as the campaign wore on:

> Trees were felled and trimmed, and the logs, often two feet thick, rolled into line. The timber revetment was usually four feet high, and the earth thrown from the ditch in front varied in thickness according to the exposure. When likely to be subjected to artillery fire it was from ten to thirteen feet thick at base, and three feet less on the upper line of the parapet. Skids or poles, resting on the top of the revetment at right angles to it, sustained a head-log, a horizontal loophole for firing under it being about three inches wide. The skids, when left in place, served to prevent the head-log from falling upon the men in the line if it were knocked off by a cannon ball. The timber in front was then slashed so as to fall outward, making an entaglement which was too heavy for removal, and which utterly broke the formation of any line attempting to pass it. Indeed, it would be only painfully and slowly that single men could clamber through it.[81]

When Sherman left the railroad as his axis of advance and marched straight toward Dallas, his strategy was to bypass the Confederate stronghold at Alatoona. From May 26th on, he consistently pursued that objective, fighting his way back east to the railroad in a series of movements designed to extend his left. On June 4, he successfully made contact with the road south of Alatoona and began disengaging McPherson in front of Dallas. [82]

During that period, the 19th Michigan alternately occupied

the front and second lines as commanders tried to keep troops fresh and maintain morale. When they were not moving up and back, they were leapfrogging to the left. When in the rear, things were a little more relaxed with time for maintaining equipment and an occasional inspection. But the front remained very near and the opening of Rebel batteries "cause a general stampeade for the breastworks."[83] The new month brought heavy and constant rains, destroying the surface of what little roads existed as thousands of men, beasts and wheels chewed up the track causing an almost impassable mire. Being short on forage, Griffin sent out his own little mounted expedition of four men, but all except one fell prey to the Rebels. By the 6th, the 19th Michigan and its division reached the vicinity of Mount Olivet church where it prepared a new position and Sherman rested his army while tracks and bridges were repaired and supplies brought forward.[84] Henry Noble tried to orient his girlfriend to the regiment's location in the field asking: "Do you study Geography" He instructed her to get out a map "and look along the line of railroad running from Chattanooga to Atlanta, Ga. and near the latter place you will see a town by the name of Marietta. Well we are about seven miles from the place a little north of west. . ."[85]

For a few days a lull existed between the combatants as informal truces were arranged by those with little rank. As happened at other times and places during the war, when cease fires were effected, soldiers traded newspapers, tobacco and other items.[86]

Short rations became severe as men went hungry without the usual opportunity to forage. After awhile, Hooker visited the lines and the cries of "hardtack, hardtack" brought results as the general apparently used his influence to secure food for his hungry soldiers.[87] Given weeks of sustained combat and rain and mud, personal hygiene and cleanliness surely suffered. Assuming private Austin's condition as typical, many of the men were probably lousy. He wrote: "I take off my clothes & skrimish with them. Sometimes I find enough so I bring on a general engagement."[88] Sherman would soon give him an opportunity to engage some bigger graybacks.

While Sherman's army consolidated and resupplied its logistics and physical strength, drenching rains continued to pour down. Confident to the last, Eli Griffin wrote: "How we shall get out of this mud I cannot tell but our Army is so large Johnston cannot keep us out of Atlanta."[89]

On the 14th, the weather broke and Sherman ordered his corps forward probing and trying to assess Confederate defenses but not looking for a fight unless he found a hole. The Rebels occupied a triangular defensive line stretching from Kennesaw Mountain on the east forward to the apex at Pine Mountain and then back again to Lost Mountain on the west. The Federals advanced with an alignment of McPherson fronting Kennesaw, Thomas in the center and Schofield against Johnston's left flank at Lost Mountain. In this general action, Johnston lost Lieutenant General Leonidas Polk, a corps commander, and deciding his advanced units were in danger of being cut-off, pulled his forces from Pine Mountain during the night and reorganized a more direct line between the two eminences which secured his flanks. But the length of the line coupled with insufficient manpower, overextended Johnston's army leaving the defense of Lost Mountain to cavalry and vulnerability.[90]

The 19th Michigan remained in camp near Mount Olivet Church until mid afternoon on the 15th when it was ordered forward to support the 1st Brigade. The two brigades advanced as part of a general movement, Sherman pressing forward hoping to break the Confederate line between Pine and Kennesaw Mountains and discovering only advanced skirmishers in front of the new Confederate position.

Butterfield's division marched southeastwardly following the Sandtown Road toward Gilgal Church. After advancing several miles, the 1st and 2nd Brigades filed off to the left and stopped, waiting to be called forward. A couple of hours passed. Then they were ordered to follow-up the 1st Brigade, advancing in line, with the 19th Michigan on the right, flanked by the 85th Indiana, 33rd Indiana and 22nd Wisconsin. They trudged forward through thickly wooded and ascending terrain. Soon the 1st Brigade came under heavy fire all along its line with its right extending across the road to the west held tenuously by the 70th Indiana. The Confederates occupied a line on higher ground a few hundred yards ahead and were delivering a devastating sheet of artillery and musket fire. With the 1st Brigade pinned down and running out of ammunition, Coburn received orders to move up in relief; he sent the 19th Michigan and 85th Indiana to bail out Colonel Benjamin Harrison's 70th Indiana.[91] As they crossed the road, one soldier believed they came under the hottest fire the regiment had ever experienced, a Rebel battery accurately dropping in rounds "at a fearful rate."[92] One of those shells made a direct hit exploding within the ranks tearing a sergeant's leg completely off above the knee and the blast peeled back the skin from hip to knee of a lieutenant in the same company. Confederate fire continued to take its toll as casualties mounted among, whom fell commanding officer Eli Griffin.[93]

After being struck in the breast by a minie ball, Major Griffin was carried to the rear on a blanket. There he received first aid. He endured great pain while being transported over a rough road to the regimental surgeon's tent where the bullet was extracted from his back; nevertheless, Griffin died early the next morning.[94]

As death is inevitable, farsighted people often have wills drawn up. It would seem especially sensible for a soldier in combat to have a will but he might feel some reluctance figuring it would be bad luck or counter a mind-set that somehow one was destined to survive it all. Obviously, Griffin had seen too many men die; fate was indiscriminate and he had searched his soul, anticipating his turn.

After Griffin's death, Lieutenant Lucius Wing wrote to the Major's father concerning the handling of his affairs, making it very evident that Griffin had anticipated the possibility. According to Quartermaster Wing, the day he left the regiment for Nashville, June 5, 1864, Griffin called him aside and said: "I am going to get killed. . ." Wing said he "tried to laugh him out of it but it was no use."[95]   The Major left written instructions for the disposition of his personal effects and property. Wing explained that he had several notes and

Lt. Col. Eli A. Griffin, the regiment's second commanding officer, died June 16, 1864 of wounds received in action the day before at Golgotha Church, Georgia. [Michigan Historical Collections]

213

estimated that the Major owed members of regiment $300 to $400. Griffin had served with the regiment for eight months; all without pay, a pathetic tribute to army politics and bureauacracy.[96]

Eli Griffin's death dealt the 19th Michigan a painful loss for he was an unusually popular and respected officer. Although with the regiment for only a short time, he drew universal praise for leadership, nobility, bravery and kind consideration. Feelings were strong, expressed in terms of love and near worship.[97] Griffin wanted that kind of idolizing and he realized the bond that had developed. Read his many letters, read his diary, read between the lines, and a discerning mind is tempted to conclude that he was determined to die a hero's death. Anything less would fall short of the regard for which he was held.

While on the west side of Sandtown Road and receiving the brunt of a fierce bombardment of enemy fire, Colonel Baird ordered both the 19th Michigan and 85th Indiana not to return the fire hoping that would cool off the situation. It worked. for the Confederates apparently satisfied they had stopped the Union advance, also stopped firing. Later in the evening these two regiments withdrew to the east side of the road rejoining the rest of the brigade and spent most of the night digging entrenchments.[98] Confused by darkness and battle, they prepared positions as best they could, but day light and the enemy exposed their errors. Their main line ran east and west and then bent sharply back north at a 45 degree angle. At this angle "the line could be taken in enfilade both westerly and northerly by opposing confederates."[99] The 19th Michigan occupied a second line, less vulnerable, yet still suffering casualties while manning it. Its losses for the two days totaled four killed and nine wounded.[100]

Captain John Baker became commanding officer upon Griffin's death. The regiment's new commander had raised Company E in St. Joseph County and consequently had nearly two years of valuable command experience. As a young man, Baker had migrated to Michigan in 1854 after having lived in Canada, (his place of birth), New York, and Wisconsin. Before the month ended, he was promoted to Major. His command ascendancy made little stir as was the case with Captain David Anderson who followed him. Anderson took over briefly while Major Baker recovered from a flesh wound inflicted at Peach Tree Creek. He returned to command in September and led the unit on its march to the sea. Neither of these two commanders drew much attention or comment in soldiers correspondence. Change in command might have become fairly routine, presumably some did not care but, more likely, it was a matter of different personalities. Colonel Gilbert was a dominant figure and commanded while everything was new; Lieutenant Colonel Griffin captured the respect and affection of the men in an unusual way.[101]

On June 16, Johnston abandoned Lost Mountain, further constricting his lines and concentrating his forces around Marietta, insuring protection of the railroad. Instead of challenging this new stronghold massed around Kennesaw Mountain, Sherman slid toward the west shifting units from his own left and testing the Confederates' left flank.[102] The rains continued to pour down dictating strategy and soaking the hides of soldiers. At least a part of the 19th Michigan received instructions to build a big fire to dry off and were issued whiskey "to warm up internally." On one occasion, after marching several miles in the rain and mud, the regiment reached a swollen creek and in the absence of a bridge, took off their shoes and socks and rolled up their pantlegs in preparing to wade across. Just before starting, a bridge was discovered and given the necessity of haste, the regiment marched barefooted for a mile.[103]

A frustrated Sherman explained his delay in a dispatch to General Grant. "I am all ready to attack the moment the weather and roads will permit troops and artillery to move with any thing like life."[104]

As the Confederates let go of Lost Mountain and pulled back their left flank to the Noses Creek, Sherman sent Hooker's corps and a division from the 23rd to pass that abandoned strong point. The two armies met each other on June 22 at a place called Culp's Farm. The 19th Michigan and its brigade advanced toward the enemy supporting the 3rd Brigade's lead. The attacking units dispersed Confederate pickets from a ridgeline and consolidated a position of their own on the terrain they had just seized. The Rebels countered as Hood came forward with determination but the Union defenses held. Before the action subsided, the 19th became engaged, occupying the division's extreme left flank and being turned back at a sharp angle from the main line. These regiments dug rifle pits with tin cups and hands since their entrenching tools had been loaned to other troops. Relieved late in the afternoon, the brigade withdrew to the rear, but not before the 19th Michigan had suffered ten more casualties, none resulting in death.[105]

Departing from his usual strategy of outflanking his opponent, Sherman went straight at Johnston on June 27 as guns cracked and roared down the line and McPherson surged ahead, only to reel back unable to break the Confederate defenses at Kennesaw Mountain. For once or so it seemed, the 19th Michigan only listened; some of the men believing they had been doing more than their share of the fighting. Given the constancy of the action, most regiments may have had similar views but it may also have reflected a high level of respect for the fighting qualities of the regiment. The night before this most recent engagement, the 19th Michigan withdrew to the second line of entrenchments. Like others, it would be rotated back through three lines of defense, the last affording an opportunity for rest, washing clothes and caring for weapons and equipment. Several men quipped that the constant roaring of cannon eliminated any opportunity to rest up. Presumably getting off the front line increased safety but with stray lead flying everywhere, it made little difference. Generally men were more cautious up close to the Rebels. Casualties in the so-called rear occurred regularly. During this part of the campaign, a minie ball went through two tents in the second line grazing a soldier and lodging in the leg of another.[106] Sergeant Hager could never understand why there were not more casualties explaining to his wife that he always stood his ground "but when we are ordered to be down, I

216

always lie as close to the ground as possible."[107]   Hager's comments explain the difference between the front and second lines; when in the front under fire a man had to stay down, when in the rear, he could be victimized by false security. However, it was all relative, each position might have its advantages. Unexpectedly even skirmishers stuck out there in front were sometimes protected from enemy artillery fire simply because they were too close to their opponents.[108]

As the campaign continued, Sherman's Army was shrinking as evidenced by the erosion of numbers in Union regiments. Company B of the 19th Michigan afforded an excellent illustration. Recruited in Allegan County, a portion of its members came from Martin, a little community of 793 residents. Henry Noble was one of that town's proud sons. "When we started from our camp at Dowagiac we had 19 men in our squad all hailing from Martin or so near there that they were called Martin Boys and we kept our numbers good for a long time only losing three until we started on this campaign. Now there are but four of us left. The rest are either killed sick or wounded."[109]   According to Sergeant Hager only 24 men were standing formation at this time. His account revealed an important factor in the battle to keep unit strength up. Hager told his wife that Company B still had 64 on the rolls which left 40 or over 60 percent who were not present for duty. There were 17 wounded, another 12 sick and the remainder absent as teamsters, hospital attendants or performing other duties. Knowingly he observed: "It takes about three men, to get one for battle."[110]

Failing on the 27th, Sherman went back to what had worked previously; shifting McPherson's Corps all the way to the right on July 2 with the intention of either luring Johnston into assaulting Thomas or forcing him back to check an envelopment of his left. Sticking to his own game plan, the Confederate commander surrendered Marietta and Kennesaw Mountain to his advisary and retreated toward the Chattahoochie; Sherman mistakenly assuming he would cross it, ordered a general advance to press him at a critical time of weakness.[111] The history of the Civil War is filled with instances where commanders failed to follow-up victory in the wake of retreating foes. Although the circumstances were a little different in the campaign (Johnston kept retreating to avoid being cut off rather than because his forces were defeated and executed withdrawals masterfully), Sherman consistently pressed hard ready to exploit any advantage.

Despite the universal admiration for those fighting commanders who vigorously pursued opponents, it was possible to blunder forward without restraint especially if the object of the chase was a shrewd general like Joe Johnston. Although officers refrained from negative comment, it appears that General William Ward, newly appointed commander of Hooker's 3rd Division, may have acted impetuously on July 3rd. Ever observant, Henry Noble charged that Ward hit the bottle too frequently which impaired his judgement and in this instance ". . . pushed us ahead until the rebels were nearly in our rear and had they known our condition might have captured us. . .as it was they opened a battery on us and for a while we hugged the ground for dear life." [112] Another private agreed with the assessment, estimating that Ward had his division three miles out in front of the rest of the army.[113] Coburn did not offer any criticism, yet reported that they were pinned down by artillery fire within three quarters of a mile of Marietta, backed off and proceeded toward the enemy by a more circuitous route.[114]

On the Nation's birthday, the regiment moved a few miles farther south inching toward the river but not engaging in any action. The connonading reminded Noble of a celebration at home and the one that he hoped would soon follow with the fall of Atlanta:

> I went up on a hill overlook both our lines and that of the rebels two of our Batteries were playing on their works and occasionally one of their guns would reply. It was quite an interesting sight to me but probably not so interesting to the parties engaged. We have in our Div several brass bands not to be excelled in any place and we have plenty of music so you see that with the

exception of the dinner dance etc. we have facilities for a celebration similar to those usually attendant in such occasions at home. Just wait until our troops get possession of Atlanta and then I will send you an invitation to a celebration which as far as noise is concerned will beat anything you ever dreampt or imagined.[115]

Johnston pulled up to defend prepared positions in front of the Chattahoochee River, again delaying the Union drive toward Atlanta. On July 8, Schofield crossed the river and started around the Confederate right, leaving the Rebel commander little choice; he fell back across the river burning bridges in his rear. Sherman spent the next week "loading up his army" ready for a renewed advance.[116]

Assuming the 19th Michigan was a representative barometer, morale remained high in spite of heavy casualties and attrition. The appearance of Rebel deserters, the sighting of Atlanta (observed from the tops of trees) and confidence in William T. Sherman were contributing factors. Private Noble knew the Confederates were strongly fortified across the river yet he was just as sure that "time & Sherman will get them out."[117] Sergeant Hager had lots of hope, no question about it, God would see them through. Peace would come, but first, men must seek forgiveness for sins commited against former slaves; the ravage of war was God's punishment. "We shall have peace as soon as the people repent of their sins, and especially of their sins against the colored race. There has been a very great change for the better, but there is much wrong yet. Let Christians use all their influence to have justice done to the black man; and not only that, try and convince the people that they have been wronged, and that God is dealing with the nation on account of this particular sin."[118]

Crossing the Chattahoochee promised to be a big psychological victory for the Union Army, with the coveted goal of Atlanta just a few miles away. While both sides waited, another unofficial truce was declared as Yankees crossed the river on trading jaunts. Hager provided his wife with a description of this quiet front, writing: ". . . the pickets on both sides set one on one bank and the other on the other - and talk across the river, which is just about as wide as the Kalamazoo River back of your barn. They are on perfectly good terms and it seems awful that after talking together on perfectly friendly terms for hours that they may be ordered to commence firing on each other."[119]

Hooker's 20th Corps brought up the rear in crossing the Chattahoochee on July 17. The 19th Michigan drew picket duty while the crossing was made and although within a stone's throw of their Rebel counterparts, no fire was exchanged. Union pickets were instructed not to shoot unless the Confederates advanced and perhaps the Rebs were aware of their orders for they milled around casually while ignoring the enemy's activity. The 19th advanced a few miles closer and camped.[120] On July 19, Sherman's armies were converging on Atlanta, McPherson on the extreme left moving south along the railroad from Decatur; farther to the west Schofield marched on a parallel axis, and Thomas representing the right began crossing Peach Tree Creek straight north of the objective.[121] Private Noble painted a graphic picture of immediacy as his regiment awaited orders to march forward. He seized the opportunity to write a letter while everywhere men waited in readiness. Except for the officers, tents had been struck and packed away on backs and a long line stretched out on either flank. Everywhere he looked men were crouched or lying down reading and writing and thinking, expressions foretold common yearnings of home or so Noble assumed.[122]

All day nothing happened but tomorrow morning as soon as it was light, they had better be ready to go. So it happened over and over again in this campaign. Wednesday morning, July 20, 1864 Coburn's brigade leading its division marched south and crossed Peach Tree Creek sometime around noon. The creek posed an obstacle of 40 feet in width and water too deep to ford. After getting across on a bridge, the brigade rested. As Coburn soon learned, two ridges, the first covered with trees and occupied by enemy skirmishers, ran parallel with Peach Tree Creek to his front. Another creek with steep banks lay in a ravine separating the two ridges, the latter barren of cover because it had been farmed. Beyond these dominant terrain features, the Rebels assembled in force. The 22nd Wisconsin, sent forward as skirmishers, repelled Confederate pickets from the first hill and pressed ahead until they gained control of the second summit. The brigade was in the center of its division, flanked by the 4th Corps on the left and Geary's division of the 20th Corps on their right.[123]

Soon a message came from the skirmish line that the Rebels were advancing, and Coburn sought Ward's authority to move up in support. Ward hesitated and supposedly questioned the accuracy of this report; Coburn soon advanced, perhaps at his own initiative.[124]

Three days earlier, General John Bell Hood had replaced Joe Johnston, guaranteeing a change in Confederate tactics. On the 20th, hoping to catch Sherman spread out, he struck suddenly, with Hooker's corps catching the brunt of his assault.

The 22nd Wisconsin stayed as long as possible before falling back to the creek bottom to rally a second line of defense. Certainly after Coburn started, the rest of the decisions were his own. He advanced in two lines, the 33rd and 85th Indiana leading and the 19th Michigan in support. After ascending the first hill and not liking the prospects of its defense, he moved the brigade down into the ravine using the creek banks as a breastwork. The Confederates stormed over the hill in a furious attack. Being in a very advanced position, Coburn's flanks were "in the air." The 33rd Indiana's left was refused and a very critical time passed as Coburn hurriedly sought the aid of others. In very timely fashion, the 1st and 3rd Brigades came up to extend his flanks.[125]

The Rebels swept down upon Coburn's brigade seven or eight lines deep but were hit with a galling fire and repulsed. "Our division had to meet the rebs in an open field and came up in less than 10 rods before we were alowed to open on them with our muskets. When we did unhitch I tell you their lines broke & they could not get them in shape again."[126] Decisively and spontaneously, the Federals leaped forward in a counter charge gaining momentum as soldiers chased the enemy, firing as they ran. Everyone was in the front line now as "charged-up" Yankess overran and captured many of their foes. In this determined pursuit, Captain Frank Baldwin commanding Company D, personally captured two commissioned officers and the guidon of a Georgia regiment. For his heroics, Baldwin received the Congressional Medal of Honor, the regiment's only recipient. [127]

The momentum carried the Yankees to the top of the hill where they stopped and consolidated their most advanced position. And Hood came three more times but with no more success than the first.[128] In one of these charges, ". . . a rebel officer lost control of his horse coming towards us. But finally he got the horse turned and away he went lickety scoot, our men firing at him furiously. But to all appearance he was not hurt."[129] The battle lasted for several hours.

The ground before them was strewn with casualties and red with blood, Both sides suffered greatly but, at last, Sherman met the Confederates in an open field, a good share of the time on the defensive, and inflicted greater casualties than he received.[130] Not one to exaggerate, Sergeant Hager stated: "We slaughtered the rebels terribly." [131] That night and the following day, members of the regiment assisted wounded soldiers and buried dead Confederates. In at least two instances, unusual discoveries were made. One of the Rebel wounded turned out to be a woman. "She was shot in the breast and through the thy & was still alive & as gritty as any reb I ever saw."[132] High minded Phinehas Hager found a wad of U.S. paper money on the body of a dead Confederate soldier. In view of his code of ethics, surprisingly he kept it sending a couple of bills to Michigan to determine if they were legitimate. "Whether I did right or not depends upon whether I ought to have given it to the Quartermaster as government property. I thought I could make as good use of it as the Q.M. could; for I don't believe the government would ever get any of it."[133]

Another fight had passed with still more casualties; this time 4 killed and 35 wounded. During the action at Peach Tree Creek, Major Baker was wounded and command fell upon senior Captain David Anderson. Among the killed was Lieutenant Paschal Pullman, who had commanded Company B just two days.[134]

Although his letters do not indicate a high degree of literacy, Sergeant Labadie found inspiration in his brigade's spirited defense and counter charge at Peach Tree Creek. To his wife he poetically memorialized the herioc occasion.

FRIDAY

At early morn the Twentieth of July
It seems but a day although its three months ago
Coburns Brigade on which they Could Rely
Were Formed in line of Battle to meet the Foe

At the Onset when Danger was Drawing nigh
The Tremmlins voice the unsteady steps
The quivering lips the reastless Eye
Told us plainly what next we might expect

At last the Word sounds down the line
Fix Bayonet Forward double quick March
Every thing Now is lively Every man up to time
To meet the Southern Shivalry the traitorous trash

Onward Onward the Surges swell
Amid the Musketry and Cannons roar
Onward towards that Fiery Hell
Our gallant Herows Bravely Bore

We met Clayborns Division in Open field
We gave them an Equal Sight
But Our firing and Bayonet charge soon made them yield
And Old Hood Swore that he could not fight

Such Yankee Devils that wore the Blue Star
Was to Much for his rughuffins to stand
Ho Boys for Atlanta at lenght he cried
Run or they will Kill you to a man

They left us their wounded Dieing and Dead
To take Care of Which of Course we did
four Hundred we Burried in front of our Brigade
And Our Hospitals Were full for Many a day

One Hundred and Six Killed Wounded and Missing
Was the loss of our Gallant Brigade
33rd Ind 85th Ind 22nd Wis and the 19th Michigan
Are the regiments the true and the Brave [135]

Notwithstanding their success, the fury of Hood's assault had not escaped the attention of General Sherman. He knew Hood would fight, and Peach Tree Creek confirmed the need to be vigilant.[136] In its wake, Hager related that the regiment had ". . . put up the best works that we have ever built."[137]

Hood kept the initiative, striking suddenly on the 22nd between Atlanta and Decatur, his attack hitting McPherson's 17th Corps in the flank, momentarily enveloping Sherman's left. Reinforcements arrived in time to stay the momentum and force the Confederates back but Hood's surprise precipitated a crisis and in that scramble, General McPherson rode recklessly to his death.[138] Sergeant Rice assessed it precisely ". . . we lost one of our best officers."[139]

Undiscouraged, the Confederate commander remained aggressive trying to defeat his opponent in detail. His strategy met with the overwhelming approval of Private Austin. "The rebs pitch onto some part of our lines almost every day & as often get a good sound whiping or men killing would sound more like it to me. . . hope they will keep charging our lines if they want to get their army used up quick for I rather they do the charging than to be one of the charging party."[140]

While Sherman moved the Army of the Tennessee from the left to the right on July 28 with the intention of cutting the railroad south of Atlanta, Hood thought he saw another moment of weakness. The Confederate offensive struck Logan's 15th Corps near Ezra Church, charging the Union lines repeatedly, each time being repulsed and suffering heavy losses.[141]

Fate determined that the 19th Michigan and 20th Corps would miss both of these actions. They were assigned to the trenches as the siege lines around Atlanta constricted, tighter and tighter. By late July and August lines were inched forward; earlier movement was measured in miles but now it was a matter of feet. Trench warfare dictated a singular strategy involving close coordination among lines of defense, added precautions against exploding shells as lines drew closer, and careful occupancy of new lines and positions generally using the cover of darkness. Employing the principle of supporting fire, the main lines fired high to provide cover as picket lines were advanced. Otherwise the front line restricted its fire until the skirmishers were driven in.[142]

It might be assumed that being on the skirmish line paralleled the preoccupancy of a typical sentinel with watchfulness and warning. Before Atlanta, skirmishers apparently were fairly active in exchanging fire with the enemy as one soldier reported firing about a hundred rounds in a single day making his combat more like a battle.[143] A skirmisher's assignment could be risky and lonely and despite the presence of an officer in command, circumstances compelled pickets to act on their volition. Sergeant Rice confessed his independent actions while manning a post in the lines just outside of Atlanta. "The pickets we relieved had built picket posts. So myself and two of Company G were in a post together and were discussing whether we should fire any or not, when the rebel picket line gave us a volley. We returned the compliment and went to the rear in a hurry. We supposed the rebels were advancing. I ran aways and thought what am I running for, and stopped and listened, and so I stepped behind a big whitewood tree. But it calmed down and I went back to my post, or at least a post."[144] Rice reveals that this was an unoccupied and different post meaning others were also moving around indiscriminately, obviously leaving a gap in the first line of defense.

Escaping active engagement in the battles of Atlanta and Ezra Church spared the potential for more heavy losses, but the war in the trenches produced a steady stream of casualties.

The horrible experience of a member of Company A, illustrated how a soldier could get caught in a combat zone where lines were extremely close and sorties had to be cut off immediately. Allegedly this skirmisher had gone forward in search of wood to fortify his post; the Rebels rushed the Union line and his own comrades mistakenly shot him not realizing he was out there.[145] Luck worked in strange ways. While here in front of Atlanta, a stray ball ripped through three tents striking a 19th Michigan Infantryman, going all the way through his head, yet incredibly, he lived.[146]

Strangely, men were fascinated by artillery, curious to know what was inside those round iron balls and where they were coming from and where they hit. While writing his wife, Private Austin teased her, suggesting she would never be able to write under the circumstancs instead would be out watching the fireworks. "This is the way with many of our men & more than one have watched to his sorrow. I am not so very particular to find out or know so much about such things as long as they dont come whare I am."[147]

An unsuspecting Sergeant Rice got hit in the rear with a piece of shrapnel causing only a very minor wound. After casually reaching behind and pulling it out ". . . the boys laughed at me and said I was getting very expert to catch pieces of shell in my breeches."[148]

It has often been observed that no man is indispensable, because there is always someone to take his place. That applied to Generals Polk and McPherson as it did to Colonels Gilbert and Griffin. Military units go on but naturally some losses are more deeply felt. On the 8th of August, 1864 the 19th Michigan lost another NCO. It happened with regularity during this campaign. The previous day, Sergeant Phinehas Hager was shot in the back while doling out rations; at the time he served as both first sergeant and company commander in the absence of all commissioned officers. Only a few soldiers mentioned his death in their correspondence, but his company commander Captain Sam Hubbard back in the rear recovering from a wound, wrote a long four page letter to Mrs. Hager expressing unusual affection and respect for his fallen comrade. When he

The grave of Phinehas Hager in the National Cemetery at Marietta, Georgia. [Sydney C. Kerksis]

227

was struck, Hager obviously sensed his time had come and in very expected fashion, asked a corporal to pray with him. Hubbard wrote:

He entered the service from a sense of duty - and at all times was in the line of duty and bore all the hardships and trials of the camp & field - with a fortitude and heriosm deserving the highest praise. No man was ever more unselfish - nor more devoted to his calling . . . During this whole bloody campaign Sgt. Hager has been with the company and had a part in every skrimish and battle in which the regiment was engaged. On all occasions he showed himself brave and competent. . . He was a model soldier - enduring all the stern trials of army life without a murmur. He was . . loved by all of his companions in arms no greater loss could we have sustained by such an effect.[149]

Not just some accolades to console a grieving widow but a fitting tribute to the kind of soldier who comprised the backbone of Sherman's army!

Confidence in Sherman, steady progress toward their objective, and the continuing flow of Rebel deserters all served to prop up morale. In one letter, Noble told of 550 Rebels coming into Union lines. About a week later he related a unique circumstance in which another 700 surrendered en masse. The desertion was engineered by representatives of both sides, with the Confederates faking a charge upon the Union lines and the Federals firing blank cartridges to give the whole affair an apparent legitimacy and deceive Rebel officers.[150]

Before circling around Atlanta and sealing off the remaining railroad arteries, Sherman sent the 20th Corps back to the Chattahoochee to secure the crossing and his own railroad supply line back to Chattanooga. The 19th Michigan defended a place called Turner's Ferry, a few miles south of the railroad bridge.[151] The Union withdrawal was accomplished as neatly as if Joe Johnston directed it. Skirmishers were doubled, camp-fires left burning, bands played to drown the noise of troop and cannon movement, taps sounded as usual and the Rebels woke up on August 26 to find abandoned Union works.[152]

Beginning with McPherson's death, the Star Corps (20th) experienced several command changes in a relatively brief span of time. First "Fighting Joe" resigned when Sherman overlooked him in selecting General Oliver O. Howard as the new commander of the Army of the Tennessee. In his place, General Alpheus S. Williams was promoted from division ranks, yet his command lasted only a month. He was superceded by General Henry Slocum on August 27.[153] Slocum commanded Sherman's defense back at the river.

While Sherman pressed toward the railroad south of Atlanta, Hood tried desparately to intercept him, striking the Army of the Tennessee on August 31 near Jonesboro. The battle continued the next day, with Hood again being repulsed.[154] Beaten, it was now Hood's turn to retreat or risk the loss of his army. During the night heavy explosions were heard in the direction of Atlanta causing great anticipation. Next morning, Slocum dispatched several units toward the city to determine the situation. Coburn commanding a task force representing the 3rd Division, approached the defenses cautiously. Finding these works abandoned, he proceeded into the city where he met the mayor offering to surrender the city and requesting protection for persons and property. As Coburn's skirmishers fanned out and moved through Atlanta, Rebel cavalry left without a clash.[155]

As most military actions have objectives, seizing Atlanta was a huge "Mission Accomplished." Sergeant Labadie and others surely delighted in sending home word of their great feat. Labadie used a discarded railroad form which had these headings already printed:

FREIGHT TRAIN FROM ATLANTA TO_____
ENGINE_____ENGINEER_____CONDUCTOR_____
To announce the fall of Atlanta, he filled in:

"*Richmond, Sept 4, 1864, Yankee Bullets, General Sherman, Col John Coburn.*" [156]

Apparently, John Coburn saw the end of the campaign as a breaking point and the right time to separate from the military for he tendered his resignation, returning to Indiana to practice law and accept a new judicial appointment. In departing, Coburn wrote a "Farewell Address", extolling the valor and achievements of his brigade. Being rightfully proud of these four regiments he wrote:

> While in the past campaign, at Resaca, Cassville, New Hope Church, Culp's Farm, Peach Tree Creek, and Atlanta you have, in the front of the fight, borne straight onward your victorious banners. At Resaca your flags were the first to wave on the enemy's ramparts, at New Hope Church the fury of your onset redeemed the day's disaster, at Peach Tree Creek your charge reached the most famous feats of arms in the annals of war, and at Atlanta your ranks were the first to climb the works of the enemy and take possession of that renowned city.[157]

The respect was mutual; members of the 19th Michigan wrote admiringly of Coburn on numerous occasions. At Timothy Turner's urging, the Colonel's farewell address was reproduced in the *Coldwater Union Sentinel* with the former Quartermaster providing editorial accolades.[158]

The war was over for John Coburn as it was for 57 members of the 19th Michigan Infantry; killed in action or succumbing to wounds received during this hard fought campaign. Another 93 were just wounded, fortunate like Coburn, they had survived. Those who remained, grew more and more conscious of the approaching end; they, too, wanted to go home.[159]

11

SHERMAN'S MARCH THROUGH GEORGIA

After the fires were put out and the smoke settled, Atlanta became a big military camp, a garrisoned city, with Sherman commanding an army of occupation. To effect some order, there were many garrison duties that needed attention, and the 19th Michigan drew an assignment as provost guards and laborers for the commissary department. During most of its stay in Atlanta, the regiment was temporarily detached from its brigade with Company B providing security at the soldiers' home, others guarded the depot, and the remainder worked for the commissary and quartermaster unloading, loading and storing freight. [1]

Being garrisoned also meant an opportunity for staff to catch up on paper work that had been neglected during a campaign of sustained combat and movement. Frequently during these lulls, enlisted men who had writing skills were assigned to company and regimental headquarters to help complete monthly returns, muster rolls, write letters and make duplicate copies of several required military reports. A corporal in Company E would have welcomed the job on a regular basis but clerks were supposed to be privates and he could not figure out a way to qualify honorably. "Today, I have been writing all day for the Lieut. have been writing for him about a week. he had so much of it to do and he not being a good writer he had me excused from other duty. he would have me detailed for the

Co. Clerk if it was not for my Stripes, if I would do some mean act and get reduced to the ranks I might get the place then if I was reduced I could not get it then so I have got to stick by the old gun a while longer."[2]

Earlier in the war, capture of opposing capitals was a popularly expressed military objective. The insistence of generals like Grant and Sherman on destroying the enemy's army and his ability to fight, introduced a new level of modern military consciousness. Although immensely successful, Sherman's recent campaign left him with some perplexing problems. Significantly, he had captured a key Southern industrial city but holding it proved to be an encumbrance. He still had to maintain a 120 mile supply line back to his base of operations at Chattanooga, and Hood had been driven off, not defeated. His first major decision led to an order that all civilians not employed by the government would have to leave, either going north or south depending on their choice. Sherman would provide rail transportation for those electing to migrate north and deliver those desiring to stay in the south into Hood's lines at Rough and Ready, Georgia some ten miles away. This measure, Sherman calculated, would reduce considerably his responsibilities of providing food and security and allow him to compress his lines and use whatever dwellings he desired. The displacement caused a harsh verbal exchange between Hood and Sherman, each castigating the other with charges of unusual brutality.[3]

This kind of total warfare insensed the people too. Noble witnessed the bitterness as civilians crowded the depot preparing to leave their homes. "Some of them are the most bitter rebels that I ever saw The young ladies in particular one of them remarked that she was going so far South that she never would see a *cursed yankee* again. A soldier told her she would have to go beyond the Gulf of Mexico for she would see them there in a short time."[4] The whole business bothered Noble as he anguished over this decision, having observed women and children sleeping on the cold barren floor of the depot and knowing that one old woman had already died from exposure.[5]

No doubt Sherman suffered too, but he had a war to fight and probably Hood's attack on his supply lines helped convince him of the necessity of his tough policy of ousting Atlanta's citizenry. By October 4, Hood's army had cut the Western and Atlanta road and seized the posts at Big Shanty and Ackworth. Sherman was unconcerned with Confederate cavalry raids against his line being convinced that horse soldiers did a poor job of breaking railroads but the presence of Hood's army could not be permitted. He acted promptly, leaving the 20th Corps to defend Atlanta and taking the rest of his command north to confront Hood. During the next couple of weeks a series of encounters occurred with Hood carefully avoiding a fullscale fight, while fragments of both armies fought hard at several locations; however, each time the Federals held tenaciously to their railroad defenses. By the 17th, Sherman had pushed Hood off his line toward Atlanta concluding that his adversary would soon decide on another strategy.[6]

Those left in Atlanta could attest to the necessity of keeping the cars running between Chattanooga and their advanced position in Georgia. With their "Hardtack line" cut, short rations became regular; horses and mules had to forage for themselves and hundreds died. Soldiers reportedly were afflicted with scurvy resulting from a poor diet. But a little less food was not nearly as depriving as the absence of mail for two weeks. And there was no point in writing either or so concluded one soldier for knowing the prevalence of rats and mice in the city, letters would probably be chewed up while delayed in some storage room waiting to be mailed. The arrival of a train on October 14 meant Sherman had things under control and a big load of mail; Private Austin received 14 letters.

The forthcoming Presidential election generated lots of interest and concern among several 19th Michigan soldiers. Certainly Lincoln recognized the importance of the soldiers' vote if he were to be reelected; the election results verified the accuracy of his assumption. But it was much more than the actual soldiers' votes that affected the outcome, their strong pro-Lincoln feelings must have influenced other Republican votes back home. What seems apparent in this small sample, is that mothers and wives wanted their men home so badly that peace at any price was quite acceptable.[7] Corporal Lake received a letter from his brother relating the anti-war feelings expressed by men he knew back home and he retorted angrily, warning that they had better not criticize those who elected Lincoln after the soldiers returned, ". . . for we had just as live fight there as here."[8] His brother also mentioned that his mother seemed supportive of the Copperheads so he addressed a portion of his letter to her instructing: ". . to elect McClellan it would be to undo all that we have done in the past four years. After loosing so many thousands of precious lives and then to let the rebels have the benefits of an Armistice. . .*No* it cannot be done."[9] Corporal Noble had a similar problem. His girlfriend of long standing apparently suggested that she wanted her lover home and if Mac could improve the prospects, then she would support him. Noble was so upset that he suggested her attitude was treasonous prompting her next letter to carry the title "Traitor" after her name.[10] With similar conviction, Private Austin wrote: "I. . . put in a ticket today for Old Abe Again if it does prolong the war. . ." Collectively they wanted to go home; that desire was swelling at a tremendous pitch, yet they wanted to win first.[11]

Following the election, Noble spoke the regiment's mind in expressing pride in Lincoln's great victory. "Our regt has voted and I am proud to say that out of three hundred and four votes polled only fouteen were for McClellan and am sorry to add that six of the fourteen were from *Co B.* We heard there were eight in our Co. that voted the Copperhead ticket but the number has dwindled down to six and that sounds too large but so it is."[12]

With Hood at bay once again and unwilling to confront the Union army in a general engagement, Sherman prepared to turn his back and launch another campaign. Readiness involved collecting a supply of 30 days of rations and reducing his army to those who were able bodied giving him a trim, highly mobile force. Those who were weak could not keep up; the sick, lame and lazy were transported to the rear. Some members of the regiment were included among the convalescents while others served as train guards for the trip back to Chattanooga. A Confederate raiding party broke the track causing the train to derail. Some of the train guards riding on top were thrown off and immediately captured by those who had set the trap. At least a couple of 19th Michigan men (one being a lieutenant) were among the captured.[13]

Back in April before the Atlanta campaign commenced, soldiers packed up overcoats and blankets for storage in McMinnville in trying to lighten the load. Now facing a winter campaign, these were retrieved, a credit to an efficient quartermaster department. Amazingly the right ones were returned but Austin remarked that they looked "as though they had been in a beggers press."[14]

Payday was a part of the preparation too. One can surmise that a shrewd General Sherman arranged for a payday knowing its importance on troop morale particularly since the government was 12 months in arrears. It is hard to believe that anyone would work for a year without pay even if he were not getting shot at. Despite the tendency of many to squander their money playing cards, some continued to send remarkable sums home. Corporal Lake received $148.00, but he kept only "8 bucks" for himself.[15]

Since he planned to abandon Atlanta, Sherman wanted to destroy anything of military value that could not be reasonably hauled away. The engineers were busy disabling the roundhouse, railroad machine shops, and depot. Candidly a soldier observed: "The way things look to me now is that this little town is going to be burned down."[16]

Being part of 20th Corps left to defend Atlanta, members of the 19th Michigan soon got used to the comforts of garrison life and hoped, although knowing better, that they could serve out their time in relative quiet. "How I hate to start but what else can I do but go. This is what I came to war for. seems as though I had enough for one season. Gen Sherman dont seem to act that way & as near as I can guess he is going to give the rebs particularly fits all winter as he has all summer."[17] Yet faith in Sherman seemed limitless, overriding personal considerations, and instilling new levels of confidence and enthusiasm. Noble shared the desire to stay put but he believed in the general. "I seems impossible after fighting as hard as we have to get possession of the place that Sherman should deem it expedient to evacuate it so soon. But as he has a head a trifle larger than mine I purpose to trust to his management. . ." [18]

Referring to Sherman as "the great Commander of the Western Armies" Corporal Lake described him as ". . . not a very tall man slim spare face sandy wiskers and a trifle round shouldered." All soldiers admired generals who acted like regular folks and Lake added: "he don't have a half a Dosin orderlies tied to his heals or to his coattails the way most big officers do, when he is looking around." [19] Lake's idolizing soared after they reached Savannah, entitling his account of the march "Sherman against the World" while consoling his mother that ". . . the rebs did not take me away but Sherman did and I was anxious to go with him." [20]

Determined to keep the ultimate objective of his campaign as confidential as possible, Sherman shared a very vague description of his mission with his troops stating: "It is sufficient for you to know that it involves a departure from our present base and a long and difficult march to a new one." [21] Yet most everyone had a pretty good idea that they were heading for the sea.

Sherman's Army of 60,000 effectives were organized in two wings; the right (15th and 17th Corps) commanded Major General Oliver Howard and the left (14th and 20th Corps) under Major General Henry Slocum. Brigadier General Judson Kilpatrick commanded the cavalry under Sherman's direct control. The armies would proceed in two columns with each corps taking separate but parallel routes. Units were expected to average 15 miles a day and live off the land with brigade commanders responsible for organizing foraging parties. Soldiers were free to take produce, livestock and especially horses and mules, but they were to stay out of people's houses. Destruction of mills, houses and other buildings was a corps commander's decision, but if civilians or guerillas attempted to obstruct the march, commanders should retaliate harshly. [22]

The march commenced on November 15 with the right wing faking a thrust at Macon and the left striking out as if enroute to Augusta. Both movements were intended to confuse General William Hardee, commanding the Confederate defense and his cavalry leader General Joe Wheeler. They had the desired effect, causing Rebels to mass troops at the wrong places.[23] Sherman burned the bridges in his rear, cut the telegraph lines, and marched forth to meet all comers, operating without a base.

He planned his offensive in three phases; the first would take his armies to Milledgeville, the second to Millen, and the last would bring him to the coast at Savannah.[24]

The 19th Michigan and its corps followed the course of the Augusta Railroad east, tearing up the tracks as they proceeded. Marching all night served notice of the kind of campaign that could be expected. Two days later they marched through Social Circle, 51 miles from Atlanta. As the column approached Madison, the 2nd Brigade guarded the trains while other units tore up rails for several miles. At Madison, the 20th Corps turned south passing through Eatonton on the 21st, following a scrap iron set of rails. After a day in camp, the march resumed at dusk and continued through the night. Slocum's forces crossed Little River on a pontoon bridge, then burned a grist mill and a saw mill to illuminate the site while engineers pulled the pontoons, the 19th Michigan being the last unit to cross. The night was cold and regiments burned fences to keep warm. Near 6:00 A.M., the Star Corps lumbered into Milledgeville.[25]

Nothing is more commonly associated with this march than flagrant destruction of property. Whatever their participation, members of the 19th Michigan are remarkably silent on the subject. Other than the guilt expressed by a virtuous Corporal Noble, not much is said implying a low level of activity. Understandably, Noble as a member of the foraging party saw more than some of the others. "I am sorry to say that our path can be traced by the ashes of buildings both public & private and that we left the few inhabitants that we found without a mouth of food and in some cases scarcely an article of clothing.

Some of the men seemed possessed of Devils for not a house did we pass but that it was plundered. . . the people behind us must leave their homes or starvation will be their doom.'' Noble blamed the officers for allowing excesses under the guise of foraging. [26]

After lying around Georgia's capital city for a day, the 19th Michigan headed due east on November 24. They crossed the Oconne River on a covered bridge which even Southerners, anxious to slow down Yankee invaders, could not find the heart to burn. The column rested until dark, then proceeded on, again burning fences along both sides of the road for warmth and light. While marching the following day, the army confronted a citizen who had responded to Beauregard's emotional appeal for resistance by burning the bridge across Buffalo Creek. Slocum's boys reciprocated by burning all his buildings. During the next week their path took them through Sandersville and Davidsboro, across the Ogeechee River and Swamp and on past Louisville toward Millen. [27]

Although the 20th Corps skirted Millen, passing a few miles to the north, it did stop momentarily while curious soldiers examined a recently abandoned Confederate military prison:

It is a square enclosure containing forty acres of ground. The fence is constructed of pine logs, twenty feet long - placed on end; on top of this are the sentry - boxes, reached by means of ladders from the outside; inside, as next to the fence, an alley forty feet wide surrounds the entire enclosure. The inner line of this alley is marked by posts set in the ground, on top of which are spiked scantling or poles. This is termed the ''dead line'' across it is certain death for any soldier to attempt a passage. . .Although in a country abounding with timber, not a board or plant was to be seen in this enclosure - not a shelter of any description, but the entire surface was dug over and covered with holes where men had burrowed like rats to shield them from the burning rays of sun. We found the bodies of several of our men lying unburied in this loathsome den;

consigning them to the parent earth, our bugles sounded, and falling in line, solemnly and sadly we moved away.[28]

The armies then began the last leg of their march moving southeastwardly along the course of the Ogeechee River frequently negotiating swamps and streams while Confederates obstructed their route by chopping down trees. The 19th Michigan and its corps struck the Charleston and Savannah Railroad ten miles out, destroying it as they approached Savannah. When within some five miles of the city on December 10, Sherman's forces pulled up in front of the Southern defenses, momentarily stalled.[29]

The Union commander curled his armies around Hardee's lines, posting the left wing on the Savannah River and the right against the Ogeechee. While his armies invested the Rebels, he sought to make contact with the fleet. Impatiently he elected to storm Fort McAlister guarding the mouth of the Ogeechee River. General William B. Hazen's division carried out the assignment magnificently and on December 13, Sherman once again had a supply line. On the 17th, he tried to bluff Hardee into a surrender but the Confederate was not fooled.[30]

The ranks would let Sherman figure out how to get into Savannah. For them reaching the coast meant a chance to rest after a tiring 300 mile march much of it accomplished at night, only four times did they even bother to pitch tents. The best thing about Fort McAlister's fall, as always, was the arrival of mail on the 17th, the first received since leaving Atlanta. While the two generals vied for an advantage, enlisted men again arranged a truce. Like the negotiations, the terms were simple. "Towards morning some of them began to call Yank etc. What do you want Johney. You ones going to shoot in the morning. Not without some of you open the ball first sayes the Yank. Well if you ones wont fire any shot we ones wont. After the compromise was made not to shoot & daylight had come two of the rebs with their cap. came halfway & some of our pickets went halfway & had a talk with the rebs. They agreed not to shoot & have kept their word good so far & it is three o clock

PM now."[31]

Before accepting the necessity of a general assault upon Hardee's line, Sherman sought to close off the Confederate's only route to their rear, a road leading east into South Carolina. The badly out-number Confederates beat him to it and slipped out the back door crossing a pontoon bridge covered with straw to deaden the sound of tramping feet. Wednesday morning, December 21, Hardee was gone.[32]

Entering this great city so suddenly and unexpectedly could be likened to an exploration. At least that is the picture conjured by Noble's account. Being detailed as a forager, Corporal Noble was on guard duty several miles away at a rice mill when news of the evacuation arrived:

> . . .I got permission from our commanding officer for seven of us to go down to river in a skiff to the city a distance of eight miles We did not start until 2 o clock PM and in two hours we were traversing the streets of the city and gazing at the new and wonderful sights that presented themselves to our astonished vision It is a very pretty place. . .much larger than I supposed It bears but few marks of the war and even the merchants were retailing their goods to our soldiers for Federal money at very reasonable rates Two rebel Gunboats were lying below the city in plain view with the rebel flag defiantly floating & refusing to surrender But they could not get out and when we came out our men had some large guns in position and were shelling them.[33]

As with McMinnville and Atlanta, the ranks would have been very contented to last out the war in Savannah but they were Sherman's veterans, front line combat soldiers and the General was anxious to launch another campaign. Members of the regiment were a little deceived by their assignment of constructing wooden barracks which suggested a prolonged encampment; Private Austin even being sent back to Tennessee with a lumbering expedition. In all probability, Sherman intended these barracks to be occupied by a small contingent which would garrison Savannah as a military post.[34]

On December 30, Sherman reviewed the 20th Corps presumably to ignite the esprit de corps, which his presence stirred, preparatory to a new campaign just authorized by Grant. Although stated with great exuberance, the claims expressed by Delos Lake represented how Sherman had these men charged with confidence. As the army advanced he boasted that ". . . the rebs are a quaking in their shoes for fear of Old Billy." Sounding like a modern day marine, a few days later Lake claimed ". . . the Rebels have such a dislike to Billy Sherman's Army that they arnt there when we go for them and we know how to go for them."[35] Attitudes of invincibility had gone full circle; regiments organized in 1861 believed it too, yet based on foolish assumptions. Sherman's legions were the elite of American fighting men eager to engage the enemy and to end the war.

December 31st - march orders, the 3rd Division of the 20th Corps swung into action marching proudly through the streets of Savannah and crossing the first channel of the river on a pontoon bridge left intact when the Confederates evacuated the city Landing on Hutchinson Island, they were obstructed by still another channel. High wind hampered construction of a pontoon

bridge and Rebel cavalry challenged the crossing causing the Union command to cancel the mission and return to their old camp. Next morning they were back on the island for another try, and this time they were reinforced with a cannon which soon began adjusting its fire on a house defended by Confederates planning to resist the crossing. The first Round ". . .burst over the house the second one was a little near and the third shot struck the side of the house and . . . bursted the ha ha ha *whop*

how the butternuts piled out of the windows and mounted their horses. . ." and spirited away.[36] The 19th Michigan beging first in line and owing to Lieutenant Colonel Baker's initiative, began crossing the river in two small boats, together having a capacity for 16 passengers. This remarkable crossing took all night and by using a scow of some type, even the horses were ferried across. During the night, brigade commander Colonel

241

Daniel Dustin discovered the availability of a steamer which he employed to transport his remaining units.[37]

On January 4, the division moved seven miles north along the Savannah River, organizing a new camp on Hardee's Plantation. They spent almost two weeks there constructing a corduroy road, drilling and waiting. To one man's thinking, the drill was just something to kill time and it disgusted him "to think how much trouble a few officers can put themselves to just in order to keep men all the time on the jump."[38]

Continuous campaigning since leaving McMinnville had, for the most part, squelched army politics within the regiment. The new year brought a promotion for one of the most amtitious noncoms in the regiment when Second Sergeant Lewis Labadie was advanced all the way to first lieutenant. Almost begrudgingly he expressed appreciation that Colonel Baker, formerly his company commander, had finally done something for him. He had coveted a commission for so long and now his pride was intense. The uniform change was one of the immediate rewards but an expensive one at $160.[39]

While Labadie's ego was being inflated, another officer had had enough. Captain Sam Hubbard had tendered his resignation, because he was ailing and in love. As in the case of other officers, some men resented his special privilege of being able to resign when they too longed to quit. Though Labadie would not recognize it at the moment, it was another significant "rank has its privilege" advantage. Despite being envious of the captain's early departure, one of the privates in his company thought they were going to have the last laugh, because he knew the woman Hubbard was going to marry. "I think if he enlists for life with the one you think he used to [court] he will hear louder guns then he ever has. . ."[40]

A twelve mile march on January 17 took Ward's division to Hardeeville, and the 2nd Brigade continued on three miles farther to encamp at Perrysburg. The town was an established landing for river traffic on the Savannah, but Noble did not think the place justified being called a town for its structures were limited to a couple of buildings, a brick kiln and an old fortress. Except for a Negro family, the natives had cleared

242

Lt. Colonel David Anderson of Matteson was the last regimental commander. He had organized Company H and served as its commanding officer. [ruth Anderson]

out. As a staging area for military operations, Perrysburg was terrible. It may have been good for the navy but these poor foot sloggers soon found their base completely surrounded by water as the whole area became inundated for several days, and pickets used row boats to get to their posts.[41]

Here again the regiment began building winter quarters but some members of Company B decided it was a lot of work for nothing and ignored the order. Another got busy confiscating some local building materials. "I took a few boards off a barn this morning because it had never taken the oath."[42]

Enroute to this site, Colonel Baker became so ill he relinquished command to Captain Anderson and returned to Savannah where he remained hospitalized for nearly three months. He rejoined the unit in late March and then within a week, seemingly jinxed, he was thrown from his horse and injured. He spent the duration hospitalized.[43]

243

David Anderson was 40 years old when he became the fourth and last commander of the 19th Michigan. Born in New York in 1824, Anderson started teaching school at age 20. Later he engaged in business. In 1854, he came west, settling in Michigan and taking up farming in Branch and Van Buren Counties. Captain Anderson became Major Anderson in October, 1864.[44] Anderson's ascendancy to command pleased an enlisted man in his company, as he observed that the Captain was ". . . an able and efficient officer, a favorite with his regiment, and will do well for a field officer."[45]

The regiment broke camp on January 29 striking out for Robertsville at 7:00 A.M. The road was encumbered with felled trees but they still succeeded in making 16 miles. The next day they arrived at Robertsville before noon; cannonading could be heard in the distance.[46]

In reality the month of January was consumed by getting units into position, gaining a "beachhead" in South Carolina, preliminary to jumping off in another major offense, through the Carolinas. Using the same organization of two wings commanded by Howard and Slocum, Sherman intended to march straight through to Goldsboro, 425 miles away, striking the two railroads that converged there and gaining linkage to the sea coast at Wilmington and New Bern. While maneuver became his trademark during the Atlanta campaign, Sherman had now become the master of the feint. On this leg of his march, he successfully led Southern commanders to conclude that Augusta and Charleston were primary targets. Basically the campaign had three intermediate objectives; the South Carolina Railroad near Blackville, Columbia, and Fayetteville. These were checkpoints along a route of devastation as Sherman's army determined to waste railroads, arsenals and everything in general.[47]

On February 2, the brigade moved out, leaving the river and marching in a northerly direction. The column brushed with light skirmishers as it proceeded, making steady daily progress past Lawtonville and reaching the Charleston and Augusta Railroad near Blackville on February 9. The entire army engaged in destroying this road accomplishing its task with incredible efficiency and speed. Each unit down through and including companies had a separate section to destroy. The 2nd Brigade could render useless two miles of track in just two hours.[48]

Again, brigades were instructed to organize foraging parties and scrounge for their food. Like the rest, Dustin's commandos confiscated available horses and mules and escorted wagons on extensive foraging operations. These were hardly regular cavalry mounts or saddle horses, and an infantryman took his chances just grateful for the transportation. Corporal Noble was again detailed as a forager and relates an experience with an uncooperative steed. "The one I got was a refractory beast and I scarely got seated on his back as I was precipated to the ground. One experiment was sufficient and I reported to my company."[49] On a different occasion while riding a mule, Noble agreed to transport a lady across a stream. In the process, the mule fell through the bridge sending both rider and passenger tumbling into the water. These incidents were humorous but the life of a forager combined much hard riding and frequent skirmishes with Rebel cavalry and required a calloused willingness to destroy personal property. And there were casualties of all kinds. Sherman's execution of 17 Rebel prisoners speaks to the bitterness of these clashes. Noble claimed that Sherman retaliated for the loss of 17 Union soldiers ". . . found dead and a paper with the words 'death to all foragers' written upon."[50]

Noble's account of his first raid in South Carolina describes the encounters and tactics of a foraging party:

> There was forty of us including an officer and we had barely got out of hearing of camp before we were attacked by a party of Wheeler's men and several of our men who were in advance were either killed or captured The attack commenced on some men that were at a plantation a short distance ahead of our party and but a few of them succeeded in making their escape. But few bullets came among us and we fell back with more haste then we had used in advancing and succeeded in

245

eluding the Rebels. We went to a plantation on which was situated the finest house that I have ever seen in the Southern States. The yard in front was laid out into paths on each side of which grew all descriptions of evergreens and an endless variety of plants and flowers The house was large & costly and bore evidence of being furnished in a costly manner Marble topped tables and bureaus large full length mirrors etc were left the owner not being able to take them all with them when he fled from the approach of the hated Yanks The men distroyed everything in the building and then set it on fire. South Carolina is doomed unless the rebels are brought to see the error of their ways and flee from the wrath to come for the men are aware that secession originated in this state and no mercy will be shown to inhabitants while we are marching through the state. I do not think there is a building left standing between here & Sa.[51]

The march resumed and on the 12th, the regiment crossed the south fork of the Edisto River without benefit of a bridge. Although very shallow, the water and mud were extremely cold with chunks of ice floating on the surface. Some men cried out in pain but Delos Lake toughed it out comparing his situation to American patriots who crossed the Delaware.[52] The column proceeded northeastwardly, bypassing Columbia on February 17, crossing the Saluda and Broad Rivers and pushing on to reach Winnsborough by noon February 21. Near their next encampment, some men discovered a piano in a cabin and Captain Shafter entertained. Unlike others, they did not choose to smash it when they left. That night they crossed the Catawba River and engaged in extensive road construction requiring exceptionally hard labor. Colonel Dustin reported that railroad ties were manually carried for distances up to a mile. Hard rains, mud and the need to corduroy roads slowed the pace for the next few days but finally the division arrived in Chesterfield on March 3. They entered North Carolina the following day, marching on through Cheraw while other units destroyed the

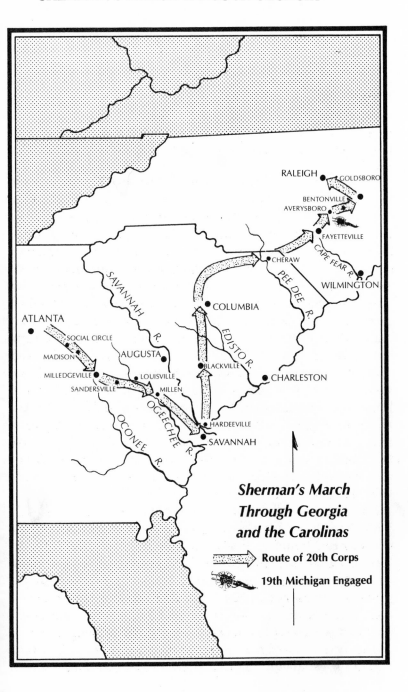

Sherman's March Through Georgia and the Carolinas

Route of 20th Corps

19th Michigan Engaged

arsenal. [53]

On March 7, the brigade covered the 20th Corps' crossing of the Great Pee Dee River. The Rebels had burned the bridge and in its place engineers positioned a pontoon structure. Upstream the Rebels conspired to prevent the crossing by pouring turpentine into the water, lighting it and hoping it would drift down and ignite the pontoon bridge. The scheme failed but did create an interesting illusion of the river being on fire. [54]

At the end of the week, March 11, Sherman's army entered Fayetteville; the last intermediate objective had been reached. The capture of Fayetteville meant Sherman had made contact with Wilmington via the Cape Fear River, the regiment would receive its first mail in 55 days, and gave Lieutenant Labadie a chance to change his shirt for the first time since January 25, 1865. The army had traveled nearly 400 miles to achieve this victory and Sherman determined the occasion worthy of a little ceremony; thus he ordered his troops to pass in review as they marched through the streets of Fayetteville. And what a sight they must have been. "Our Corps marched into the city with our war worne colors unfurled to the breeze and the 85th Ind and the 22nd Wisc brass band playing at the head of our brigade as we passed by Gen Sherman he couldn't help but notice our ragged clothes and barefoot men I had on a pair of lincy and woley pants (as they use to be called) striped like State prison pants. . .I almost barefooted no socks of any account an old hat cocked up on four sides top of it all out and I have not shaved for over one year." [56]

Sherman paused briefly to resupply and then anxiously pushed on toward his ultimate goal of Goldsboro and a juncture with General John Schofield coming up from New Bern. By the 15th, his army had crossed the Cape Fear River moving north as though marching toward Raleigh aware, however, that Joe Johnston's presence in North Carolina would make deception much more difficult. Out of respect for his old adversary, Sherman advanced cautiously keeping his striking columns relatively close and unencumbered by trains. For the first time during the campaign, the Confederates had consolidated their forces in Sherman's front. [57]

During the day, Kilpatrick skirmished with Hardee's rear guard as he withdrew north. On the 16th, resistence stiffened as the Rebels seized the initiative, threatening to overrun this advanced Union position. The call went out for help and portions of Slocum's corps hurried forward. At the time, Ward's division was corduroying roads as it advanced north on the Raleigh Road. Abandoning the task, Colonel Dustin pushed his lead brigade hard toward Aversboro. A two-mile march brought them to the action where they were immediately deployed, with the 19th Michigan and 85th Indiana going off to the left in line. Soon the other two regiments were sent forward, spreading out from the road left with the 19th Michigan, 85th Indiana, 22nd Wisconsin, and 33rd Indiana in line. Captains LeRoy Cahill and John Clark commanded a skirmish line manned exclusively by 19th Michigan soldiers. In front of the main line on a knoll, three batteries unlimbered. [58] "As their works were low they did not shield them much and our batteries were making sad havoc among them For the credit of our batteries I will say they done some of the most accurate shooting that I ever saw. . ." [59]

While the 1st Brigade slid down the line feeling for the Rebel right flank, Dustin's brigade went forward. Particularly in front of the 19th Michigan and 85th Indiana, the ground separating the opposing armies was very open. Once in the open, the Confederates cut loose with a heavy sheet of fire causing the advancing line to sag toward the left seeking the cover of several farm buildings and some woods. [60] "Our Brig halted when within easy musket range of their works and we had a fair chance to shoot rebs and they had an equal chance to shoot Yanks." [61] At that range it was a deadly affair. "I saw one man Confederate at least with a hole made through his breast as slick as you could have bored it with an auger." [62]

With the Confederate battery silenced and the 1st Brigade about to roll up the enemy's flank, the assault began. The 1st and 2nd Brigades overran the position, and the 19th Michigan was the first to reach the Rebel line. Their skirmishers charged in among the overwhelmed Confederates. Two lieutenants were killed and an artillery captain captured in the close encounter.[63] One of the skirmishers delighted in recounting how he had ". . . fired a good many shotts at the scared Johnies as they run back from one tree & stump to an other . . Such a running of rebs is not seen every day."[64]

The 20th Corps pressed the Confederates vigorously, forcing them to bypass a second line of prepared works and retreat further to a main line already occupied by other Southern troops.[65] Dustin's 2nd Brigade pursued the enemy across Raleigh Road to the right through a swamp. Finally the Confederates' third line stopped the Union momentum. As the action quieted, the 19th Michigan assumed a reserve role.[66]

The 2nd Brigade suffered 55 casualties in the two days' action, 85 percent occurring within the 85th Indiana and the 19th Michigan. Charging through an open field against entrenched positions accounts for the heavy losses of these two regiments. The only officers killed were Captain Leonard Gibbon and Lieutenant Charles Pursell, 19th Michigan company commanders, both shot in the head, an indication of the direct fire they were under. The only other 19th Michigan battlefield deaths were two color bearers making obvious the high risk occupations within a Civil War regiment. Seventeen others were wounded, in a sense lucky, certainly more fortunate than some. Corporal Bill Beebe felt so. Grazed across the breast, he walked off the field laughing at his narrow escape.[67]

Early in the morning, vacant trenches were discovered, for the Rebels during the night had slipped away. The left wing proceeded toward Goldsboro with the 14th Corps leading. The going was slow as units struggled to cross the Black River on a bridge only partially intact and their route forced them to pass through a series of swamps. Corps trains became so strung out that the front of the supply column was seven hours ahead of the rear. All day on the 18th, Dustin's brigade served as train guards.[68]

Finally Joe Johnston saw an opportunity. He knew by now that Sherman's objective was Goldsboro, not Raleigh, and the Union general had overconfidently dispersed his army. In preparation for a surprise attack on Slocum's lead corps,

Johnston began concentrating his forces near Bentonville, some 20 miles west of Goldsboro. General Wade Hampton's cavalry stubbornly contested the Union advance giving Confederates valuable time to mass. The Federals were reluctant to believe that the enemy in their front was anything more than cavalry.[69]

Slocum's realization of the trap about to be sprung was nearly too late and he sent couriers scurrying in several directions with urgent appeals for help. Before reinforcements arrived, Johnston struck driving most of the 14th Corps.[70]

The 19th Michigan was at the front of the column and could hear rumbling cannon ahead when the alarm sounded. They literally ran the four miles to Bentonville reaching the battlefield in the shortest possible time, just as their comrades were being driven in disorder. "When we came up a seene of confusion greeted our eyes officers riding in all directions men running back some badly scared and a few wounded. . ."[71] Deployed on the left flank, the brigade waited for an expected attack that never came.[72] The 20th Corps' presence stabilized the Union defense.[73]

By the end of the next day, March 20, Sherman had most of his right wing at Bentonville content to wait it out and allow Johnston the opportunity to withdraw. Both commanders knew Schofield had arrived at Goldsboro on the 21st, so Johnston accommodated his foe and retreated. The following day, Sherman's army resumed its march and arrived in Goldsboro on March 23.

Behind Sherman's army lay a 400 mile path of destruction. It seems certain that some units were more directly involved than others in devastating the land, just as the degree to which men carried out their vengeance varied. Accounts describing the destruction of property are missing from the correspondence of 19th Michigan soldiers. They made general comments regarding its extensiveness but did not relate personal involvement. Granted they may not have chosen to record it, yet it could be expected that someone would have boasted of their "heroics". It is apparent that they generally approved of the practice. South Carolina symbolized the worst kind of "secesh"; the desire to even a score with her represented a special rationale for destruction. Major Anderson felt that malice as he recounted the army's feats on its devastating march through the cradle of secession. His vengeful attitude could not be mistaken as he informed a local newspaper editor that South Carolina had been dealt a "just and merited punishment." [74] "They had it coming," expressed a basic justification.

One can sense pride of accomplishment in Private Lake's bragging: "we burnt every house, barn, mill, that we passed." [75] But "we" in all likelihood meant Sherman's army and not the regiment specifically. And strangely enough this very pious soldier could sound like a typical bummer yet in another letter, reprimand his brother for deserting moral standards by going out dancing. [76]

Although the judgment involves speculation, it appears that the main army had less direct involvement in confiscating, burning, pillaging and destroying property than those assigned to foraging parties or belonging to the cavalry or other units operating on the fringe. Operating independently, these units took extra liberties beyond their mission.

For the most part, Henry Noble served as a forager after the 19th Michigan left Atlanta. He fought an entirely different war than the rest of the boys. His conviction toward restoring the Union remained unswerving; however the routine activities of foraging parties confronted his morality. To his first love he wrote: "Ruth I have been disgusted with the manner in which this raid has been conducted and it is a disgrace to our cause the way the citizens of South Carolina has been treated under the plea that it was the state where secession originated The men committed depredations without restraint and not a single dwelling within miles of our line of march but was plundered and in some instances burned by men whose consciences were deadened to tears & entreates of helpless women & children" [77] Visions of guilt played heavily on his mind as he recalled an incident, presumably fairly typical, when foragers arrived at the home of a widow whose husband had died in the Confederate army. Left along to provide for six children, the family struggled to survive. The Yankees acted more like bandits than American soldiers taking everything including the last goose. Frightened and crying hysterically, mother and six children, the oldest about eight, pleaded for mercy. No one was listening and in a desperate grasp for strength, the poor women cried out: "my dear friends I hope you will remember me when you die." [78]

A campaign was over; Sherman had marched straight through rebeldom, linked up with Schofield, and eagerly awaited orders to strike at Richmond and engage Lee's Army of Northern Virginia.

THEY DIED TO MAKE MEN FREE

12

GOING HOME

For most dutiful soldiers, there was only one way to go home honorably and alive, and that was to defeat the Confederate armies. The longing to go home was by far the most powerful and persistent frame of mind of Civil War soldiers. Some began contemplating it the same month they entered service back in the fall of 1862. By March, 1865, the desire was intense.

At Goldsboro, Sherman paused briefly to refit his army. Lacking normal logistical support during a sustained campaign, the 19th Michigan was forced to wear Confederate uniforms.[1] On April 10th, Sherman went after Johnston and arrived at Raleigh, North Carolina, April 13. The next day a truce was arranged and the two generals began discussing surrender terms. Because their agreement reached on the 18th was unacceptable, the final surrender was delayed until April 26.[2]

One glorious announcement followed another: first came the news of Lee's surrender, then Johnston's. Having been previously disappointed so often by rumors, soldiers initially responded with cautious reservation. But once confirmed, they broke into unrestrained jubilation, regiment after regiment, cheered at the top of their lungs.[3] Amidst the celebration came the tragic news of Lincoln's death. Although saddened, 19th Michigan soldiers did not express their grief very profoundly.[4]

At the end of the month, the regiment began its march

toward the nation's capital and passed through Richmond and by several already famous Virginia battlefields. It reached its camp near Alexandria on May 19. On the 24th, the 19th Michigan participated in the Grand Review:

> Through the streets of Washington saw Generals Sherman Grant & Meade the president & a man they said was secretary Stanton The streets were lined on either side with crowds of men women & children and near the staging the Generals & president were standing there was a perfect sea of bonnets and hats. Handerkerchiefs were waved at us & across the street in one place a rope was stretched and a frame of some description suspended to the middle and on a canvass was written in large letters 'All Hail To Our Western Heroes' with the several battles we have participated in & the places we have captured written below Flowers were woven in various shapes and wreaths encircled the frame and it was decorated off in fine style.[5]

One would assume that the Grand Review would have been a special occasion and a time of great pride for these seasoned veterans. But the urge to go home apparently dominated most attitudes. These 19th Michigan soldiers did not perceive themselves as heroes. They did not want to soak up the glory. They just wanted to get it over with. Major Anderson was obviously upset with their lackadaisical attitude in preparation for the review. He ordered inspections for May 21, 22, and 23 directing that the regiment would not ". . . tarnish a reputation purchased by toil, by Suffering, and by blood."[6] Private Austin was unimpressed by the event. To his wife he wrote: "I suppose it would be a little interesting to you if you could see the army on review. I have got enough of it & dont know as I would care if I never see another review."[7] Both he and Noble were hoping they would be home for the Fourth of July.[8]

During these last months, seemingly the only sustaining source of military pride came from an abiding faith in General Sherman. These soldiers believed he would fight it through to the finish. Even after they thought their war was over and then learned they were going to pursue Johnston near Raleigh, a confident Austin would write: "I suppose we are going to hunt old Johnson. If we find him & he wants to fight us OLD BILLY will make it hot for his icebox."9

On June 10, the regiment was mustered out of Federal service and started for home. It traveled west by rail to Cleveland. At Pittsburg they were given a warm reception and a splendid meal. They crossed Lake Erie aboard the *"Morning Star"* and arrived in Detroit around 1:00 P.M.10 Here they received a rousing welcome as citizens gathered to greet them. In promoting their return, The *Detroit Free Press* referred to the 19th ". . . as the captured and cut-up regiment."11 They were given a hero's reception complete with a sumptuous meal and a parade down Jefferson Avenue with cheering spectators lining the street.12

During the next week, the men waited impatiently for the paymaster to arrive. Many elected to go home and wait. Finally on June 25, they all reassembled at Detroit, received their remaining pay, and disbanded. They had served 2 years, 9 months and 21 days.13

When Companies C and H arrived back in Coldwater, no organized rally had been planned. Instead they dispersed into the arms of loved ones and friends. The editor of the newspaper regretted this lack of recognition and announced that the community would soon properly pay its respects with a big Fourth of July celebration.14

They were home, at least some of them. The regiment had begun with 995 officers and men; it returned with 391, about 200 of whom were original members. During the war, 1206 officers and men were enrolled. Losses are accounted for as follows: 54 killed in action, 31 died of wounds, 7 died in Confederate prisons, 132 died of disease, 182 were discharged for disability.15

Many years later when old gray-bearded 19th Michigan veterans gathered, members recalled their great adventure; each year it surely became a little more glorious. Henry A. Ford was designated historian, yet despite his literary talents, never wrote a history of the regiment's experience. One of the best attempts came from the pen of Malcolm B. Duffie. At one of those reunions he shared his "Recollections" in verse.

RECOLLECTIONS

Respectfully Dedicated To The Living And The Dead Of The Nineteenth Michigan Volunteer Infantry

One more year, my dear old comrades,
Has been numbered with the past;
Since we met in glad reunion,
Since we saw each other last.
Let us pledge to meet together,
(If by any means we can.)
While remains a living member
Of the Nineteenth Michigan.

Let us talk of Old Kentucky,
Of that night at "Honey Run,"
Of those days of weary marching,
Of our sorrows and our fun.
How with gallant Colonel Coburn,
That devoted Hoosier man,
On the field of Thompson's Station,
Stood the Nineteenth Michigan!

Of your life in Libby Prison;
How you sought again the front
After leaving old McMinnville,
To receive the battle's brunt.
How that day at dark Resaca,
Riding foremost in the van,
Fell the brave old Colonel Gilbert
Of the Nineteenth Michigan!

GOING HOME

Standing like a wall of granite
In the breach from day to day,
You upheld your country's honor,
You have held her foes at bay!
Then as ebbed the tide of battle,
When the foeman broke and ran,
Close behind, with cheer exultant,
Pressed the Nineteenth Michigan!

On the skirmish line we see you,
Slowly moving 'cross that field,
Now supporting yonder batt'ry,
Which you ne'er was known to yield!
Where the fight did rage the fiercest,
Hand to hand and man to man,
There did wave the riddled colors
Of the Nineteenth Michigan!

In the archives of your country,
In the temple reared to fame;
On a tablet, - high uplifted,
You have carved an honored name.
Grayhaired vet'rans tell the children
How and where the fight began;
Pointing out the spot defended
By the Nineteenth Michigan!

On the picket line we find you;
There, unsheltered from the rain;
In the woods, out in that cornfield,
By those cedars down the lane.
Step by step the foe retreated,
Inch by inch, and span by span.
Ev'ry mile from Chattanooga
Fought the Nineteenth Michigan!

259

THEY DIED TO MAKE MEN FREE

On, still on, though faint and weary,
Hungry, cold, yea, even sick!
'Cross the winding Chattahoochee,
Thro' the fight at Peach Tree Creek!
Onward, still, from burned Atlanta,
In pursuit of Treason's clan,
To the sea with Billy Sherman,
Marched the Nineteenth Michigan!

On, again, from quaint Savannah,
Marching to and from the sea,
Onward, through the Carolinas,
You have borne our banner, free.
History will tell the story,
If you will it's pages scan,
Of the charge at Averysborough
By the Nineteenth Michigan!

Then you will remember, comrades,
How our batt'ry on the hill
Shook the earth, when General Johnston
Charged our lines at Bentonville!
All along, 'neath grassy hillocks,
Death still holds them under ban;
Sleeping there, the fallen heroes,
Of the Nineteenth Michigan!

Let us, comrades, strive to muster
In that camp on yonder shore,
Where no foe can ever enter,
And where war shall come no more.
When are gathered out the jewels
In accord with Heaven's plan,
May there enter in the Kingdom
All the Nineteenth Michigan! [16]

THEY DIED TO MAKE MEN FREE

Chapter I -- A CALL TO ARMS:
"THREE HUNDRED THOUSAND MORE"

1. Michigan Adjutant General's Office, *Annual Report of the Adjutant General of the State of Michigan for the Year 1862* (Lansing, 1862), 8.

2. U.S., Secretary of Interior, *Population of the United States in 1860* (Washington, 1864), 236-246. Franklin Rice, *Diary of 19th Michigan Volunteer Infantry During Their Three Years Service in the War of the Rebellion* (Big Rapids, n.d.), September 5, 1862 (Hereafter cited as Rice, *Diary*). The author has only examined a typescript of this book. An extensive search failed to locate a copy. When George May edited his bibliography of *Michigan Civil War History,* he located copies at the Michigan State Library and the Burton Historical Collection of the Detroit Public Library. George S. May (ed.), *Michigan Civil War History: An Annotated Bibliography* (Detroit, 1961), 47. The author contacted both libraries and found these copies missing. Given complete reliance on a typescript, chronological diary entries rather than page numbers are cited.

3. *Three Rivers Reporter,* July 26, 1862, 1.

4. Crisfield Johnson, *History of Branch County, Michigan* (Piladelphia, 1879), 135; *American Biographical History of Eminent and Self Made Men* (Cincinnati, 1878), I, 40; *Coldwater Daily Reporter,* June 28, 1961, Sec. 2, 1; *Western Chronicle* (Centerville), September 10, 1862, 3; Microcopy, United States Census for 1860, Branch County, Michigan, National Archives, Washington, D.C.

5. *Coldwater Daily Reporter,* June 28, 1961, Sec. 2, 1.

6. *Three Rivers Reporter,* July 26, 1862, 1.

7. Regimental Descriptive Book, Record of Enlistments, 19th Michigan Infantry, National Archives, Washington, D.C.

8. Michigan Adjutant General's Office, *Record of Service of Michigan Volunteers in the Civil War* (Kalamazoo, 1905), IXX, 16, 20, 56 and 100 (Hereafter cited as *Record of Service.*).

9.	Regimental Descriptive book, record of Enlistments, 19th Michigan Infantry, National Archives, Washington, D.C.

10.	*Three Rivers Reorter*, July 26, 1862, 2.

11.	*Kalamazoo Gazette*, August 1, 1862, 2. *Western Chronicle* (Centreville), August 13, 1862, 3.

12.	Regimental Descriptive Book, Record of Enlistments, 19th Michigan Infantry, National Archives, Washington, D.C.

13.	*Cass County Republican*, August 7, 1862, 2.

14.	*Ibid.*, July 31, 1862, 3.

15.	*Ibid.*, August 7, 1862, 2 and July 31, 1862, 3. *Three Rivers Reporter*, August 9, 1862, 5.

16.	*Cass County Repubican*, August 7, 1862, 2.

17.	*Kalamazoo Gazette*, July 25, 1862, 3. *Western Chronicle* (Centreville), August 5, 1862, 3.

18.	*Cass County Republican* August 14, 1862, 2.

19.	*Three Rivers Reporter*, August 2, 1862, 2.

20.	*Kalamzoo Gazette*, August 1, 1862, 2.

21.	E.A. Brown to his brother Captain Darius Brown, 12th Michigan Infantry Regiment, August 24, 1862. Letter is privately owned by Dr. Robert Pennell, Newtonville, Massachusetts.

22.	Ibid.

23.	John Robertson, *Michigan in the War* (Lansing, 1882), 450 (Hereafter cited as Robertson, *Michigan in the War*). *Western Chronicel* (Centreville), July 30, 1862, 2.

24.	Regimental Descriptive book, Record of Enlistments, 19th Michigan Infantry, National Archives, Washington, D.C.

25.	Rice, *Diary*, August 5, 1862.

26.	*Cass County Republican*, July 31, 1862, 3.

27.	*Three Rivers Reporter*, August 2, 1862, 3.

28.	*Allegan Journal*, September 1, 1862, 2.

29.	*Ibid.* See also Charles Prentiss Letter, August 31, 1862. All Prentiss letters and his diary are privately owned by Archie Nevins, Kalamazoo, Michigan.

30.	Rice, *Diary* August, 18, 1862; *Allegan Journal*, August 25, 1862, 2; Ira Carpenter Letter, *Constantine Weekly Mercury & St. Joseph County Advertiser*, August, 24, 1862, 2.

31.	Ira Carpenter Letter, *Constantine Weekly Mercury & St. Joseph County Advertiser*, August 24, 1862, 2.

32.	*Ibid.; Kalamazoo Gazette*, August 29, 1862, 2-3.

33.	Ira Carpenter Letter, *Constantine Weekly Mercury & St. Joseph County Advertiser*, August 24, 1862, 2; Samuel Hewitt Letter, *Allegan Journal*, September 15, 1862, 1.

34.	*Detroit Free Press*, July 23, 1862, 1.

35. Alfred Mathews, *History of Cass County, Michigan* (Chicago, 1882), 183 (Hereafter cited as Mathews, *History of Cass County*).

36. Ira Carpenter Letter, *Constantine Weekly Mercury & St. Joseph County Advertiser*, August 24, 1862, 2. *Kalamazoo Gazette*, August 29, 1862, *J.* The letter that appeared in the *Gazette* presumably was written by Lieutenant Henry A. Ford, who prior to the war was editor of that newspaper.

37. Mathews, *History of Cass County*, 182, 185 and 186. L.H. Glover, *A Twentieth Century History of Cass County* (Chicago, 1906), 155, 160 and 174 (Hereafter cited as Glover, *Twentieth Century History of Cass County*).

38. *Cass County Republican*, July 31, 1862, 3.

39. James W. Gilbert to Captain M. Mayer, October 14, 1862, located in the Bentley Historical Library, Michigan Historical Collections at The University of Michigan, Ann Arbor, Michigan.

40. *Detroit Free Press*, July 23, 1862, 1.

41. Henry A. Ford Letter, *Kalamazoo Gazette*, August 29, 1862, 2. Henry Noble Letter, August 23, 1862, located in the Bentley Historical Library, Michigan Historical Collections at The University of Michigan, Ann Arbor, Michigan. All Noble Letters and diaries are located there. Ira Carpenter Letter, *Constantime Weekly Mercury & St. Joseph County Advertiser*, August 24, 1862, 2.

42. Cyrus Wheeler Letter, September 3, 1862, located in the Bentley Historical Library, Michigan Historical Collections at The University of Michigan, Ann Arbor, Michigan. All Wheeler letters are located there.

43. Robertson, *Michigan in the War*, 392; Henry Ford Letter, *Kalamazoo Gazette*, August 29, 1862, 2.

44. Delos Lake Letter, August 22, 1862, located in The Huntington Library, San Marino, California. All Lake letters are located there.

45. Microcopy, United States Census for 1860, Allegan, Berrien, Branch, Cass and Kalamazoo Counties, National Archives, Washington, D.C. *Dowagiac Daily News*, October 13, 1948, 1. Knowledge of relationships is also gleaned from soldiers' correspondence. For Delos Lake, the regiment's organization must have seemed like a family reunion for he discovered a cousin among the ranks. Delos Lake Letter, August 22, 1862.

46. Background data on the initial command and staff cadre was derived from the following sources: *American Biographical History of Eminent and Self Made Men* (Cincinnati, 1878), 1, 40; Orville W. Collidge, *A Twentieth Century History of Berrien*

County (Chicago, 1893), 155; Charles D. Rhodes, "William Rufus Shafter," *Michigan History Magazine*, XVI (1932), 375; Microcopy, United States Census for 1860, Allegan, Berrien, Branch, Cass and Kalamazoo Counties, National Archives, Washington, D.C.; Glover, *History of Cass County*, 260; Cecil K. Byrd (ed.), "Journal of Israel Cogshall, 1862 - 1863", *Indiana Magazine of History*, XLII (1946), 69 (Hereafter cited as "Cogshall Journal); *Kalamazoo Gazette*, July 25, 1862, 3; *Record of Service.*

47. Mathews *History of Cass County*, 184 and 191. Glover, *Twentieth Century History of Cass County*, 159 and 195.

48. Charles Prentiss Letter, August 31, 1862. Phinehas Hager Letter, August 23, 1862, located in the Bentley Historical Library, Michigan Historical Collections at The University of Michigan, Ann Arbor, Michigan. All Hager letters are located there.

49. Henry A. Ford Letter, *Kalamazoo Gazette*, August 29, 1862, 2. Smauel Hewitt Letter, *Allegan Journal*, September 15, 1862, 1.

50. Phinehas Hager Letter, August 23, 1862.

51. Samuel Hewitt Letter, *Allegan Journal*, September 15, 1862, 1.

52. Phinehas Hager Letter, August 23, 1862. Henry Noble Letter, August 23, 1862.

53. Charles Prentiss Letter, August 28, 1862.

54. Henry Noble Letter, August 23, 1862 and others.

55. Cyrus Wheeler Letter, September 3, 1862. Since there was only one Jones in Company B, Wheeler must have been referring to Martin M. Jones. *Record of Service*, 51.

56. Charles Prentiss Letter, August 28, 1862.

57. *St. Joseph Traveler*, September 3, 1862, 3.

58. Phinehas Hager Letter, August 23, 1862.

59. Ira Carpenter Letter, *Constantine Weekly Mercury & St. Joseph County Advertiser*, September 11, 1862, 1.

60. Delos Lake Letter, September 7, 1862.

61. *Cass County Republican* September 18, 1862, 3.

62. *Three Rivers Reporter,* September 20, 1862, 3.

63. *Cass County Republican*, September 18, 1862, 3.

Chapter II -- GETTING INTO THE WAR

1. *The War of the Rebellion: A Compilation of the Official Records of the Union and Confederate Armies* (69 vols. and index; Washington, 1880 - 1901), XVI, Pt. II, 459. (Hereafter cited as OR. All references are to series I).

2. *Ibid.*, 476 and Whitelow Reid, *Ohio in the War: Her Statesmen,*

Her Generals, and Soldiers (Cincinnati, 1863), I, 91 - 92. (Hereafter referred to as Reid, *Ohio in the War*).

3.   OR, XVI, Pt. II, 500.
4.   *Ibid.*, 472 and 494. See also E. B. Long, *The Civil War Day By Day* (Garden City, 1971), 266. (Hereafter cited as Long, *The Civil War Day By Day*).
5.   Long, *The Civil War Day By Day*, 258 and 261. OR, XVI, Pt. II, 467-68 and 505.
6.   *St. Joseph Traveler*, September 17, 1862, 3.
7.   Henry Noble Diary, September 14, 1862.
8.   Henry A. Ford Letter, *Kalamazoo Gazette*, October 3, 1862, 2. Charles Prentiss Letter, September 17, 1862.
9.   Samuel Hubbard Letter, *Allegan Journal*, October 20, 1862, 1. See also Charles Fonda Letter, *Three Rivers Reporter*, September 27, 1862, 2.
10. Charles Prentiss Letter, September 17, 1862; Henry Noble Letter, September 20, 1862.
11. Samuel Hubbard Letter, *Allegan Journal*, October 20, 1862, 1.
12. Charles Fonda Letter, *Three Rivers Reporter*, September 27, 1862, 2; Henry A. Ford Letter, *Kalamazoo Gazette*, October 3, 1862, 2; Henry Noble Letter, September 20, 1862.
13. OR, XVI, Pt. II, 471-72.
14. Henry A. Ford Letter, *Kalamazoo Gazette* October 3, 1862, 2.
15. Samuel Hubbard Letter, *Allegan Journal*, October 20, 1862, 1. Reference is to Corporal Robert Patterson.
16. Charles Prentiss Letter, September 27, 1862.
17. Ibid.
18. Charles Fonda Letter, *Three Rivers Reporter*, September 27, 1862, 2.
19. Samuel Hewitt Letter, *Allegan Journal*, October 13, 1862, 1.
20. *Ibid.*
21. *Ibid.*
22. Rice, *Diary*, October 1, 1862.
23. Charles Prentiss Letter, October 12, 1862 and letter from unidentified member of 19th Michigan, *Three Rivers Reporter*, October 11, 1862, 2.
24. Charles Prentiss Letter, October 2, 1862.
25. Charles Prentiss Letter, October 12, 1862; Sherman Stephens Letter, *Allegan Journal*, November 10, 1862, 1.
26. John Bennett Letter, *Three Rivers Reporter*, October 11, 1862, 2. Private Delos Lake came to the same conclusion after observing mules floating in the river on more than one occasion. He and his tent mates secured the lieutenant's permission to fetch fresh

water from a spring a couple of miles from camp. Delos Lake Letter, October 8, 1862.

27. *OR*, XVI, Pt. II, 621 - 22. Henry M. Cist, *The Army of the Cumberland* (New York, 1898), 72. (Hereafter cited as Cist, *Army of the Cumberland*).

28. *Kalamazoo Gazette*, October 24, 1862, 2. (Letter is signed "Heinrich", assumed to be written by Henry A. Ford).

29. *Ibid.*

30. John S. Griffis Letter, October 15, 1862, located in the Bentley Historical Library, Michigan Historical Collections at The University of Michigan, Ann Arbor, Michigan. All Griffis letters are located in the Bentley Historical Library.

31. *Kalamazoo Gazette*, October 24, 1862, 2.

32. Samuel Hewitt Letter, *Allegan Journal*, November 10, 1862, 1.

33. Edmund Amidon Letter, *Sturgis Journal*, November 6, 1862, 1.

34. Henry Noble Letter, November 9, 1862.

35. Rice, *Diary*, October 18, 1862.

36. Judson Austin Letter, November 15, 1862 located in the Bentley Historical Library, Michigan Historical Collections at The University of Michigan, Ann Arbor, Michigan. All Austin letters are located in the Bentley Historical Library.

37. Charles Prentiss Letter, October 21, 1862.

38. Edmund Amidon Letter, *Sturgis Journal*, November 6, 1862, 1.

39. Phinehas Hager Letters, November 1 and 6, 1862.

40. Ibid., November 1, 1862.

41. Ibid.

42. Ibid.

43. Ibid., November 7, 1862.

44. Charles Prentiss Letter, November 5, 1862.

45. Ibid., November 9, 1862.

46. *Kalamazoo Gazette*, October 24, 1862, 2.

47. Phinehas Hager Letter, November 6, 1862.

48. Charles Prentiss Letter, November 9, 1862.

49. Ibid., November 5, 1862. Reference is to Privates Dave Anderson and Vernon Rose.

50. Ibid.

51. Phinehas Hager Letter, November 5, 1862.

52. Charles Prentiss Letter, November 9, 1862.

Chapter III -- GARRISONED AT NICHOLSVILLE

1. *OR*, XVI, Pt. II, 993. The Michigan Adjutant General, John Robertson, incorrectly recorded that the 19th Michigan Infantry

was attached to the 1st Division, Army of the Ohio until January, 1863. Robertson, *Michigan in the War*, 392.

He compounded the error by stating that it was a part of the 1st Division, Army of the Ohio in compiling: *Record of Service*, 1. These inaccuracies probably resulted because the regiment was captured on March 5, 1863 and all of the records were destroyed. See Regimental Letter and Order Book, 19th Michigan Infantry, December 20, 1863, National Archives, Washington, D.C.

2. George Irving Reed (ed.), *The Encyclopedia of Biography of Indiana* (Chicago, 1899), II, 62 - 66. (Hereafter cited as Reed, *Encyclopedia of Biography of Indiana*).

3. *Ibid.*, 63. See also Henry C. Bradsby, *History of Vigo County, Indiana, With Biographical Selections* (Chicago, 1891), 337; *American Biographical History of Eminent and Self Made Men* (Michigan Volume) (Cincinnati, 1878), 40; Frank L. Byrne (ed.), *The View From Headquarters; Civil War Letters of Harvey Reid* (Madison, 1965), xii (Hereafter cited as Byrne, *Letters of Harvey Reid*); Gil R. Stormont, *History of Gibson County, Indiana, Her People, Industries and Institutions* (Indianapolis, 1914), 211.

4. Samuel Hewitt Letter, *Allegan Journal*, December 8, 1862, 2.

5. Ira Carpenter Letter, *Constantine Weekly Mercury & St. Joseph County Advertiser*, December 4, 1862, 2; Samuel Hewitt Letter, *Allegan Journal*, December 8, 1862, 2.

6. Charles Conner Letter, November 21, 1862, located in the Regional History Collection at Western Michigan University, Kalamazoo, Michigan. All Conner letters are located there.

7. Judson Austin Letter, December 27, 1862.

8. Samuel Hewitt Letters, *Allegan Journal*, December 8, 1862, 2; January 5, 1863; Charles Prentiss Letter, November 17, 1862.

9. Ezra J. Warner, *Generals in Blue* (Baton Rouge, 1964), 255 - 56. (Hereafter cited as Warner, *Generals in Blue*].

10. Samuel Hewitt Letter, *Allegan Journal*, December 8, 1862, 2.

11. Henry Noble Letter, November 27, 1862.

12. Ibid.

13. Samuel Hewitt Letter, *Allegan Journal*, January 5, 1863, 1.

14. Charles Prentiss Letter, November 28, 1862.

15. Henry Noble Letter, November 27, 1862. See also Samuel Hewitt Letter, *Allegan Journal*, January 5, 1863,1.

16. Charles Conner Letter, November 21, 1862.

17. Samuel Hewitt Letter, *Allegan Journal*, January 5, 1863, 1.

18. Phinehas Hager Letter, November 28, 1862.

19. Judson Austin Letter, November 23, 1862.

20. Charles Prentiss Letter, December 6, 1862.

21. Henry Noble Letter, November 27, 1862.
22. Samuel Hewitt Letter, *Allegan Journal*, December 8, 1862, 2.
23. Rice, *Diary*, November 24, 1862.
24. Henry Noble Letter, November 27, 1862.
25. Ira Carpenter Letter, *Constantine Weekly Mercury & St. Joseph County Advertiser*, December 4, 1862, 2.
26. *Ibid.*
27. George T. Shaffer Letter, January 20, 1863, located in the Bentley Historical Library, Michigan Historical Collections at The University of Michigan, Ann Arbor, Michigan. All Shaffer letters are located in the Bentley Historical Library.
28. Regimental Descriptive Book, Co. B, 19th Michigan Infantry, National Archives, Washington, D.C.
29. Charles Prentiss Letter, January 4, 1863.
30. Ibid., November 22, 1862. Prentiss does not elaborate on what he has written to his wife concerning Sergeant Hager. This must have been mentioned in another letter which is not among the Prentiss correspondence.
31. Phinehas Hager Letter, November 28, 1862.
32. Ibid.
33. Ibid.
34. Samuel Hubbard Letter, August 8, 1864, located in the Bentley Historical Library, Michigan Historical Collections at The University of Michigan, Ann Arbor, Michigan
35. Phinehas Hager Letter, December 11, 1863.

Chapter IV -- WINTER QUARTERS AT DANVILLE

1. John Griffis Letter, December 12, 1862.
2. Samuel Hewitt Letter, *Allegan Journal*, January 5, 1863, 1.
3. "Cogshall Journal", 71.
4. Proceedings of a General Court Martial Held at Danville December 20 - 23, 1863. Records of the Judge Advocate General's Office, Court Martial Case Files, Number KK 701, Record Group 153, Captain George H. White, National Archives, Washington, D.C. (Hereafter referred to as Proceedings of General Court Martial). Private Harrison Rockafellow who carried Captain White's message to Colonel Gilbert told the court that White said the Colonel ". . . had made a shitass of himself."
5. Frederick A. Virkus (ed.), *Compendium of American Genealogy* (Chicago, 1937), VI, 256, *The DAR Lineage Book* (Washington, D.C., 1932), CIXX, 52. Robertson, *Michigan in the War*, 798. Although Adjutant Robertson was very protective of officers'

reputations, there is no evidence that Clark was dismissed from the 4th Michigan.

6.   Judson Austin Letter, November 25, 1862.

7.   Charles Prentiss Letter, November 22, 1862.

8.   George Shaffer Letter, January 20, 1863.

9.   Proceedings of General Court Martial. White had become the "fall guy" as Private Austin saw it. "They have got one of our Caps arrested for nothing. Some of our men got up a paper and lots of the boys & Sargants signed it. paper was to get the old Doctor out of the reg. The Col. got hold of the paper and found out that Cap. White knew the paper was going around & did not offer to stop it so the old Col. arrested the Cap. Took his sword away and put him in close quarters & put a guard over him. Judson Austin Letter, November 19, 1862.

10.   Charles Prentiss Letter, November 22, 1862; George Shaffer Letter, January 20, 1863; John Griffis Letter, January 9, 1863.

11.   George Shaffer Letter, January 20, 1863.

12.   John Griffis Letter, January 9, 1863.

13.   George Shaffer Letter, January 20, 1863. The Colonel's brand of leadership and his determination to whip the regiment into shape as noted by Lieutenant Shaffer, was also illustrated by his approach toward encouraging church attendance. Following a poor showing at a sermon preached by Chaplain Cogshall, Gilbert announced that the men had a choice, either attend services or report for a formation and hear the articles of war read. A stubborn and resentful Private Austin heard the "Army laws read" and observed that they were "mighty strict." Judson Austin Letters, November 16 and 19, 1862.

14.   Ibid.

15.   *Cass County Republican*, January 1, 1863, 1.

16.   *Ibid.*

17.   Proceeding of General Court Martial.

18.   Ibid.

19.   Ibid.

20.   Ibid.

21.   Ibid.

22.   Ibid.

23.   Ibid.

24.   Henry Noble Letter, December 19, 1862.

25.   Charley Prentiss Letter, December 15, 1862.

26.   Ibid., December 18, 1862.

27.   Ibid., December 15, 1862.

28.   Ibid.

29. Ibid.
30. Phinehas Hager Letter, December 25, 1862.
31. Ibid.
32. Edmund Amidon Letter, *Sturgis Journal*, January 8, 1863, 1.
33. "Cogshall Journal", 72. *OR*, XX, Pt. I, 142.
34. Cist, *Army of the Cumberland*, 84.
35. *OR*, XX, Pt. I, 154-156.
36. *Ibid.*, 142.
37. "Cogshall Journal", 72.
38. Edmund Amidon Letter, *Sturgis Journal*, January 8, 1863, 1.
39. "Cogshall journal", 72.
40. *OR*, XX, Pt. I, 156.
41. *Ibid.*, 158.
42. *Ibid.*
43. Rice, *Diary*, January 5, 1863.
44. Phinehas Hager Letter, January 6, 1863.
45. Ibid., January 4, 1863.
46. Ira Carpenter Letter, *Constantine Weekly Mercury & St. Joseph County Advertiser*, January 8, 1863, 1.
47. Samuel Hewitt Letter, *Allegan Journal*, January 5, 1863.
48. Charles Prentiss Letter, December 15, 1862. See also John Griffis Letter, December 12, 1862.
49. Ira Carpenter Letter, *Constantine Weekly Mercury & St. Joseph County Advertiser*, January 8, 1863, 1.
50. Charles Prentiss Letter, January 9, 1863 and Rice, *Diary*, January 8, 1863.
51. Judson Austin Letter, January 8, 1863.
52. Phinehas Hager Letter, January 22, 1863.
53. Ibid.
54. Henry Noble Letter, January 6, 1863.
55. John Griffis Letter, January 9, 1863.
56. John Griffis Letter, January 18, 1863.
57. Judson Austin Letter, January 11, 1863. See his letter dated February 10, 1863 for reference to polishing materials.
58. Phinehas Hager Letter, January 18, 1863.
59. Charles Prentiss Letter, January 14, 1863.
60. Phinehas Hager Letter, January 18, 1863.
61. Ibid.
62. *Constantine Weekly Mercury & St. Joseph County Advertiser*, February 26, 1863, 2.
63. Phinehas Hager Letter, January 22, 1863.

Chapter V -- "I AM TIRED OF A SOLDIER'S LIFE"

1. Henry Noble Letter, February 17, 1863.
2. Wood Gray, *The Hidden Civil War: The Story of the Copperheads* (New York, 1964), 118.
3. *Ibid*, 118-133.
4. *Ibid.*, 133.
5. Charles Prentiss Letter, February 10, 1863.
6. Ibid., February 8, 1863.
7. Ibid., February 10, 1863.
8. Ibid., January 30, 1863.
9. Regimental Descriptive Book, Register of Desserters, 19th Michigan Infantry, National Archives, Washington, D.C.
10. Judson Austin Letter, February 10, 1863. In a letter dated February 10, 1863, Charles Prentiss also names Eldridge Morey and Martin Jones as two of the regiment's desserters.
11. Edmund Amidon Letter, *Sturgis Journal*, March 5, 1863, 2.
12. Judson Austin Letter, February 11, 1863.
13. Phinehas Hager Letter, February 15, 1863.
14. Ibid. Stephen Knapp was discharged March 27, 1863, *Record of Service*, 53.
15. Charles Prentiss Letter, February 19, 1863.
16. Phinehas Hager Letter, February 15, 1863.
17. Judson Austin Letter, February 20, 1863.
18. John Griffis Letter, February 10, 1863.
19. Phinehas Hager Letter, February 18, 1863.
20. George Shaffer Letter, February 26, 1863.
21. Charles Prentiss Letter, February 10, 1863.
22. Lewis Labadie Letter, February 22, 1863, located in the Burton Historical Collection, Detroit Public Library, Detroit, Michigan. All Labadie letters are located there. Reference is to William Snooks.
23. Charles Prentiss Letter, February 24, 1863.
24. Phinehas Hager Letter, March 1, 1863.
25. Ibid., January 26, 1863.
26. John R. McBride, *History of the Thirty-Third Indiana Veteran Volunteer Infantry* (Indianapolis, 1900), 71. (Hereafter cited as McBride, *History of Thirty-Third Indiana*).
27. Phinehas Hager, January 29, 1863.
28. Delos Lake Letter, January 30, 1863.
29. Byrne, *Letters of Harvey Reid*, 20-21.
30. Rice, *Diary*, January 21, 1863. See also Charles Prentiss Letter, February 7, 1863; "Cogshall Journal", 72-73.

31. Samuel Hewitt Letter, *Allegan Journal*, March 2, 1863, 1; Judson Austin Letter, February 5, 1863.

32. John Griffis Letter, February 10, 1863.

33. Samuel Hewitt Letter, *Allegan Journal*, March 2, 1863, 1; John Griffis Letter, February 10, 1863; "Cogshall Journal", 73.

34. Charles Conner Letter, February 14, 1863.

35. "Cogshall Journal", 73.

36. Henry Noble Letter, February 26, 1863.

37. Charles Prentiss Letter, February 17, 1863; Phinehas Hager Letter, February 18, 1863.

38. George Shaffer Letter, February 26, 1863.

39. Phinehas Hager Letter, February 15, 1863.

40. "Cogshall Journal", 71 and 73-74.

41. John Griffis Letter, February 14, 1863. Griffis was referring to Orin Laylin who hailed from Wayne Township, Cass County.

42. Charles Conner Letter, February 14, 1863; John Griffis Letter, February 14, 1863; Phinehas Hager Letter, February 15, 1863, and others. *Small Arms Used By Michigan Troops in the Civil War* (Lansing, 1966), 34, erroneously suggests that the 19th Michigan retained their Austrian Rifle Muskets until they were reorganized in June, 1863 following their capture at Thompson's Station.

43. Charles Prentiss Letter, February 10, 1863.

44. Ira Carpenter Letter, *Constantine Weekly Mercury & St. Joseph County Advertiser*, February 26, 1863, 2.

45. Henry Noble Letter, February 26, 1863.

46. Charles Prentiss Letter, February 24, 1863.

47. Phinehas Hager Letter, February 18, 1863.

48. Ibid., March 1, 1863.

49. Ibid. Augustus Lilly had served initially as first sergeant of Company B and John Shafter was sergeant major of the regiment

50. Henry Noble Letter, February 26, 1863.

51. Rice, *Diary*, February 24, 1863.

52. Henry Noble Letter, February 26, 1863.

Chapter VI -- "ENGAGEMENT AT THOMPSON'S STATION

1. William M. Lamers, *The Edge of Glory: A Biography of General William S. Rosecrans, U.S.A.* (New York, 1961), 244-256. (Hereafter cited as Lamers, *The Edge of Glory*).

2. *OR*, XXIII, Pt. I, 77.

3. *Ibid.*, 85.

4. *Ibid.*, 86.

5.   *Ibid.*, 84, 106.

6.   Reid, *Ohio in the War*, II, 873.

7.   *Ibid.*, 872 - 73.

8.   Carlos Baker Letter, *Allegan Journal*, April 13, 1863, 1 - 2.

9.   Byrne, *Letters of Harvey Reid*, 29 - 30.

10.   *OR*, XXIII, Pt. I, 86.

11.   Carlos Baker Letter, *Allegan Journal*, April 13, 1863, 1 - 2.

12.   *OR*, XXIII, Pt. I, 77 - 78 and 86.

13.   *Ibid.*, 94 and 98.

14.   *Ibid.*, 86 and 97.

15.   Byrne, *Letters of Harvey Reid*, 32.

16.   *Ibid.*, 33.

17.   *OR*, XXIII, Pt. I, 86 and 104.

18.   *Ibid.*, 87, 88, 106 and 107.

19.   *Ibid.*, 87 and 116. McBride, *History of the Thirty-Third Indiana*, 91. John Wyeth, *That Devil Forrest: Life of General Nathan Bedford Forrest* (New York, 1959), 135. (Hereafter cited as Wyeth, *That Devil Forrest*). Wyeth estimated the Confederates had some 6,000 troops present at Thompson's Station. Yet the precise strength of Van Dorn's command is difficult to determine. In making his official report, Van Dorn did not indicate the numerical size of his army. *OR*, XXIII, Pt. I, 116 - 118. According to Braxton Bragg's tri-monthly return, dated February 28, 1863, Van Dorn's command numbered 5,807. *OR*, XXIII, Pt. II, 654. Two days later, Bragg informed General Joseph E. Johnson that Van Dorn had "over 7,000 effective men." *OR*, XXIII, Pt. II, 656.

20.   *OR*, XXIII, Pt. I, 88, 94, 99, 101 and 102. See also John A. Wilkins Letter, March 7, 1863 located in the Indiana State Historical Library, Indianapolis, Indiana; McBride, *History of the Thirty-Third Indiana*, 76.

21.   Charles P. Lincoln, "Engagement at Thompson's Station, Tennessee", Military Order of the Loyal Legion of the United States, Commandery of the District of Columbia (1893), 9. (Hereafter cited as Lincoln, "Thompson's Station").

22.   *OR*, XXIII, Pt. I, 88, 104, 107 and 112; Lincoln "Thomspon's Station", 7 - 8; Byrne, *Letters of Harvey Reid*, 33.

23.   Lincoln, "Thompson's Station", 7 - 8.

24.   Byrne, *Letters of Harvey Reid*, 34.

25.   Regimental Letter and Order Book, June 13, 1863, 19th Michigan Infantry, National Archives, Washington, D.C.

26.   *OR*, XXIII, Pt. I, 120.

27.   Lincoln, "Thompson's Station", 9.

28.   Byrne, *Letters of Harvey Reid*, 34.

29. *Ibid.*
30. Lincoln, "Thompson's Station", 10.
31. *OR*, XXIII, Pt. I, 107 - 108, and 112; Byrne, *Letters of Harvey Reid*, 36 - 37.
32. *OR*, XXIII, Pt. I, 81-82, 89, 95, 99-100, 105, 108 and 114.
33. John Griffis Letter, April 11, 1863.
34. *OR*, XXIII, Pt. I, 122.
35. Wyeth, *That Devil Forrest*, 140.
36. Lincoln, "Thompson's Station", 10.
37. Robertson, *Michigan in the War*, 393; *OR*, XXIII, Pt. I, 89; Charles Stow Letter, *Sturgis Journal*, April 9, 1863, 2. Corporal Charles Adair, Company F was the hero of one of these seizures; he not only captured a flag but three members of the Confederate color guard. *Record of Service*, 4.
38. John Griffis Letter, April 11, 1863.
39. Ibid.
40. Rice, *Diary*, March 5, 1863.
41. Judson Austin Letter, September 12, 1863. Thompson's Station was frequently referred to as Spring Hill.
42. George W. Adams, *Doctors in Blue: The Medical History of the Union Army in the Civil War* (New York, 1961), 102 and Francis A. Lord, *Civil War Collectors Encyclopedia* (New York, 1965), 54 - 55.
43. *OR*, XXIII, Pt. I, 89, 103, and 104.
44. *Ibid.*, 117.
45. *Ibid.*, 90 and 120.
46. *Ibid.*, 121.
47. *Ibid.*, 91 and 119.
48. Rice, *Diary*, March 5, 1863.
49. *OR*, XXIII, Pt. I, 81.
50. *Ibid.*, 82.
51. *Ibid.*, 115.
52. *Ibid.*, 112.
53. *Ibid.*, 117.
54. *Ibid.*, 116 and 120.
55. *Ibid.*, 82 - 83 and 114 - 115. See also John W. Rowell, *Yankee Cavalrymen: Through the Civil War With the Ninth Pennsylvania Cavalry* (Knoxville, 1971), 120 - 121 (Hereafter cited as Rowell, *Yankee Cavalrymen*) and Carlos Baker Letter, *Allegan Journal*, April 13, 1863, 1 - 2.
56. *OR*, XXIII, Pt. I, 91. Casualties of individual companies of the 19th Michigan Infantry compiled from date in *Record of Service*.
57. *OR*, XXIII, Pt. I, 118.

58. Rowell, *Yankee Cavalrymen*, 66-67 and 105.
59. *OR*, XXIII, Pt. I, 105.
60. *Ibid.*, 88, 95 and 99.
61. *Ibid.*, 107 and 112.
62. *Ibid.*, 116.
63. *Ibid.*, 115.
64. Byrne, *Letters of Harvey Reid*, 36.
65. *OR*, XXIII, Pt. I, 95 and 99.
66. John A. Wilkins Letter, March 7, 1863.
67. Frank K. Moore (ed.), *The Rebellion Record: A Diary of American Events*, Boston, 1900, VI, 442-443. (New York: 1861-63; 1864-68).
68. Frederick D. Williams (ed.), *The Wild Life of the Army; Civil War Letters of James A. Garfield* (East Lansing, 1964), 247.
69. Colonel Emerson Opdycke Letter, March 8, 1863, located in Library of Congress, Washington, D.C., Series 4, Volume 6 of the James A. Garfield Papers.
70. *OR*, XXIII, Pt. II, 112.
71. Warner, *Generals in Blue*, 174.
72. Carlos Baker Letter, *Allegan Journal*, April 13, 1863, 1-2.
73. *OR*, XXIII, Pt. I, 84 and 91.
74. Israel Cogshall Letter, *Detroit Advertiser and Tribune*, May 6, 1863, 2.
75. "Cogshall Journal", 76.
76. Judson Austin Letter, *Allegan Journal*, April 20, 1863, 2.
77. *Ibid.*
78. Edmund Amidon Letter, *Sturgis Journal*, April 2, 1863, 2.
79. *OR*, XXIII, Pt. I, 109.
80. B.H. Polk Letter to Mrs. William R. Shafter, March 25, 1863, William R. Shafter Papers, The Stanford University Libraries, Stanford, California.
81. *OR*, XXIII, Pt. I, 84.
82. Wyeth, *That Devil Forrest*, 147.
83. Charles Stow Letter, *Sturgis Journal*, April 9, 1863, 1.

Chater VII -- PRISONERS OF WAR

1.   Rice, *Diary*, March 6, 1863; Charles Stow Letter, *Sturgis Journal*, April 9, 1863, 1.
2.   John Griffis Letter, April 11, 1863; Judson Austin Letter, April 10, 1863.
3.   Rice, *Diary*, March 10, 1863.
4.   George Livingston Letter, *St. Joseph Traveler*, Apirl 16, 1863, 1.

5. *Ibid*. See also Rice, *Diary* March 8.
6. Judson Austin Letter, April 10, 1863.
7. Ibid. Both Stow and Griffis remembered it as one of the worst nights they had every experienced. Charles Stow Letter, *Sturgis Journal*, April 9, 1863, 1; John Griffis Letter, April 11, 1863.
8. Rice, *Diary*, March 10, 1863.
9. *Ibid*. See also Judson Austin Letter, April 10, 1863.
10. Rice, *Diary*, March 22, 1863.
11. *St. Joseph Traveler*, March 19, 1863, 2.
12. Charles Prentiss Letter, March 23, 1863.
13. Ira Carpenter Letter, *Constantine Weekly Mercury & St. Joseph County Advertiser*, April 16, 1863, 1.
14. "Cogshall Journal", 77.
15. *Ibid*.
16. *OR*, XXIII, Pt. I, 179.
17. "Cogshall Journal", 77.
18. *Ibid.*, 78.
19. *Ibid*.
20. *Ibid*. See also Charles Prentiss Letter, March 15, 1863. Although Cogshall does not cite the dead comrade's name, he states that he was a member of Company C from Batavia. Based on those two clues, the soldier must have been Erastus R. Green.
21. Charles Prentiss Letter, March 23, 1863.
22. Charles Prentiss Diary, March 25, 1863.
23. *OR*, XXIII, Pt. I, 188.
24. Charles Prentiss Letter, April 22, 1863.
25. *OR*, XXIII, Pt. I, 179.
26. *Ibid*. Actually there were three casualties, all in the 22nd Wisconsin, *OR* XXXIII, Pt. I, 186. Yet, two were accidently inflicted, as men carelessly attempted to break their loaded rifles and render them useless to their captors. Byrne, *Letters of Harvey Reid*, 47.
27. Charles Prentiss Letter, April 12, 1863.
28. Rice, *Diary*, March 6 - 30, 1863; Charles Prentiss Diary, March 25 - April 11, 1863; Charles E. Stow Letter, *Sturgis Journal*, April 9, 1863, 1.
29. George W. Livingston Letter, *St. Joseph Traveler*, April 16, 1863, 1.
30. Rice, *Diary*, March 22, 1863.
31. Franklin Rice easily provides the best description of the prison experience of the regiment, Rice, *Diary*, March 22 - 30, 1863.
32. Judson Austin Letter, April 10, 1863.
33. Ibid. See Also George Livingston Letter, *St. Joseph Traveler*, April 16, 1863, 1.

34. Rice, *Diary*, April 23, 1863.
35. Charles Prentiss Letter, May 5, 1863.
36. John Griffis Letter, May 1, 1863.
37. *Record of Service*, 42.

Chapter VIII -- 'ON OUR ROAD BACK TO DIXIE''

1. "Cogshall Journal'', 82; Henry Noble Letter, June 9, 1863.
2. Judson Austin Letter, June 27, 1863.
3. Henry Noble Letter, June 9, 1863.
4. Ibid.
5. Rice, *Diary*, June 8, 1863; Henry Noble Diary, June 11, 1863; "Cogshall Journal'', 82.
6. Henry Noble Letter, June 14, 1863.
7. Ibid.
8. Ibid. See also Charles Prentiss Letter, June 12 and June 21, 1863; Phinehas Hager Letter, July 29, 1863.
9. Henry Noble Letter, June 14, 1863.
10. Cyrus Wheeler Letter, June 17, 1863.
11. Ibid.
12. Henry Noble Letter, June 14, 1863.
13. Henry Noble Diary, June 18 - 20; Charles Conner Letter, June 23, 1863.
14. Henry Noble Letter, June 20, 1863.
15. Reid, *Letters of Harvey Reid*, 74 - 75; Charles Prentiss Diary, June 22, 1863.
16. Cist, The *Army of the Cumberland*, 151 - 152, 154 - 155; Stanley F. Horn, *The Army of Tennessee* (Norman, 1968), 231. (Hereafter cited as Horn, *Army of Tennessee*).
17. Cist, *The Army of the Cumberland*, 156.
18. Henry Noble Letter, June 24, 1863.
19. "Cogshall Journal'', 83.
20. Ira Carpenter Letter, *Constantine Weekly Mercury & St. Joseph County Advertiser*, July 23, 1863, 2.
21. Horn, *Army of Tennessee*, 236.
22. Charles Prentiss Diary, June 28 - 29, 1863.
23. Phinehas Hager Letter, July 4, 1863.
24. Henry Noble Letter, June 24, 1863.
25. Charles Prentiss Letter, July 4, 1863; Henry Noble Diary, July 4, 1863; "Cogshall Journal'', 84; Rice, *Diary*, July 4, 1863.
26. Charles Prentiss Letter, July 4, 1863; Rice, *Diary*, July 4, 1863; *Record of Service*, 85.
27. Phinehas Hager Letter, September 11, 1863.

28. Charles Prentiss Diary, August 3, 1863.
29. Regimental Letter and Order Book, 19th Michigan Infantry, Special Order No. 5, Headquarters; 3rd Brigade, 1st Division, Reserve Corps, National Archives, Washington, D.C.
30. Ibid.
31. Regimental Letter and Order Book, 19th Michigan Infantry, Special Order No. 2, Headquarters, National Archives, Washington, D.C.; Report of Approximate Strength of and Vacancies Occurring Among Commissioned Officers, State Archives of Michigan, Lansing, Michigan.
32. Charles Prentiss Letter, July 14, 1863.
33. Charles Prentiss Letter, July 21, 1863.
34. Henry Noble Letter, July 19, 1863.
35. Judson Austin Letters, July 21 and 24, 1863; McBride, *History of the Thirty-Third Indiana* 101-102.
36. Henry Noble Letter, August 12, 1863.
37. Charles Prentiss Letter, July 14, 1863.
38. Phinehas Hager Letter, July 29, 1863.
39. Phinehas Hager Letter, September 24, 1863.
40. Phinehas Hager Letter, July 24, 1863. Reference is to Sergeant David O. Brown and David Anderson.
41. Ira Carpenter Letter, *Constantine Weekly Mercury & St. Joseph County Advertiser*, July 23, 1863, 2.
42. George Shaffer Letter, June 17, 1863.
43. The 1860 Branch County census lists John R. Champion, Margaret Champion, Lucy Gilbert, Grace Gilbert and Rosanna Gilbert all residing in the Henry B. Adams household. The Gilberts were three of the Colonel's children.
44. Phinehas Hager, August 10, 1863.
45. Regimental Letter and Order Book, 19th Michigan Infantry, July 21, 1863, National Archives, Washington, D.C.
46. Francis Thompson Letter, *Mishawaka Enterprise*, (Indiana) August 8, 1863, 2.
47. Charles Prentiss Letter, July 21, 1863. Different from what could be expected in a modern army, Civil War soldiers apparently wore many non-issued items of clothing. Austin reported that they were only required to wear their caps during inspections, dress parades and guard mounts; however, many had lost theirs and soldiers wore a variety of civilian hear gear. "I wear my old hat every day it is as good as a nightcap. have got the little arrow you gave me stuck on the side of it think it is just about as military as any of their hats it laps down on all sides just in fashion" Judson Austin Letter, July 29, 1863.

48. Phinehas Hager Letter, August 19, 1863.

49. Phinehas Hager Letter, August 2, 1863.

51. Henry Noble Letter, August 10, 1863.

52. Charles Prentiss Diary, August 18 and 20, 1863; Phinehas Hager Letter, August 19, 1863.

53. Charles Prentiss Diary, August 23, 1863; Judson Austin Letter, August 27, 1863.

54. Isaac Edwards Letter, August 26, 1863. All Edwards letters are owned by Mrs. Guy Thomas, Dowagiac, Michigan. The funerals that Edwards attended were those of Daniel Knapp from Litchfield, age 19 and James Bradford of Mundon, 25 years old. *Record of Service*, 53 and 15. His description of a military funeral represented the usual ceremony. On an earlier occasion, a soldier stated that the men joined in singing two hymns. Judson Austin Letter, February 15, 1863.

55. Charles Prentiss Diary, August 25, 1863; Judson Austin Letter, August 23, 1863.

56. "Cogshall Journal", 86.

57. *Ibid.*, 86 - 87.

58. Charles Prentiss Letter, July 2, 1863; Judson Austin Letters, July 13 and September 12, 1863. Besides prayer meetings which were organized by enlisted men, soldiers like Delos Lake, took personal measures to increase their piety. In an attempt to clean up their language, Lake and his tentmates implemented a rule that required the payment of 3 cents for each time one of them swore. Lake was appointed treasurer and had collected 75 cents. Delos Lake Letter, October 8, 1864.

59. Ibid.; Charles Prentiss Letters, July 6 and 14, 1863.

60. Phinehas Hager Letter, September 11, 1863.

61. Phinehas Hager Letter, August 2, 1863.

62. Regimental Letter and Order Book, Special Field Order #219, August 9, 1863, 19th Michigan Infantry, National Archives, Washington, D.C.

63. "Cogshall Journal", 87.

64. Charles Prentiss Diary, August 30, 1863.

65. Henry Noble Letter, September 24, 1863.

66. Ibid.; Judson Austin Letter, September 26, 1863.

67. Cist, *The Army of the Cumberland*, 230 - 232.

68. McBride, *History of the Thirty-Third Indiana*, 102; Henry Noble Letter, September 10, 1863; John Griffis Letter, October 11, 1863.

69. *OR*, XXX, Pt. II, 723.

70. Phinehas Hager Letter, October 7, 1863; Henry Noble Letter,

October 8, 1863.
71. Phinehas Hager Letter, October 7, 1863.
72. *Constantine Weekly Mercury & St. Joseph County Advertiser*, October 22, 1863, 2.
73. *OR*, XXX, Pt. II, 706.
74. *Constantine Weekly Mercury & St. Joseph County Advertiser*, October 22, 1863, 2.
75. *Ibid.*
76. *Ibid.*; *OR* XXX, Pt. II, 706.
77. *OR*, XXX, Pt. II, 706, 720, 722 - 725; Shelby Foote, *The Civil War: A Narrative* (New York, 1963), Vol. II, 761; *Constantine Weekly Mercury & St. Joseph County Advertiser*, October 22, 1863, 2.
78. *Constantine Weekly Mercury & St. Joseph County Advertiser*, October 22, 1863, 2.
79. *OR*, XXX, Pt. II, 707.
80. Phinehas Hager Letter, October 7, 1863.
81. Ibid.
82. Lamers, *The Edge of Glory*, 377.
83. *OR*, XXX, Pt. II, 714 - 16.
84. *Ibid.*, 697 - 99 and 717.
85. *Ibid.*, 714, and 719 - 20. Baldwin must have been a little concerned about his reputation for his entire report to Colonel Gilbert was published in the local newspaper. *Constantine Weekly Mercury & St. Joseph County Advertiser*, November 5, 1863, 2. Hooker had ordered John Coburn to take two regiments north to Christiana and help defend that place. Coburn proceeded by rail as far as Wartrace and hesitated. Uncertain and fearful of being cut off, Coburn cautiously returned to the Duck River. It was his failure to unload his infantry and defend the Garrison Creek Bridge that provoked Butterfield. *OR*, XXX, Pt. II, 698 - 99. Though not wanting to second guess Coburn, it appears that Thompson's Station may have influenced his behavior.
86. *OR*, XXX, Pt. II, 712.
87. *Ibid.*, 713. Hooker did not identify the two officers in his report; Coburn may well have been one of them.

Chapter IX -- DUTY AT McMINNVILLE

1. *OR*, XXXI, Pt. I, 847-848.
2. *Ibid.*
3. *Ibid.*, XXX, Pt. II, 727.
4. George Shaffer Letter, October 28, 1863.
5. Henry Noble Letter, November 4, 1863.

282

6. John Griffis Letter, October 30, 1863.
7. Judson Austin Letter, October 25, 1863.
8. Lewis Labadie Letter, November, 1863.
9. Judson Austin Letter, April 4, 1864.
10. Henry Noble Letter, November 9, 1863.
11. Ibid., November 4, 1863.
12. Lewis Labadie Letter, January 17, 1864.
13. George Shaffer Letter, November 11, 1863.
14. Phinehas Hager Letter, November 4, 1863.
15. Ibid., November 15, 1863.
16. Robertson, *Michigan in the War*, 840; Coolidge, *History of Berrien County*, 713.
17. Eli Griffin Letter, January 15, 1864, located in the Bentley Historical Library, Michigan Historical Collections at The University of Michigan, Ann Arbor, Michigan. All Griffin letters and diaries are located there.
18. Phinehas Hager Letter, January 20, 1864.
19. Eli Griffin Letter, February 11, 1864.
20. Phinehas Hager Letter, February 21, 1864; Lewis Labadie Letter, February 21, 1864.
21. Regimental Letter and Order Book, March 31, 1864, 19th Michigan Infantry, National Archives, Washington, D.C.
22. Phinehas Hager Letter, March 6, 1864.
23. Eli Griffin Letter, November 20, 1863.
24. John Griffis Letter, March 17, 1864; Phinehas Hager Letter, March 18, 1864; William Lefler Letter, *Constantine Weekly Mercury & St. Joseph County Advertiser*, April 7, 1864, 2.
25. Regimental Letter and Order Book, 19th Michigan Infantry, Special Order No. 21, National Archives, Washington, D.C.
26. Rice, *Diary*, March 24, 1863; Henry Noble Letter, November 16, 1863; John Griffis Letter, February 25, 1864.
27. Rice, *Diary*, March 24, 1863; William Lefler Letter, *Constantine Weekly Mercury & St. Joseph County Advertiser*, April 7, 1864, 2.
28. Regimental Letter and Order Book, 19th Michigan Infantry, December 17, 19, 28 and 29, 1863, National Archives, Washington, D.C.
29. Eli Griffin Letter, February 11, 1864.
30. *The Cass County Republican*, October 22, 1863, 2.
31. *Ibid.*, October 8, 22 and November 26, 1863, 3; Samuel Keasy Letter, *Constantine Weekly Mercury & St. Joseph County Advertiser*, January 14, 1864, 2; Samuel Hewitt Letter, *Allegan Journal*, January 18, 1864, 2.

32. Regimental Letter and Order Book, 19th Michigan Infantry, Special Field Order #219, August 9, 1863, National Archives, Washington, D.C.; Phinehas Hager Letter, March 18, 1864.

33. Lewis Labadie Letter, December 14, 1863; Eli Griffin Letter, January 29, 1864 and others.

34. Regimental Letter and Order Book, 19th Michigan Infantry, December 17, 1863, National Archives, Washington, D.C.

35. Ibid., January 4, 1864.

36. Ibid., December 28, 1863.

37. Ibid., March 17, 1864.

38. Ibid., December 20, 1864.

39. Ibid., March 20, 1864.

40. Ibid., Corporal Slipper was 44 when he enlisted making him one of the oldest in the regiment. *Record of Service*, 83.

41. William Lefler Letter, *Constantine Weekly Mercury & St. Joseph County Advertiser*, April 7, 1864, 2.

42. *Record of Service*, 6; Rice, *Diary*, February 5, 1863.

43. Rice, *Diary*, February 5, 1863.

44. Regimental Service Records indicates that Herb Amfield, Eldin Bird, Sambo Calvin, James Gross, George Mason, Jacob Stone, Beny Washington, Dennis Woody and Jack Woody were all enlisted while the regiment was at McMinnville. Regimental Service Records, 19th Michigan Infantry, State Archives of Michigan, Lansing, Michigan.

45. Phinehas Hager Letter, January 20, 1864. Hager is referring to Captain Hubbard and Lieutenant Lilly. Colonel Gilbert, Major Griffin and Adjutant Brown were using a female cook. There is no evidence that she was ever mustered into the ranks! Eli Griffin Letter, January 2, 1864.

46. Eli Griffin Letter, January 9, 1864.

47. Statement written by Captain George Shaffer, commanding Company A. Presumably Shaffer was making a report to the quartermaster to account for lost property which Woody took along. Document in private collection of author.

48. John Griffis Letter, March 17, 1864.

49. Eli Griffin Letter, February 8, 1864.

50. Eli Griffin Letter, January 29, 1864.

51. Ibid., November 20, 1863, November 30, 1863, December 6, 1863 and January 2, 1864.

52. George Shaffer Letter, November 27, 1863. See also his letter written December 23, 1863.

53. Regimental Letter and Order Book, 19th Michigan Infantry, November 28 and 30, 1863, National Archives, Washington, D.C.

54. Phinehas Hager Letter, March 6, 1864.
55. George Shaffer Letter, November 1, 1863.
56. Ibid., November 1, 1863.
57. William Lefler Letter, *Constantine Weekly Mercury* & *St. Joseph County Advertiser,* April 7, 1864, 2.
58. Phinehas Hager Letter, February 17, 1864.
59. John Griffis Letter, March 17, 1864.
60. Eli Griffin Letter, December 20, 1863.
61. Ibid., March 13, 1864.
62. Ibid., November 10, 1863 and *Record of Service,* 21.
63. Phinehas Hager Letters, December 28, 1863 and February 9, 1864.
64. Regimental Letter and Order Book, 19th Michigan Infantry, July 22, 1863 and Report of Aggregate Strength of, and Vacancies Occurring Among Commissioned Officers, National Archives, Washington, D.C. When the 19th Michigan left McMinnville in April, 1964, the 23rd Missouri, which had been away, came back to relieve them. It appears that Gilbert did not like bing superseded any better the second time. David Coe (ed.) *Mine Eyes Have Seen the Glory: Combat Diaries of Union Sergeant Hamlin Alexander Coe* (Cranbury, 1975), 110. (Hereafter cited as Coe, *Diary.*)
65. Regimental Letter and Order Book, 19th Michigan Infantry, March 31, 1864, National Archives, Washington, D.C.
66. George Shaffer Letter, November 11, 1863; Eli Griffin Letters, December 6 and 13, 1863 and Regimental Letter and Order Book, 19th Michigan Infantry, February 17, March 20 and April 21, 1864, National Archives, Washington, D.C.
67. Eli Griffin Letters, December 6 and 13, 1863.
68. Ibid., February 27, 1864.
69. Ibid., December 13, 1863.
70. Ibid., November 30 and December 13, 1863.
71. Ibid., November 14, 1863 and February 27, 1864.
72. Ibid., December 13, 1863.
73. Ibid., November 30, 1863.
74. Phinehas Hager Letter, November 15, 1863; Henry Stark Letter, January 8, 1864. Stark's letter is in the Hager collection.
75. Lewis Labadie Letter, November 1863.
76. George Shaffer Letter, November 11, 1863.
77. Judson Austin Letter, November 14, 1863; Henry Noble Letter, November 16, 1863.
78. George Shaffer Letter, December 23, 1863.
79. Judson Austin Letter, November 14, 1863.

80. Phinehas Hager Letter, February 14, 1864.
81. *Record of Service*, 20, 40, 61, 80, 85, 89 and 94. Those who joined Shafter's 17th U.S. Colored received a promotion in the process; Sergeant Major Fletcher Marsh to captain, Sergeant Henry Canfield to first lieutenant, Corporal Terrence Goodwin to second lieutenant, Corporal Francis Snow to second lieutenant and Sergeant Orlando Van Hise to first sergeant.
82. Eli Griffin Letter, November 14, 1863. Griffin reports this same dislike for the regiment's two top officers in a letter written to his father, December 13, 1863. His own perception of a very favorable attitude toward him by other officers is most directly expressed in his November 20, 1863 letter.
83. Ibid., November 10, 1863. Sergeant Ham Coe expressed a similar opinion of the Colonel's disposition after finishing a task at Regimental headquarters. "I was relieved at the Colonel's today, and I was heartily glad of it, for he is a cross old — — ——." Coe, *Diary*, 107.
84. Eli Griffin Letter, December 12, 1863.
85. Phinehas Hager Letter, November 29, 1863.
86. George Shaffer Letter, December 23, 1863.
87. George Shaffer Letters, November 1 and 11, 1863 and December 23, 1863. In his November 1 letter, Shaffer reveals that he was not the only officer being held against his wishes. Supposedly, Lieutenant LeRoy Cahill's resignation was refused despite his inability to use one hand resulting from a crippling wound at Thompson's Station. Ultimately Shaffer would have his way; promoted to captain, then discharged from the regiment to accept a commission as major of the 28th Michigan Infantry Regiment. *Record of Service*, 80.
88. *Record of Service*, 80.
89. Regimental Letter and Order Book, 19th Michigan Infantry, March 31, 1864, National Archives, Washington, D.C.
90. Henry Noble Letter, November 4, 1863.
91. Regimental Letter and Order Book, 19th Michigan Infantry, March 31, 1864, National Archives, Washington, D.C.
92. Phinehas Hager Letter, November 1, 1863. In spite of Bassett's military failures and dismissal, he returned to Allegan and was elected mayor, attesting to his political power and suggesting why Gilbert might find him more difficult to deal with. Judson Austin Letter, April 7, 1864.
93. Phinehas Hager Letter, November 20, 1863. Gilbert's own arrest by Colonel Robinson may have been indirectly related to his failure to pursue Shafter's misconduct. If Captain Hubbard had

decided to make an issue of the matter, he may have discussed the situation with Robinson for at the time he was temporarily assigned to headquarters "examining claims against the government, for property *destroy, or used by the government.*" Phinehas Hager Letter, December 28, 1863. Furthermore, it was Sergeant Hager's opinion that Captain Hubbard was highly regarded by the post commander. Phinehas Hager Letter, December 28, 1863. Finally in this vein of speculation, it may not have been coincidentally the Hager kept predicting that Colonel Gilbert was heading for trouble. Phinehas Hager Letter, November 4, 15 and 19, 1863.

94. Regimental Letter and Order Book, 19th Michigan Infantry, March 31, 1864, National Archives, Washington, D.C.

95. John N. Shafter's Compiled Military Service File, National Archives, Washington, D.C. The Shafter boys' father was an influencial citizen in Kalamazoo County having been actively engaged in township government. One of their uncles had served as Chief Justice of the California Supreme Court, another was a distinguished attorney. Their mother was related to Charles Sumner. Samuel W. Durant, *History of Kalamazoo County, Michigan* (Philadelphia, 1880), 357-58 and 383.

96. John N. Shafter's Compiled Military Service File.

97. Phinehas Hager Letter, January 22, 1864.

98. Judson Austin Letter, January 23, 1864.

99. Regimental Letter and Order Book, 19th Michigan Infantry, March 31, 1864, National Archives, Washington, D.C.

100. John N. Shafter's Compiled Military Service File.

101. Ibid.

102. Ibid.

103. *Record of Service*, 80.

104. Regimental Letter and Order Book, 19th Michigan Infantry, November 17, 1863, National Archives, Washington, D.C.

105. Ibid., January 4, 1864.

106. Ibid., March 20, 1864.

107. Phinehas Hager Letter, February 21, 1864.

108. Henry Noble Letters, January 18 and 20, 1864.

109. Judson Austin Letter, January 15, 1864.

110. Ibid., March 16, 1864.

111. Ibid., March 4, 1864.

112. Eli Griffin Letter, November 20, 1863.

113. Judson Austin Letter, January 2, 1864.

114. Henry Noble Letter, January 1, 1864.

115. Judson Austin Letter, March 25, 1864.

116. Eli Griffin Letter, January 6, 1864; Rice, *Diary*, January 6, 1863; Phinehas Hager Letter, April 4, 1864.
117. Regimental Letter and Order Book, 19th Michigan Infantry, January 14 and March 4, 1864, National Archives, Washington, D.C.
118. Ibid., November 17, 1863.
119. Henry Noble Diary, February 9, 1864.
120. Phinehas Hager Letter, February 9, 1864.
121. Judson Austin Letter, March 16, 1864.
122. Ibid.
123. Phinehas Hager Letter, November 9, 1863.
124. Eli Griffin Letters, November 11, 1863 and February 26, 1864;
125. Eli Griffin Letters, November 11, 1863 and February 26, 1864; Phinehas Hager Letter, February 20, 1864 and many others.
126. Lewis Labadie Letter, December 14, 1863.
127. Isaac Edwards Letter, December 14, 1863.
128. Lewis Labadie Letter, November, 1863.
129. Phinehas Hager Letter, December 6, 1863.
130. Ibid., February 2, 1864.
131. Regimental Letter and Order Book, 19th Michigan Infantry, February 22, 1864, National Archives, Washington, D.C.
132. Eli Griffin Letter, March 22, 1864.
133. General Order No. 2, February 24, 1864. Located in the Eli Griffin Letters.
134. Eli Griffin Letter, March 12, 1864; William Lefler Letter, *Constantine Weekly & St. Joseph County Advertiser* April 7, 1864, 2.
135. Judson Austin, April 14, 1864.
136. Ibid., April 18, 1864.

Chapter X -- THE ATLANTA CAMPAIGN

1. Phinehas Hager Letters, April 24 - 25, 1864; Judson Austin Letter April 24, 1864.
2. Judson Austin Letter, April 25, 1864.
3. Phinehas Hager Letter, April 30, 1864.
4. Henry Noble Letter, May 1, 1864.
5. Judson Austin Letter, May 1, 1864.
6. John Griffis Letter, May 5, 1864.
7. Henry Noble Letter, April 30, 1864.
8. Phinehas Hager Letter, April 25, 1864.
9. Ibid., April 30, 1864.
10. Ulysses S. Grant, *Personal Memoirs of U.S. Grant* (New York, 1864), II, 42.
11. Henry Noble Diary, April, 1864; Rice, *Diary*, April 24, 1864;

Byrne, *Letters of Harvey Reid,* 130.

12. Henry Noble Diary, April 1864; Rice *Diary*, April 25 - 30, 1864; Phinehas Hager Letter, April 30, 1864.
13. Judson Austin Letter, May 2, 1864.
14. Phinehas Hager Letter, April 25, 1864; Henry Noble Letter, April 30, 1864; John Griffis Letter, May 5, 1864.
15. Jacob D. Cox, *Atlanta* (New York, 1882), 245 - 249. (Hereafter cited as Cox, *Atlanta*).
16. Eli Griffin Letter, May 9, 1864.
17. Ibid., May 1, 1864.
18. Judson Austin Letter, May 4, 1864; Henry Noble Diary, April, 1864; Phinehas Hager Letter, May 5, 1864; John Griffis Letter, May 5, 1864.
19. Henry Noble Diary, May, 1864; Rice, *Diary*, May 7, 1864; Judson Austin Letters, May 5 and 6, 1864.
20. Eli Griffin Letter, May 9, 1864.
21. Phinehas Hager Letter, May 5, 1864.
22. Judson Austin Letter, May 6, 1864; Phinehas Hager Letter, May 5, 1864; Eli Griffin Letter, May 9, 1864.
23. Eli Griffin Letter, May 9, 1864.
24. Judson Austin Letter, May 5, 1864.
25. William T. Sherman, *Memoirs of W.T. Sherman* (New York, 1875), II, 33 - 34 (Hereafter cited as Sherman, *Memoirs.*)
26. Lucius Phettenplace Letter, *Coldwater Union Sentinel*, June 3, 1864, 2 and Rice, *Diary*, May 7, 1864.
27. *OR*, XXXVIII, Pt. II, 447-48 and Rice, *Diary*, May 10, 1864.
28. Lewis Labadie Letter, May 10, 1864.
28. Sherman, *Memoirs*, II, 34 - 35.
30. Eli Griffin Letter, May 9, 1864.
31. Cox, *Atlanta*, 36; and 40-42.
32. *OR*, XXXVIII, Pt. II, 378; Eli Griffin Diary, April 13, 1864; Coe, *Diary*, 129 - 130.
33. Coe, *Diary*, 130.
34. Cox, *Atlanta* 43 - 46.
35. *OR*, XXXVIII, Pt. II, 378 - 379.
36. Lucius Phettenplace Letter, *Coldwater Union Sentinel*, June 3, 1864, 2.
37. Henry Noble Diary, May 14, 1864.
38. Lucius Phettenplace Letter, *Coldwater Union Sentinel*, June 3, 1864, 2.
39. Cox, *Atlanta*, 47 and *OR*, XXXVIII, Pt. II, 379.
40. Sherman, *Memoirs*, II, 35.
41. *OR*, XXXVIII, Pt. II, 28 322 and 434.

42. *OR*, XXXVIII, Pt. II, 276, 305, 435 and Pt. III, 812.

43. *OR*, XXXVIII, Pt. II, 379.

44. *Ibid.*, 118, 119, and 435. Although it is unclear, the impression is left that this gun crew was either killed, captured or fled in the face of this attack. Hood on the other hand, states that they were forced to abandon their guns because of effective Federal artillery fire. J.B. Hood, *Advance and Retreat* (Bloomington, 1959), 96.

45. *OR*, XXXVIII, Pt. II, 379.

46. *OR*, XXXVIII, Pt. II, 322, 340, 341, and 415.

47. Henry Noble Letter, May 21, 1864.

48. Eli Griffin Diary, May 15, 1864; Rice, *Diary*, May 15, 1864; Henry Noble Letter, Mary 21, 1864.

49. Henry Noble Letter, May 21, 1864.

50. Rice, *Diary*, May 15, 1864.

51. *OR*, XXXVIII, Pt. II, 278 and 305; S.F. Fleharty, *A History of The 102d Illinois Infantry Volunteers* (Chicago, 1865), 60. (Hereafter cited as Fleharty, *History of 102d Illinois*).

52. Griffin Diary, May 15, 1864; Henry Noble Letter, May 21, 1864; *OR*, XXXVIII, Pt. II, 322, *Coldwater Union Sentinel*, June 3, 1864, 2.

53. Griffin Diary, May 15, 1864; *OR* XXXVIII, Pt. II, 380; *The Detroit Free Press*, June 26, 1864, 3; Coe, *Diary*, 105, 106 and 131.

54. Judson Austin Letter, May 15, 1864.

55. *OR*, XXXVIII, Pt. II, 395.

56. *Ibid.*, 305 and 435.

57. *Ibid.*, 322 - 323; Fleharty, *History of 102d Illinois*, 58.

58. Judson Austin Letter, May 15, 1864.

59. *OR*, XXXVIII, Pt. II, 323; Eli Griffin Letter, May 16, 1864.

60. *OR*, XXXVIII, Pt. III, 813; Eli Griffin Diary, May 15, 1864.

61. *OR*, XXXVIII, Pt. II, 120, 227, and 456 - 457.

62. Robertson, *Michigan in the War*, 394.

63. Soldier's Letter (unidentified member of 19th Michigan), *Coldwater Union Sentinel*, June 10, 1864, 2.

64. Judson Austin Letter, May 16, 1864; Soldier's Letter (unidentified member of 19th Michigan), *Sturgis Journal*, June 2, 1864, 2.

65. Eli Griffin Diary, May 16, 1864; William Cook Letter, *Coldwater Union Sentinel*, July 17, 1864, 2.

66. *OR*, XXXVIII, Pt. II, 380 and Coe, *Diary*, 132 - 135.

67. *OR*, XXXVIII, Pt. II, 380 - 81 and 416; Henry Noble Letter, May 21, 1864.

68. Judson Austin Letter, May 16, 1864.

69. Sherman, *Memoirs II*, 41-43 and Cox, *Atlanta* 64-65 and 69.

70. *OR*, XXXVIII, Pt. II, 381-382; Eli Griffin Diary, May 23-24. 1864; Sherman, *Memoirs*, II, 43-44.
71. *OR*, XXXVIII, Pt. II, 382.
72. Henry Noble Letter, May 29, 1864.
73. Eli Griffin Diary, May 24, 1864; *OR*, XXXVIII, Pt. II, 383.
74. Eli Griffin Letter, May 29, 1864 located in the State Archives of Michigan, Lansing, Michigan.
75. Ibid., Henry Noble Letter, May 29, 1864.
76. Eli Griffin Letters, May 20 and 29, 1864.
77. Phinehas Hager Letter, June 1, 1864.
78. Ibid.
79. Ibid.
80. Eli Griffin Diary, May 26 - 29, 1864.
81. Cox, *Atlanta*, 82.
82. Sherman, *Memoirs*, II, 45 - 46.
83. Henry Noble Diary, May 27, 1864; Eli Griffin Diary, May 26 - June 6, 1864.
84. Eli Griffin and Henry Noble Diaries, June 1 - 6, 1864.
85. Henry Noble Letter, June 7, 1864.
86. Judson Austin Letter, June 7, 1864.
87. Henry Noble Diary, June 11 - 12, 1864.
88. Judson Austin Letter, June 13, 1864.
89. Eli Griffin Letter, June 13, 1864.
90. Cox, *atlanta*, 97-100; Sherman, *Memoirs*, II, 51; Sydney C. Kerksis, "Action at Gilgal Church, Georgia, June 15-16, 1864," *The Atlanta Historical Bulletin*, Fall, 1970, 9.
91. *OR*, XXXVIII, Pt. II, 384; Sherman, *Memoirs*, II, 54.
92. Henry Noble Letter, June 17, 1864.
93. Ibid. Both Sergeant Frederick Clay and Lieutenant George Livingston died; Clay immediately, the lieutenant lingered on until July 1, 1864. *Record of Service*, 23 and 58. See also Henry Noble Diary, June 16, 1864 and *OR*, XXXVIII, Pt. II, 385. There are two versions of where Griffin was hit. Coburn reported that he was shot on the west side of the road but Sergeant Paschal Pullman stated he was, hit by a stray bullet while standing behind Company B after the regiment had crossed back to the east side of the road. Paschal Pullman Letter, June 19, 1864, located at The University of Michigan, Ann Arbor, Michigan.
    The University of Michigan, Ann Arbor, Michigan.
94. Paschal Pullman Letter, June 19, 1864.
95. Lucius Wing Letter, June 26, 1864 located in the Bentley Historical Library, Michigan Historical Collections at The University of Michigan, Ann Arbor, Michigan.

96. Ibid.
97. Henry Noble Diary, June 17, 1864, and Letter, June 22, 1864; Paschal Pullman Letter, June 19, 1864; Phinehas Hager Letter July 14, 1864; Coe *Diary* 154; Soldier's Letter (unidentified member of 19th Michigan), *Sturgis Journal*, June 30, 1864, 2 and others.
98. *OR*, XXXVIII, Pt. II 385.
99. Sydney Kerksis, "Action at Gilgal Church, June 15-16, 1864," *The Atlanta Historical Bulletin*, Fall, 1970, 12.
100. Robertson, *Michigan in the War*, 395.
101. *Bonner Springs Chieftain*, (Kansas), May 3, 1900.
102. Sherman, *Memoirs*, II, 54 - 56.
103. Henry Noble Diary, June 18 - 19, 1864.
104. Sherman, *Memoirs*, II, 57.
105. *OR*, XXXVIII, Pt. II, 385 - 86; Robertson, *Michigan in the War*, 395.
106. Henry Noble Letter, July 2, 1864.
107. Phinehas Hager Letter, July 11, 1864.
108. Judson Austin Letter, July 10, 1864.
109. Henry Noble Letter, July 7, 1864.
110. Phinehas Hager Letter, July 11, 1864.
111. Sherman, *Memoirs,* II, 62 and 65.
112. Henry Noble Letter, July 7, 1864.
113. Judson Austin Letter, July 3, 1864.
114. *OR*, XXXVIII, Pt. II, 388.
115. Henry Noble Letter, July 7, 1864.
116. Sherman, *Memoirs*, II, 70-71.
117. Henry Noble Letter, July 7, 1864. See also Phinehas Hager Letter, July 11, 1864, and Henry Noble Letter July 2, 1864.
118. Phinehas Hager Letter, July 14, 1864.
119. Ibid.
120. Henry Noble Letter, July 19, 1864.
121. Sherman, *Memoirs*, II, 72.
122. Henry Noble Letter, July 19, 1864.
123. *OR*, XXXVIII, Pt. II, 389 and 404.
124. *Ibid.* Coburn claims that Ward initially rejected his request to advance because it was against Hooker's orders but then changed his mind. Major Levin Miler, commanding the 33rd Indiana, maintained that Coburn came back from division headquarters having been told that he was unnecessarily alarmed but when sustained firing was heard from the skirmishers, the brigade commander acted without further consultation. An enlisted man in the 19th Michigan saw it similarly: "No

commanding officer seemed to be present. Our gallant Colonel Coburn ordered his brigade forward.'' Coe, *Diary*, 178 - 179.

125. *OR*, XXXVIII, Pt. II, 389 - 390 and 427.
126. Judson Austin Letter, July 21, 1864.
127. Minnie D. Millbrook, *A Study In Valor: Michigan Medal of Honor Winners in the Civil War* (Lansing, 1966), 54.
128. *OR*, XXXVIII, Pt. II, 390.
129. Rice,*Diary*, July 20, 1864.
130. *OR*, XXXVIII, Pt. II, 390; Coe, *Diary*, 179; Cox, *Atlanta*, 158.
131. Phinehas Hager Letter, July 23, 1864.
132. Judson Austin Letter, July 21, 1864.
133. Phinehas Hager Letter, July 23, 1864.
134. Robertson, *Michigan in the War*, 395; Phinehas Hager Letter, July 23, 1864.
135. Lewis Labadie Papers.
136. Sherman, *Memoirs*, II, 73.
137. Phinehas Hager Letter, July 23, 1864.
138. Sherman, *Memoirs*, II, 82 - 83.
139. Rice, *Diary*, July 22, 1864.
140. Judson Austin Letters, July 31 and August 19, 1864.
141. Sherman, *Memoirs*, II, 88 - 90.
142. Henry Noble Letter, August 14, 1864; Rice, *Diary*, August 5, 1864
143. Judson Austin Letter, August 19, 1864.
144. Rice, *Diary*, July 22, 1864.
145. Judson Austin Letter, July 23, 1864.
146. Ibid., August 4, 1864.
147. Ibid., August 12, 1864.
148. Rice, *Diary*, July 24, 1864.
149. Samuel Hubbard Letter, August 8, 1864 located in the Bentley Historical Library, Michigan Historical Collections at The University of Michigan, Ann Arbor, Michigan.
150. Henry Noble Letters, August 14 and 22, 1864.
151. Sherman, *Memoirs*, II, 104; *OR*, XXXVIII, Pt. II, 392.
152. Judson Austin Letter, August 29, 1864.
153. *OR*, XXXVIII, Pt. II, 21.
154. Sherman, *Memoirs*, II, 107.
155. *OR*, XXXVIII, Pt. II, 392 - 93.
156. Lewis Labadie Letter, September 4, 1864.
157. Colonel Coburn's Farewell Address to the Soldiers of the 2d Brig 3d Div. 20th Army Corps, author's manuscript collection.
158. Timothy Turner Letter, *Coldwater Union Sentinel*, October 21, 1864, 1; Reed, *Encyclopedia of Biography of Indiana*, II, 1899, 63
159. Robertson, *Michigan in the War*, 394 - 95; *Annual Report of the*

Adjutant General of the State of Michigan for the Year 1864 (Lansing, 1865), 173.

Chapter XI -- SHERMAN'S MARCH THROUGH GEORGIA AND THE CAROLINAS

1.   *OR*, XLIV, 343 - 344; Delos Lake Letter, September 11, 1864.
2.   Delos Lake Letter, November 6, 1864; Rice, *Diary*, September 13, 14 and 27, 1864.
3.   Sherman, *Memoirs*, II, 118 - 124.
4.   Henry Noble Letter, September 15, 1864.
5.   Ibid., September 25, 1864.
6.   Cox, *Atlanta*, 224 - 239; Sherman, *Memoirs*, II, 144 - 158.
7.   Henry Noble Letters, October 11 and 19, 1864; Delos Lake Letter, October 18, 1864; Judson Austin Letters, October 14 and 23, 1864.
8.   Delos Lake Letter, October, 30, 1864.
9.   Ibid.
10. Henry Noble Letter, November 10, 1864.
11. Judson Austin Letter, November 8, 1864.
12. Henry Noble Letter, November 10, 1864. Rice confirms the same number of Copperhead votes cast. *Rice Diary*, November 7, 1864.
13. Sherman, *Memoirs*, II, 158 - 159; Judson Austin Letter, October 29, 1864; Henry Noble Letter, November 7, 1864.
14. Judson Austin Letter, October 30, 1864.
15. Ibid., October 30 and 31, 1864; Delos Lake Letter, November 6, 1864.
16. Judson Austin Letter, November 7; Sherman, *Memoirs*, II, 177.
17. Judson Austin Letter, November 1, 1864.
18. Henry Noble Letter, November 1, 1864; David P. Cunningham, *Sherman's March Through The South* (New York, 1865), 241.
19. Delos Lake Letter, September 11, 1864.
20. Ibid., December 26, 1864.
21. Sherman, *Memoirs*, II, 174.
22. *Ibid.*, 174 - 175.
23. B.H. Liddell Hart, *Sherman: Soldier, Realist, American* (New York, 1960), 336-337. (Hereafter referred to as Hart, *Sherman*].
24. Sherman, *Memoirs*, II, 177, 190, and 192 - 193.
25. Delos Lake Letters, December 16 and 26, 1864; Rice, *Diary*, November 15, 1864.
26. Henry Noble Letter, December 18, 1864.
27. Rice, *Diary*, November 23 - 29, 1864; Delos Lake Letter, December 26, 1864.

28. David Anderson Letter, *Coldwater Union Sentinel*, January 13, 1865, 3.
29. *Ibid.*; Rice, *Diary*, December 4 - 10, 1864.
30. Hart, *Sherman*, 341 - 345.
31. Judson Austin Letter, December 18, 1865; Delos Lake Letters, December 16 and 26, 1864.
32. Sherman, *Memoirs*, II, 216 - 217; Henry Noble Letter, December 23, 1864.
33. Henry Noble Letter, December 23, 1864.
34. Rice, *Diary*, December 23, 1864; Henry Noble Letter, January 1, 1865; Judson Austin Letter, December 27, 1864.
35. Sherman, *Memoirs*, II, 238; Delos Lake Letters, January 23 and 26, 1865.
36. Delos Lake Letter, January 23, 1865.
37. Ibid., *OR*, XLVII, Pt. I, 802.
38. Judson Austin Letter, January 12, 1865.
39. Lewis Labadie Letter, January 1, 1865.
40. Judson Austin Letter, January 8, 1865.
41. *OR*, XLVII, Pt. I, 802; Henry Noble Letter, January 19, 1865; Henry Noble Diary, January 17 - 18, 1865.
42. Judson Austin Letter, January 21, 1865; Henry Noble Diary, January 18, 1865.
43. *OR*, XLVII, Pt. I, 819; *Bonner Springs Chieftain*, (Kansas), May 3, 1900; Lewis Labadie Letter, April 1, 1865.
44. *Portrait and Biographical Record of Kalamazoo, Allegan and Van Buren Counties*, (Chicago, 1892), 723 - 24.
45. Alfred Cheney Letter, *Coldwater Union Sentinel*, August 26, 1864, 3.
46. *OR*, XLVII, Pt. I, 803; Henry Noble Diary, January 29, 1865.
47. Sherman, *Memoirs*, II, 268-272; John G. Barrett, *Sherman's March Through The Carolinas* (Chapel Hill, 1956), 39. (Hereafter cited as Barrett, *Through The Carolinas*).
48. *OR*, XLVII, Pt. I, 803 - 804.
49. Henry Noble Diary, February 14, 1865.
50. Henry Noble Letter, no date but content identifies it as being written in February or early March, 1865. His diary for February 25, 1865 mentions the same incident. A soldier in Company I and Jim Martin, Company B, were among those captured while foraging. Rice, *Diary* January 31, 1865; Judson Austin Letter, April 1, 1865; *Record of Service*, 61.
51. Henry Noble Letter, January 31, 1865.
52. Delos Lake Letter, March 26, 1865.
53. *OR*, XLVIII, Pt. I, 804 - 806; Rice, *Diary*, February 21 - 22 and

March 3, 1865.

54. *OR*, XLVII, Pt. I, 806; Judson Austin Letter, March 31, 1865.
55. Delos Lake Letter, March 26, 1865; Lewis Labadie Letter, March 12, 1865.
56. Delos Lake Letter, March 26, 1865.
57. Sherman, *Memoirs*, II, 299 - 300; Barrett, *Through The Carolinas*, 148.
58. *OR*, XLVII, Pt. I, 585, 783, and 807 - 808.
59. Henry Noble Letter, March 24, 1865. The contribution of these batteries drew special praise from corps commander Alpheus Williams. *OR*, XLVII, Pt. I, 808.
60. *OR*, XLVII, Pt. I, 808.
61. Henry Noble Letter, March 24, 1865.
62. Rice, *Diary*, March 16, 1862.
63. *OR*, XLVII, Pt. I, 808; Henry Noble Letter, March 24, 1865.
64. Judson Austin Letter, March 27, 1865.
65. Hartwell Osburn, *Trials and Triumphs: The Record of the Fifty-Fith Ohio Volunteer Infantry* (Chicago, 1904), 199. In his report, Colonel Dustin stated that there were no Rebels defending the second line when his brigade came upon it. *OR*, XLVII, Pt. I, 808.
66. *OR*, XLVII, Pt. I, 808.
67. *Ibid.*, 65; Malcolm Duffie Letter, *The Detroit Free Press*, April 9, 1865, 1.
68. *OR*, XLVII, Pt. 1, 809.
69. Barrett, *Through The Carolinas*, 157 - 167.
70. *Ibid.*, 167 - 169.
71. Henry Noble Letter, March 24, 1865; *OR*, XLVII, Pt. 1, 809; Barrett, *Through The Carolinas*, 169.
72. *OR*, XLVII, Pt. I, 809.
73. Barrett, *Through The Carolinas*, 177 - 185.
74. David Anderson Letter, *Coldwater Union Sentinel*, April 28, 1865, 2.
75. Delos Lake Letter, March 12, 1865.
76. Ibid., December 26, 1864.
77. Henry Noble Letter, March 14, 1865.
78. Ibid.

Chapter XII -- GOING HOME

1. Malcolm Duffie, *The Detroit Free Press*, April 9, 1865, 1.
2. Barrett, *Through The Carolinas*, 226, 240, 245, 267 and 271-72.
3. Rice, *Diary*, April 18, 1865; Henry Noble Letter, April 20, 1865.
4. Henry Noble Diary, April 18, 1865 and Rice, *Diary*, April 18, 1865

5. Henry Noble Letter, May 26, 1865.
6. Regimental Letter and Order Book, 19th Michigan Infantry, May 21, 1865, National Archives, Washington, D.C.
7. Judson Austin Letter, April 23, 1865.
8. Ibid.; Henry Noble Letter, June 18, 1865.
9. Judson Austin Letter, April 9, 1865.
10. Rice, *Diary*, June 9 - 13, 1865.
11. *The Detroit Free Press*, June 13, 1865, 1.
12. *Ibid.*, June 14, 1865.
13. Rice, *Diary*, June 14 - 25, 1865.
14. *Coldwater Union Sentinel*, June 30, 1865, 3.
15. *Ibid.; Record of Service*, 3.
16. Malcolm B. Duffie, "Recollections." Presumably Duffie's poetry was reproduced in either a newspaper or reunion program. The copy examined and reference to its being read at a 19th Michigan reunion, were preserved in a scrapbook and owned by Mrs. Leslie Woodward, Coldwater, Michigan.

BIBLIOGRAPHY

MANUSCRIPTS

Allen, C. Emerson, Diary, Bentley Historical Library, Michigan Historical Collections, The University of Michigan, Ann Arbor, Michigan.

Austin, Judson, Letters, Bentley Historical Library, Michigan Historical Collections, The University of Michigan, Ann Arbor, Michigan.

Brown, E. A.: Letter to Darius Brown, August 24, 1862, privately owned by Robert Pennell, Newtonville, Massachusetts.

Colonel Coburn's Farewell Address to the Soldiers of the 2d Brig. 3d Div. 20th Army Corps, privately owned by William M. Anderson, Galesburg, Illinois.

Conner, Charles, Letters, Regional History Collections Western Michigan University, Kalamazoo, Michigan.

Dugan, Jeremiah, Letter, August 12, 1864, Regional History Collections, Western Michigan University, Kalamazoo, Michigan.

Edwards, Isaac, Letters, privately owned by Mrs. Guy Thomas, Dowagiac, Michigan.

Gilbert, James W.: Letter to Mr. Mayer, October 14, 1862, Bentley Historical Library, Michigan Historical Collections The University of Michigan, Ann Arbor, Michigan.

Griffin, Eli, Letters and Diaries, Bentley Historical Library, Michigan Historical Collections, The University of Michigan, Ann Arbor, Michigan.

Griffis, John, Letters, Bentley Historical Library, Michigan

BIBLIOGRAPHY

Historical Collections, The University of Michigan, Ann Arbor, Michigan.

Hager, Phinehas, Letters, Bentley Historical Library, Michigan Historical Collections, The University of Michigan, Ann Arbor, Michigan.

Hubbard, Samuel, Letter, August 8, 1864, Bentley Historical Library, Michigan Historical Collections, The University of Michigan, Ann Arbor, Michigan.

Huntley, Alden B. Diary, Regional History Collections, Western Michigan University, Kalamazoo, Michigan.

Labadie, Lewis, Letters, Burton Historical Collection, Detroit Public Library, Detroit, Michigan.

Lake, Delos, Letters, The Huntington Library, San Marino, California.

Lamb, Joseph, Letter, December 19, 1862, Regional History Collections, Western Michigan University, Kalamazoo, Michigan.

McCormick, Thomas, Letters, Regional History Collections, Western Michigan University, Kalamazoo, Michigan.

Noble, Henry, Letters and Diaries, Bentley Historical Library, Michigan Historical Collections, The University of Michigan, Ann Arbor, Michigan.

Opdycke, Emerson, Letter, March 8, 1863, Library of Congress, Washington, D.C., Series 4, Volume 6 of the James A. Garfield Papers.

Penland, Hiram F., Letters, Bentley Historical Library, Michigan Historical Collections, The University of Michigan, Ann Arbor, Michigan.

BIBLIOGRAPHY

Polk, B.H.: Letter to Mrs. William R. Shafter, March 25, 1863, William R. Shafter Papers, The Stanford University Libraries, Stanford, California.

Post, Ebenezer, Letters, Bentley Historical Library, Michigan Historical Collections, The University of Michigan, Ann Arbor, Michigan.

Prentiss, Charles, Letters and Diary, privately owned by Archie Nevins, Kalamazoo, Michigan.

Proceedings of a General Court Martial Held at Danville December 20 - 23, 1863. Records of the Judge Advocate General's Office, Court Martial Case Files, Number KK 701, Record Group November 153, Captain George H White, National Archives, Washington, D.C.

Pullman, Paschal, Letter, June 19, 1864, Bentley Historical Library, Michigan Historical Collections, The University of Michigan, Ann Arbor, Michigan.

Regimental Records, 19th Michigan Infantry, National Archives, Washington, D.C.

Regimental Records, 19th Michigan Infantry, State Archives of Michigan, Lansing, Michigan.

Shaffer, George, Letters, Bentley Historical Library, Michigan Historical Collections, The University of Michigan, Ann Arbor, Michigan.

Shaffer, George, Statement Accounting for Lost Property, August 31, 1864, privately owned by William M. Anderson, Galesburg, Illinois.

Shafter, John, Compiled Military Service File, National Archives, Washington, D.C.

BIBLIOGRAPHY

Shafter, John, Letter, September 2, 1864, Bentley Historical Library, Michigan Historical Collections, The University of Michigan, Ann Arbor, Michigan.

United States Census for 1860, Allegan, Berrien, Branch, Cass, and Kalamazoo Counties, National Archives, Washington, D.C.

Wilkins, John A., Letter, March 7, 1863, Indiana State Historical Library, Indianapolis, Indiana.

Wing, Lucuis, Letter, June 26, 1864, Bentley Historical Library, Michigan Historical Collections, The University of Michigan, Ann Arbor, Michigan.

Wheeler, Cyrus, Letters, Bentley Historical Library, Michigan Historical Collections, The University of Michigan, Ann Arbor, Michigan.

Woodward, Abram P., Diary, privately owned by Don E. Truax, Canby, Oregon.

NEWSPAPERS

Allegan Journal
Bonner Springs Chieftain (Kansas)
Cass County Republican
Coldwater Daily Reporter
Coldwater Union Sentinel
Constantine Weekly Mercury & *St. Joseph County Advertiser*
Detroit Advertiser and Tribune
Detroit Free Press
Dowagiac Daily News
Kalamazoo Gazette
Mishawaka Enterprise (Indiana)
St. Joseph Traveler
Sturgis Journal

BIBLIOGRAPHY

Three Rivers Reporter
Western Chronicle (Centreville)

PRINTED PRIMARY SOURCES

Baughman, Theodore. *Baughman The Oklahoma Scout. Personal Reminiscences.* Chicago: Bedford, Clark & Co., 1886.

Bradley, G.S. *The Star Corps.* Milwaukee: Jermain & Brightman, Book & Job Printers, 1865.

Byrd, Cecil K. (ed.) "Journal of Israel Cogshall", *Indiana Magazine of History* XLII (March 1946), 69-87.

Byrne, Frank L. (ed) *The View From Headquarters: Civil War Letters of Harvey Reid.* Madison: The State Historical Society of Wisconsin, 1965.

Cist, Henry M. *The Army of the Cumberland.* New York: Charles Scribner's Sons, 1898.

Coe, David (ed.) *Mine Eyes Have Seen the Glory: Combat Diaries of Union Sergeant Hamlin Alexander Coe.* Cranbury: Associated University Presses, Inc. 1975.

Cox, Jacob D. *Atlanta.* New York: Charles Scribner's Sons, 1882.

Fleharty, S.F. *A History of The 102d Illinois Infantry Volunteers.* Chicago: Brewster & Hanscom, Printers, 1865.

Grant, Ulysses S. *Personal Memoirs of U.S. Grant.* 2 vols. New York: Charles Webster & Co., 1885-86.

Hood, J.B. *Advance and Retreat.* Bloomington: Indiana University Press, 1959.

BIBLIOGRAPHY

Lincoln, Charles P. "Engagement at Thompson's Station, Tennessee," Military Order of the Loyal Legion of the United States, Commandery of the District of Columbia, 1893.

McBride, John R. *History of the Thirty-Third Indiana Veteran Volunteer Infantry.* Indianapolis: Wm. B. Burford, Printer & Binder, 1900.

Michigan Adjutant General's Office, *Annual Report of the Adjutant General of the State of Michigan, for the Year 1862.* Lansing: John A. Keir & Co., 1862.

_____*Annual Report of the Adjutant General of the State of Michigan for the Year 1863.* Lansing: John A. Keir & Co., 1864.

_____*Annual Report of the Adjutant General of the State of Michigan for the Year 1864.* Lansing: John A. Keir & Co., 1865.

_____*Annual Report of the Adjutant General of the State of Michigan for the Year 1865.* 3 vols. Lansing: John A. Keir & Co., 1866.

_____*Record of Service of Michigan Volunteers in the Civil War.* Vol. XX. Kalamazoo: Ihling Bros. & Everard, 1905.

_____*Michigan in the War.* Compiled by Jno. Robertson. Lansing: W.S. George & Co., 1882.

Moore, Frank K. (ed.) *The Rebellion Record: A Diary of American Events.* 11 vols. New York: G. P. Putnam, 1861 - 63; D. Van Nostrand, 1864 - 68.

Osborn Hartwell. *Trials and Triumps; The Record of the Fifth-Fifth Ohio Volunteer Infantry.* Chicago: A.C. McClurg &

Co., 1904.

Population of The United States in 1860 Washington: Government Printing Office, 1864.

Rice, Franklin D. *Diary of 19th Michigan Volunteer Infantry During Their Three Years Service in the War of the Rebellion.* Big Rapids: n.p., n.d.

Sherman, William T. *Memoirs of W.T. Sherman.* 2 vols. New York: D. Appleton & Co., 1875.

The DAR Lineage Book. CIXX Washington, D.C.; National Society of the Daughters of the American Revolution, 1932.

Virkus, Frederick A. (ed.) *Compendium of American Genealogy.* Chicago: Institute of American Genealogy, 1937.

War of the Rebellion: A Compilation of the Official Records of the Union and Confederate Armies. 69 vols. Washington, D.C.: The Government Printing Office, 1880-1901.

Williams, Frederick D. (ed.) *The Wild Life of the Army: Civil War Letters of James A. Garfield.* East Lansing: Michigan State University Press, 1964.

Wyeth, John. *That Devil Forrest: Life of General Nathan Bedford Forrest.* New York: Harper & Brothers, 1959.

SECONDARY SOURCES

Adams, George W. *Doctors in Blue: The Medical History of the Union Army in the Civil War.* New York: The Crowell-Collier Co., 1961.

American Biographical History of Eminent and Self Made Men. Vol. I. Cincinnati: Western Biographical Publishing

BIBLIOGRAPHY

Co., 1878.

Baldwin, Alice B. *Memoirs of the Late Frank D. Baldwin, Major General, U.S.A.* Los Angeles: Wetzel Publishing Co., Inc., 1929.

Barrett, John G. *Sherman's March Through The Carolina's.* Chapel Hill: The University of North Carolina Press, 1956.

Bradsby, Henry C. *History of Vigo County, Indiana, With Biographical Selections.* Chicago: S. B. Nelson & Co., 1891.

Collidge, Orville W. *A Twentieth Century History of Berrien County.* Chicago: The Lewis Publishing Co., 1906.

Cunningham, David P. *Sherman's March Through The South.* New York: Sheldon & Co., 1865.

Durant, Samuel W. *History of Kalamazoo County, Michigan.* Phiadephia: Evers and Abbott, 1880.

Dyer, John P. *"Fighting Joe" Wheeler.* University, Louisiana; Louisiana University Press, 1941.

Foote, Shelby. *The Civil War: A Narrative.* 3 vols. New York: Random House, 1958, 1963, 1974.

Glover, L. H. *A Twentieth Century History of Cass County.* Chicago: The Lewis Publishing Co., 1906.

Hart, B. H. Liddell. *Sherman: Soldier, Realist, American.* New York: Frederick A. Praeger, 1960.

Horn, Stanley F. *The Army of the Tennessee.* Norman: University of Oklahoma Press, 1968.

BIBLIOGRAPHY

Johnson, Crisfield. *History of Branch County.* Philadelphia: Everts & Abbott, 1879.

Kerksis, Sydney C. "Action at Gilgal Church, Georgia, June 15 -16, 1864," *The Atlanta Historical Bulletin*, (Fall, 1970), 9 - 17.

Lamers, William M. *The Edge of Glory: A Biography of General William S. Rosecrans*, U.S.A. New York: Harcourt, Brace & World, Inc., 1961.

Long, E.B. *The Civil War Day By Day.* Garden City: Doubleday & Co. 1971.

Lord, Francis A. *Civil War Collectors Encyclopedia.* New York: Castle Books, 1965.

Mathews, Alfred. *History of Cass County, Michigan.* Chicago: Waterman, Watkins & Co., 1882.

May, George S. (ed.) *Michigan Civil War History: An Annotated Bibliography.* Detroit: Wayne State University Press, 1961.

Millbrook, Minnie D. *A Study In Valor: Michigan Medal of Honor Winners in the Civil War.* Lansing: Michigan Civil War Centennial Observance Commission, 1966.

Portrait and Biographical Record of Kalamazoo, Allegan and Van Buren Counties. Chicago: Chapman Bros., 1892.

Reed, George Irving (ed.) *The Encyclopedia of Biography of Indiana.* Vol. II. Chicago: Century Publishing and Engraving Co., 1899.

Reid, Whitelow. *Ohio in the War: Her Statesmen, Her Generals, and Soldiers.* 2 vols. Cincinnati: Moore,

BIBLIOGRAPHY

Wilstach & Baldwin, 1868.

Rhodes, Charles D. "William Rufus Shafter", *Michigan History Magazine,* XVI (Autumn, 1932), 375 - 83.

Rowell, John W. *Yankee Cavalrymen: Through the Civil War With the Ninth Pennsylvania Cavalry.* Knoxville, The University of Tennessee Press, 1971.

Small Arms Used by Michigan Troops. Lansing: Michigan Civil War Centennial Observance Commission, 1966.

Stormont, Gil R. *History of Gibson County, Indiana, Her People, Industries and Institutions.* Indianapolis: B.F. Bowen & Co., 1914.

Warner, Ezra. *Generals in Blue.* Baton Rouge: Louisiana State University Press, 1964.

Wood, Gray. *The Hidden Civil War: The Story of the Copperheads.* New York: The Viking Press, 1964.

INDEX

317